W9-CRN-121

The Pastmasters

The Pastmasters

ELEVEN MODERN PIONEERS OF ARCHAEOLOGY

V. Gordon Childe, Stuart Piggott, Charles Phillips, Christopher Hawkes, Seton Lloyd, Robert J. Braidwood, Gordon R. Willey, C. J. Becker, Sigfried J. De Laet, J. Desmond Clark, D. J. Mulvaney

Edited by Glyn Daniel and Christopher Chippindale

WITH 22 ILLUSTRATIONS

THAMES AND HUDSON

© Antiquity Publications Ltd, contributors and their estates 1958, 1980, 1981, 1982, 1983, 1984, 1985, 1986, 1989

First published in the United States in 1989 by Thames and Hudson Inc., 500 Fifth Avenue, New York, New York 10110
Library of Congress Catalog Card Number 88–50229

Typeset in Great Britain by Antiquity Publications Ltd/Alan Sutton Publishing Ltd

Printed and bound in Singapore

Contents

Sources of Photographs

Introduction

The past, once past, is past. We study only the past as we are able to see it from the present. The present gives us present points of view, whether we are aware of them or not. The history of archaeology, even the history of ideas about a single site like Stonehenge, shows how closely conceptions about the distant past have followed the opinions and the spirit of each age – as well as an increasing range of empirical evidence.

This is why the history of archaeology matters for the subject as it is today, and why it has a role in making the subject as it will be tomorrow. Current archaeological ideas relate, in each generation, to many things besides the evidence that we have from that real past which has gone for ever. The evidence from new work makes new patterns; well-published records from old work are re-made into new patterns and revised interpretations; but those new patterns are not absolute, timeless verities – they derive from current interests and current points of view. They will pass in time and in their turn. This is true of all historical studies; it is true *a fortiori* of archaeology, where so much has to be inferred from the enigmatic evidence of mute objects.

Few archaeologists have known this better than Glyn Daniel, my predecessor as editor of ANTIQUITY. In a series of books (Daniel 1942; 1950, revised as Daniel 1975; 1961, revised as Daniel and Renfrew 1988; 1967; and others), he set out essentials of the history of archaeology. He encouraged others to take a serious concern in the subject. And between 1980 and 1986 he published in ANTIQUITY a series of ten retrospective essays by senior archaeologists, the essays that are here collected together in book form.

The first essay, by Gordon Childe (b. 1892), was published in ANTIQUITY rather earlier – in 1958, the year after Childe's death. I include it here because it is the prelude to the rest, by eminent members of that generation of archaeologists who were born in the first twenty years of the century. It was Childe's ideas, more than anyone else's, that provided the intellectual overall framework for Old World archaeology in the period.

The next three authors, Stuart Piggott, Charles Phillips, and Christopher Hawkes, worked for the most part on the later prehistory of Britain and its European context. Piggott, professor at Edinburgh, is best known for his work on the Neolithic. Phillips succeeded O.G.S. Crawford, ANTIQUITY's founder-editor, as Archaeology Officer to the Ordnance Survey, and continued its topographic fieldwork and mapping. Hawkes, professor at Oxford, concentrated on the Iron Age. Seton Lloyd, the next Briton, spent his life in near eastern archaeology, latterly as professor at the Institute of Archaeology in London. Robert Braidwood, the first American author, also worked in the Near East, and became professor at the Oriental Institute at Chicago. The second American, Gordon Willey, professor at Harvard, is an Americanist who has particularly specialized in Maya archaeology. The next two essays are by Europeans, C.J. Becker from Denmark, professor at Copenhagen, and Sigfried De Laet from Belgium, professor at Ghent, who have concentrated on the archaeology of their own regions, and within ranged widely there through the range of periods. The two final essays have canvasses of continental scale: Desmond Clark worked in Africa, latterly as professor at the University of California, Berkeley; John Mulvaney discovered the prehistory of Australia, and became professor in Canberra.

There is no purpose in my summarizing here what the rest of the book says. But there is a larger pattern, beyond the sum of eleven individual stories, and it may be useful to set down here some things that strike an archaeologist of a generation forty years junior in the work of these pastmasters, who led the subject from the 1930s to the 1970s.

These men – and notice they are all men – worked in a subject that was small and precarious. When a professional institute for archaeologists was contemplated in Britain about 1980, the number of people employed in the subject was estimated at under a thousand – but that was towards a hundredfold increase on the number in 1930. Many things follow from that domestic scale of archaeology – even on the world stage.

A first was the diversity of backgrounds and training, in the absence of routine university courses in archaeology. Lloyd trained as an architect, for example. Piggott made himself the leading young British prehistorian before he got round to a university course, and was appointed to the professorship in Edinburgh before he finished it. Some training once acquired, jobs were practically non-existent: in Britain, a small scatter of university jobs, a few museum posts, the Abercromby chair in Edinburgh, the post of archaeology officer in the Ordnance Survey. There may be more archaeologists chasing jobs today, but at least there are now some jobs for them to chase.

So it is that the same names come up so often in these essays – and often the names of other contributors. Archaeology, even world archaeology, was a small world. As Piggott explains, it took only a few cars of young turks, packing a meeting in Norwich arranged at a time inconvenient for the *ancien régime*, to seize control of the Prehistoric Society in 1935, and to make it into a real force in British and world archaeology. (In 1985, the Prehistorics celebrated its fiftieth birthday with a jubilee meeting at Norwich, with those turks become the respected elder statesmen of a most distinguished society: what would they have thought if new young turks had decided the time had come themselves to take revolutionary control against that now *ancien régime*?)

In a small world, one individual can have a special influence, and the name that seems to come up most often in these essays is Gordon Childe's, from his teaching in Edinburgh and then at the new Institute of Archaeology in London. Professor Charles Thomas, of that middle generation between the pastmasters' and my own, remarks, in comment on one of the Childe biographies:

In thinking back, I am also certain that younger people have overlooked, and will overlook, the remarkable personal influence exercised by Childe – not unlike a man who throws a handful of gravel into a pond, with some lumps making big ripples, other lumps tiny ones, and a few sinking without trace. What sticks in my mind from Institute days is not in fact any of the Danubian I–IV stuff, *Most ancient East*, or any of the (now obsolete) *context*. It is the *approach*, the methodology and the concepts, and I taught first-year classes for ten years at Edinburgh University entirely upon the V.G.C. base. Childe may not have had all that many diploma pupils, but *en masse* they played a very significant part in turning British archaeology outward from big Wheeler-digs, the notions of the county societies that most of us grew up with, and most textbooks – such as they were – before the revised *Prehistoric communities of the British Isles*.

Chance as well as Childe had its role, as it does in all lives – perhaps a controlling role in many of these. Willey went to the University of Arizona at Tucson, rather than the University of California at Berkeley, because the high-school counsellor could not find archaeology in the Berkeley handbook. Clark went to work in Africa because there were no jobs in Britain; his mother said, 'It's only for three years,' and he stayed a lifetime.

The collection begins with the oldest contributor, an Australian, and ends with the youngest, an Australian. Gordon Childe's and John Mulvaney's retrospects make a fascinating pair, with their similarities – they both started in Classics – and in their many contrasts. Just after the First World War Childe came from peripheral Australia to Europe, where the great issues of archaeology could be addressed; his life's work was to establish a chronology and an order for European archaeology that would make sense of its disparate material by reference to the surer structures of the most ancient Near East. Just after the Second World War, Mulvaney came to Europe for his training, and then went back to Australia; there, with a growing number of colleagues, he has shown that Australia is at least as central to world prehistory as is Europe. Chronology, thanks to physical-science dating methods, is increasingly an early point of departure, rather than a goal at which research aims in the distance. In Australia there is cave-art as old as the painted caves of Europe; there is human settlement by modern man, *Homo sapiens sapiens*, at much the same period in Australia and in Europe; and there are pecked and polished stone axes – one of the classic artifacts that define the Neolithic of Europe – from Australasian contexts that are 20,000 and more years older than anything like them in Europe. The way of life of native Australians is seen no longer as a failure to invent agriculture and reach to a civilization on the near eastern or central American model, but as a different kind of adaptation to a difficult ecology so effective that it endured in stability for millennia. And archaeology has now taken an active role in relations between native and newcomer in Australia, between Aboriginal and European views of time and of human life: that might have surprised Childe, whose ardent interest in radical Australian politics had not much of this aspect to it; and it might have even pleased him, in showing how alive prehistory is today, and alive in politics too. Thus far has archaeology travelled, and on to that much larger a stage, in space, in time, in contemporary relevance, over the decades that these retrospects span.

Understated in all these lives is the routine workload of heavyweight academics. There are great excavations and field projects, like Sutton Hoo, Jarmo, and Kalambo Falls; academic papers by the many score; standard books written on the archaeology of countries and continents – De Laet on the Low Countries, Piggott on India (in the spare time from military service), Hawkes and Piggott on Europe, Childe several times on Europe and beyond, Willey on both Americas, Clark on Africa, Mulvaney on Australia; the great questions of human history answered as best ingenuity and evidence have permitted – the African origins of man and of modern man, the Near Eastern origin of agriculture, the New and Old World origins of civilization, the origin of the distinctive character of European society; graduate and undergraduate teaching; conferences, congresses, committees. Any number of medals, prizes and honours have not seemed worth mentioning in these self-portraits, and nor have the appalling quantities of artifacts and paperwork that have been dealt with in trenches and tents and studies, year by year. Unmentioned also, though it lies behind everything these pastmasters accomplished, is that characteristic flexibility of mind that great researchers have: to know in detail a mass of empirical data and yet not to be trapped by that knowledge; rather, still to remain curious, to be able to see what new data, of a different character, is required, to know where best to search for it, to discover unexpected insights in old and forgotten places.

A final impression. These seem to me to have been less anxious times intellectually – though these careers span the years of the depression and the Second World War. Archaeologists today use a great range of analytical techniques, and try to integrate the various stories which these tell into a coherent account that satisfies ambitions of history, of anthropology, or of human ecology, as well as those of archaeology itself. The techniques available to these pastmasters were fewer, the quantity of data to be explored was smaller, and the ambitions were less grandiose: most of the task was to establish what material there was and what chronology it made. But were they really quieter, easier times? I cannot know what it was like to be of these pastmasters' generation; I can only see them as the young men they were from the distant viewpoint of today. Like one of the early voyagers delighted by the happiness of the native Americans in Virginia, theirs appears to me a marvellous time to have been an archaeologist, 'the people most gentle, loving and faithful, void of all guile and treason, and such as live after the manner of the Golden Age'. And perhaps – the guile of the *coup d'état* at the Prehistoric Society notwithstanding – it was sometimes like that.

Some of the authors have made slight amendment or addition to the texts of their essays as those were first published in ANTIQUITY.

Two authors have since published full autobiographies, Charles Phillips (1987) and Seton Lloyd (1987); so did Glyn Daniel himself (1986), following his own advice that far more archaeologists ought to write autobiographies. Robert Braidwood and Gordon Willey contributed also to another book of retrospective essays, focussing on individual research projects (Willey 1974), that complements this volume.

References

DANIEL, G.E. 1942. *The three ages.* Cambridge:Cambridge University Press.
1950. *A hundred years of archaeology.* London: Duckworth.
1961. *The idea of prehistory.* London: C.A. Watts.
1967. *The origins and growth of archaeology.* Harmondsworth: Penguin.
1975. *A hundred and fifty years of archaeology.* London: Duckworth.
1986. *Some small harvest: the memoirs of Glyn Daniel.* London: Thames and Hudson.
DANIEL, G.E. and A.C. RENFREW. 1988. *The idea of prehistory.* Second edition. Edinburgh: Edinburgh University Press.
LLOYD, S. 1987. *The Interval.* Faringdon: Lloyd Collon.
PHILLIPS, C.W. 1987. *My life in archaeology.* Gloucester: Alan Sutton.
WILLEY, G.R. (ed.). 1974. *Archaeological researches in retrospect.* Cambridge (MA): Winthrop.

1

V. Gordon Childe

The most original and useful contributions that I may have made to prehistory
are certainly not novel data rescued by brilliant excavation from the soil or by
patient research from dusty museum cases, nor yet well founded chronological
schemes nor freshly defined cultures, but rather interpretative concepts and
methods of explanation. So it is the genesis and development of these to which
this autobiographical note is devoted.

Like Gustav Kossinna I came to prehistory from comparative philology; I
began the study of European archaeology in the hope of finding the cradle of
the Indo-Europeans and of identifying their primitive culture. Reading my
Homer and my Veda with the guidance of Schrader and Jevons, Zimmer and
Wilamowitz-Moellendorf I was thrilled by the discoveries of Evans in
Prehellenic Crete and of Wace and Thompson in Prehistoric Thessaly. Indeed I
hoped to find archaeological links between the latter area and some tract north
of the Balkans whence similar links might lead also to Iran and India. This
search – naturally fruitless – was the theme of my B.Litt. thesis at Oxford and
set me trying to discover what I could in the libraries of Oxford and London
about the already celebrated 'Pre-Mycenaean' pottery of the Ukraine and
hence of its analogues in the Balkans, Transylvania and Central Europe; for at
that time cultures tended to be identified with, not only by, pottery!
My Oxford training was in the Classical tradition to which bronzes, terra-
cottas and pottery (at least if painted) were respectable while stone and bone
tools were banausic. Starting again from this point in 1922 – after a sentimental
excursion into Australian politics – I got the idea of a chronological
framework at least for central Europe based on the sequence of pottery styles
established stratigraphically by Palliardi in southern Moravia on the analogy of
Evans's Nine Minoan Periods and the four Thessalian periods of Wace and
Thompson; it provided the skeleton of four Danubian periods adumbrated in
'When did the Beaker Folk arrive?' (1925a) and the first edition of *The dawn of
European civilisation* (1925b), and expanded later to six in *The Danube in
prehistory* (1929). And these relative ceramic periods were to be given absolute
values by influences from the Aegean, again reflected mainly in
pottery.

At the same time my original quest lured me on northwards to Jutland and
eventually to Scotland – rumours of the Abercromby Chair accelerating my
progress in the latter direction! In so doing I accumulated a volume of facts and

a number of notions that were unfamiliar to English prehistorians; for these came either from the Classical school or were disciples of de Mortillet, wedded to the typology of flints ; the influence of Abercromby and Bryce was virtually confined to Scotland. From Continental literature I absorbed the German concept of a culture, defined but not constituted by distinctive pottery and representing a people. (Abercromby and Petrie had both grasped the notion, but never got it across to the official keepers of British Archaeology.) I came across Schliz's article, 'Die schnurkeramische Kultur', and subsequently its elaborations by Wahle and Reinerth; at that time the significance of the loess for Neolithic settlement and of forest as a barrier thereto were strangely unfamiliar in Britain though Myres had long been preaching a geographical approach. Eventually I stumbled upon Gams and Nordhagen and so introduced the idea of post-glacial climatic changes to English readers who had of course ignored Geikie. So to the British public many of the ideas presented in *The dawn* in 1925 were as novel as the various Continental cultures disconcertingly thrust on to the map of a supposedly uniform Neolithic Europe – indeed on to four superimposed maps.

Still *The dawn* aimed at distilling from archaeological remains a preliterate substitute for the conventional politico-military history with cultures, instead of statesmen, as actors, and migrations in place of battles. The sole unifying theme was the irradiation of European barbarism by Oriental civilization, a traditional dogma in Britain my faith in which had been consolidated as much by a reaction against the doctrines of Kossinna and Hubert Schmidt (which were recognized as slogans of Germanic imperialism more easily after the victory of World War I than they are after the disillusionment of World War II) as by the Diffusionist thesis of Elliot Smith and Perry which at the time was arousing quite sectarian passions among anthropologists and prehistorians. Yet the sea-voyagers who diffused culture to Britain and Denmark in the first chapters in the first *Dawn* (1925) – and they were relegated to a secondary position in the second edition of *The dawn* (1927) – though they do not hail from Egypt, yet wear recognizably the emblems of the Children of the Sun.

On the other hand, the principal channel of diffusion was already the Danube thoroughfare though, inspired by J. L. Myres and behind him Schrader and Jevons, I looked with over-credulous eyes for footprints of Steppe horsemen in the marshes of the Pripet. But the footprints of migrants and missionaries alike remained isolated culture traits torn from their contexts while typological equivalence, even in pottery, was accepted as a chronological horizon of continental dimensions. This was childish, not Childeish. Yet, after all, the Three Ages had been explicitly abandoned as a chronological framework; they did not, like Pleistocene and Holocene, label divisions of sidereal time, as many English and German prehistorians seemed still to think, but chapter headings in local archaeological records. Distinctively Childeish was the endeavour to make these labels informative by adopting food-production as the differentia of the Neolithic. The expression at least is derived

from Elliot Smith, but its selection was an attempt to endow – or re-endow;
for originally the beginning of food-production had been supposed to coincide
with that of stone polishing – a convenient typological division of the
archaeological record with a human, or at least economic, significance. The
next step was taken in *The Bronze Age* (1930).

By that time I had elaborated my chronological scheme in *The Danube in
prehistory* and become Professor at Edinburgh. As such I felt obliged to lecture
on the Old Stone and Iron Ages and to give my students at least a survey of the
beginnings of food-production, the rise of civilization and – on the assumption
I accepted – the bases of the absolute chronology of European prehistory. I had
to apply the culture concept to an age when cultures were accepted as defining
periods of global time (Menghin and Rellini were doing this already, but it was
five years or more before Aurignacian was contrasted with a partly contemporary Perigordian and Gravettian). And I had also to assemble the data for
Mesopotamian and Indian prehistory; for the first scientific excavations in
those provinces were just starting and their results known only from brief
reports in the *Antiquaries Journal*, the *Journal of the Royal Asiatic Society*, or the
Illustrated London News. This necessity was the pretext for *The most ancient East:
the Oriental prelude to European prehistory* (1928). Its compilation contributed to
the writing of *The Bronze Age* and familiarized me with archaeological data
which can be illumined from written texts as well as, or instead of, just
illustrating the latter.

In *The Bronze Age*, each chapter heading in the archaeological record
likewise became informative. If the criterion for inclusion be the *regular* use of
bronze or even copper for the principal cutting tools and weapons, that implies
regular trade and social division of labour. I had not yet read Spengler but I
assumed that metal was the first *indispensable* article of commerce (as contrasted with luxuries which, at a pinch, society could do without and had
admittedly been traded even in the Old Stone Age) and that metal workers
were always professionals, who did not grow their own food. (I had not yet
realized the distinction, so happily expounded by C. S. Coon, between
part-time and full-time specialists.) The former assumption is necessarily *a
priori* and is not contradicted even by the Melanesians' *kula* traffic; the
professionalism of smiths I inferred from ethnographic evidence, but the status
of metal workers in a Sumerian temple-city and an Indian village community
is not too easy to reconcile with this assumption. Still the regularization of –
intertribal or international – trade gives an economic significance to the
chapter-heading even if its sociological implication be not quite so certain.

By this redefinition of the Bronze Age I was finally committed to an
economic interpretation of archaeological data, and I drew the appropriate
corollaries. Obliged by unexpected new discoveries to rewrite *The most ancient
East*, I not only read excavation reports but visited Mesopotamia and India. I
saw how the beginnings of literacy in the three great river valleys coincided
with the erection of the first monumental tombs and temples and the

aggregation of population in regular cities. Indeed at Ur and Erech I saw how rustic villages had grown into vast townships just as English villages had grown into manufacturing towns. Now the latter transfiguration was familiarly attributed to an 'industrial revolution'. Demographically the birth of literacy in the Ancient East also corresponded to a revolution, the Urban Revolution. The upward kink in the population graph, deduced from the monuments, must be due at least partly to the emergence in addition to the farmers of a new order of professionals who did not grow or catch their own food. (The epithet 'urban' may have unduly exaggerated the numerical importance of this order; of course primary producers enormously preponderated throughout the ancient world, and in Egypt it is not proven that professionals were aggregated in cities or towns under the Old Kingdom though Frankfort's arguments to the contrary are quite inconclusive.) But if the Urban Revolution had added an order of professionals to the farmers, the latter were themselves the offspring of a revolution. The adoption of food-production must have been, and, from the available data, had been, followed by a still greater expansion of population than on the foregoing analogy would amply justify the term 'Neolithic Revolution'. So in *New light on the most ancient East* (1934), despite the occasional invocation of undocumented events in the wings, a truly historical pageant of economic development was presented on the stage.

In the same year I visited for the first time the USSR and secured some typical Russian works on prehistory. From Kruglov and Podgayetsky, Krichevskĭ and Tretyakov I learned how neatly even the Marrist perversion of Marxism explained without appeal to undocumented external factors the development of certain prehistoric cultures in the Union. So I at least took over the Marxist terms, actually borrowed from L. H. Morgan, 'savagery', 'barbarism' and 'civilization' and applied them to the archaeological ages or stages separated by my two revolutions: Palaeolithic and Mesolithic can be identified with savagery; all Neolithic is barbarian; the Bronze Age coincides with civilization, but only in the Ancient East.

About the same time I had been asked to write the prehistoric and early Oriental chapter in a projected Marxist History of Science. Though I did not attempt to master hieroglyphic or cuneiform I read a number of articles in *Isis* and some books on ancient science, above all Neugebauer, and that just when pictographic account tablets from Erech and Jemdet Nasr were figuring in excavation reports. Moreover, I adopted the quite respectable view that the lore, successfully applied by craftsmen, has contributed quite as much to modern Natural Science as the rather futile speculations of literate astrologers, hepatoscopes and alchemists. So craft processes and products that archaeologists can observe can stand beside mathematical tablets and surgical papyri as genuine documents in the history of science which no longer begins with the invention of writing. (For this attitude I earned the special commendation of Sarton, its editor, in *Isis*.)

Since 'means of production' figure so conspicuously in the archaeological record, I suppose most prehistorians are inclined to be so far Marxists as to wish to assign them a determining role among the behaviour patterns that have fossilized. They can do so even in the USA without invoking the 5th Amendment, since it was to the 'mode of production' ('means' plus 'relations') that Marx attributed such a dominating influence. By 1936 I had advanced beyond this in so far as I insisted on the need for concentrating the surplus to accomplish the Urban Revolution and so recognized the Hegelian rationality of the political and religious totalitarianism that characterized the ancient Oriental States. (The term 'totalitarian' I adopted later from Heichelheim while its applicability to the Indus civilization was only demonstrated by Wheeler's excavations after 1945.)

With the aid of the foregoing concepts in *Man makes himself* (1936) the archaeological record is interpreted as documenting a directional process wherein men by applications of science steadily increased their control over non-human nature so that their species might multiply and incidentally secrete laws and political institutions, religions and art. That falls short of Marxism in so far as it failed to emphasize that and how science can only be applied, means of production only operated, within an institutional framework that is not itself entirely economic. Still it is genuine history extracted mainly from unwritten documents.

In the new *Dawn* of 1939 I paid lip-service to 'Marxism' in a standardized scheme for the description of cultures: first the food quest, then secondary industries and trade, only thereafter social and religious institutions in so far as they can be inferred or deduced. Though the cultures, thus described, were supposed to stand for societies, they did not develop autonomously; the events remained external as before, movements of peoples, and the unifying theme was still irradiation by Oriental and Aegean civilization so that nothing distinctively European emerged. (Embittered hostility to and fear of the archaeological buttresses of Hitlerism enhanced my reluctance to recognize the positive aspects of all European barbarisms.) I took from Marxism the idea of the economy as the integrating force in society, but I was just as much influenced by Malinowski's functionalism and tried to stick the archaeological bits together by reference to their possible role in a working organism. Still there are passages which, despite extreme compression, hint at truly historical conjunctures of environmental change, internal economic progress and external stimuli. Such historical explanation found more scope later when Iversen's *Landnam*, and Grahame Clark's 'Farmers and forests in Neolithic Europe' (1945) had cleared the wooded barriers to settlement and revealed even prehistoric man as an agent in environmental change.

But this release from geographical determinism came only after *What happened in history* (1942) which was a real contribution to archaeology as a concrete and readable demonstration designed for the bookstall public that history as generally understood can be extracted from archaeological data. I wrote it to convince myself that a Dark Age was not a bottomless cleft in which all traditions of culture were finally engulfed. (I was convinced at the time that European Civilization – Capitalist and Stalinist alike – was irrevocably heading for a Dark Age.) So I wrote with more passion and consequently more pretentions to literary style than in my other works. It presented a smoothly continuous historical narrative based equally on archaeological and textual data. It bears witness to the truth that no chasm, not an unconformity even, divides prehistory from history, and so validates archaeology's claim to provide unwritten historical documents as informative and reliable as written texts. And it gave its testimony before a public far wider than a couple of thousand readers interested in the past; over 300,000 copies have been sold. Still the conceptual framework and explicative mechanisms have advanced but little since *Man makes himself* and discredited fictions like 'Economic Man' still haunt its pages.

It was only later that I reread Soviet prehistorians in the brief interval during which a sympathetic attitude to the USSR was not only useful for getting information on an archaeological province that was crucial for my own special interests, but was also commended by public opinion and the State. In this atmosphere I came to appreciate better the value of even the perversion of Marxism, subsequently branded as Marrism. Its principles I applied in *Scotland before the Scots* (1946). The cautious application of working hypotheses that were frankly stated there did give a picture of Scotland's development which was far more realistic and far more historical than had been achieved with migrationist hypotheses in *The prehistory of Scotland* (1935). Yet I just had to admit migrations and the impact of foreign cultures: the internal development of Scottish society in accordance with 'universal laws' simply could not explain the archaeological data from Scotland; reference to Continental data actually documented the solvent effects of external factors.

My incredibly bad chapter in *The European inheritance* (edited by Barker, Clark and Waucher, 1954) was dominated by an old-fashioned overestimation of the Orient's role, and utterly missed the individuality of prehistoric Europe, while in *Prehistoric migrations in Europe* (1950) a return to my original quest for the Indo-Europeans completely failed to locate the cradle, while its plausible identification of the Indo-Europeans in Europe with Urnfield-folk was refuted within ten years by the Ventris–Chadwick decipherment of the Mycenaean script and the discovery of earlier wheeled vehicles north of the Alps.

In pursuit of an early interest in philosophy, which since 1913 has fascinated me as much and as unprofitably as the Indo-European Urheimat, I was led to a sociological approach to epistemology and the discovery of Durkheim and a deeper appreciation of his master, Marx. Now at last I rid my mind of transcendental laws determining history and mechanical causes, whether economic or environmental, automatically shaping its course. Incidentally I realized that the environment that affected a prehistoric society was not that reconstructed by geologists and palàeobotanists but that known or knowable by the society with its then existing material and conceptual equipment. (Neither arable land nor ores figure in the historical environment of a Palaeolithic horde.) A society's scientific knowledge in turn is limited by its economic and social organization. (It would be misleading to attribute a knowledge of bronze-casting to a society unless an adequate supply of metal was guaranteed, for neither memories fading into myths nor the secrets of a single family deserve the adjective scientific.) This completed my equipment for venturing upon a prehistory of Europe that should be both historical and scientific.

In rewriting *New light on the most ancient East* in 1954 and *The dawn of European civilisation* in 1956, I began to recognize how right Hawkes had been in 1940 when in his *The prehistoric foundations of Europe* he had insisted that, by the Bronze Age, Europe had achieved a kind of culture distinctively its own. I saw not only that this was so but also why. I invoke no agencies external to the observed data, no eternal laws transcending the process as empirically given, but historical conjectures of well-established environmental circumstances and equally well-known patterns of human behaviour legitimately inferred from their archaeological results. The archaeological data are interpreted as the fossilized remnants of behaviour patterns repeatedly illustrated in ethnography and written records. Together with the relevant features of the non-human environment they are presented as instances of more general known processes. So the specific events are explained as individual and perhaps unique con-junctures of known universal factors. Such explanation is scientific as well as historical. It is just so that a geologist would explain the peculiarities of a particular site, where a dam is to be built or a mine shaft sunk, as the resultant of general characters of the minerals exemplified there and the equally general processes of folding, faulting, erosion . . . to which they have been exposed at this precise spot. For natural, like human, history explains particulars by describing them as exemplifying universal laws, and these laws are no longer regarded as imposed upon nature from outside, but as generalized descriptions of what has been observed inside; so 'laws of nature' are not necessary but very highly probable. At the same time, as soon as an event is seen to conform to such a law, it is recognized as rational and logically necessary, or, in a word, understood. Admittedly laws of human behaviour are so far less highly probable than the laws of chemistry and physics that the term law is deceptive. Yet they are or would be of the same kind.

Now I confess that my whole account may prove to be erroneous; my formulae may be inadequate; my interpretations are perhaps ill-founded; my chronological framework – and without such one cannot speak of con-junctures – is frankly shaky. Yet I submit the result [*The prehistory of European society, 1958*] was worth publishing. It is a final answer to those who told us: 'the true prelude to European history was written in Egypt, Mesopotamia and Palestine while the natives of Europe remained illiterate barbarians'. It exemplifies better than any other work I know how what everyone will accept as history could be extracted from archaeological finds; whether the particular extract be accepted or no, it should help to confirm the status of archaeology among historical disciplines. At the same time it illustrates what scientific history ought in my opinion to be like. Incidentally it emphasizes once more the urgency of establishing a reliable chronology; a great deal of the argument depends on a precise date for the beginning of Unětice that is at best very slightly the most probable guess out of perfectly possible guesses ranging over five centuries.

References

CHILDE, V.G. 1925a. When did the Beaker-folk arrive?, *Archaeology* 74: 159–78.

1925b. *The dawn of European civilisation*. London: Kegan Paul, Trench, Trubner.

1927. *The dawn of European civilisation*. 2nd edition. London: Kegan Paul, Trench, Trubner.

1928. *The most ancient East: the Oriental prelude to European prehistory*. London Kegan Paul, Trench, Trubner.

1929. *The Danube in prehistory*. Oxford: Clarendon Press.

1930. *The Bronze Age*. Cambridge: Cambridge University Press.

1934. *New light on the most ancient East: the Oriental prelude to European prehistory*. London: Kegan Paul, Trench, Trubner.

1935. *The prehistory of Scotland*. London: Kegan Paul, Trench, Trubner.

1936. *Man makes himself*. London: Watts.

1939. *The dawn of European civilisation*. 3rd edition. London: Kegan Paul, Trench, Trubner.

1942. *What happened in history*. Harmondsworth: Penguin.

1946. *Scotland before the Scots: being the Rhind lectures for 1944*. London: Methuen.

1950. *Prehistoric migrations in Europe*. London.

1954. Prehistory, in E. Barker, G. Clark & P. Vaucher (eds.), *The European inheritance*: 3–38. Oxford: Clarendon Press.

1957. *The dawn of European civilisation*. 5th edition. London: Kegan Paul, Trench, Trubner.

1958. *The prehistory of European society*. Harmondsworth: Penguin.

CLARK, J.G.D. 1945. Farmers and forests in Neolithic Europe, *Antiquity* 20: 57–71.

HAWKES, C.F.C. 1940. *The prehistoric foundations of Europe*. London: Methuen.

2

Stuart Piggott

It has long been a source of pleasure to us both that the author of another of these Archaeological Retrospects, Charles Phillips, should share with me independent boyhood contacts with the Vale of White Horse, then in Berkshire but since 1974 in Oxfordshire (Phillips 1980). Piggotts had been around in Marcham, Hatford and West Challow since the early seventeenth century, and the families died out or slipped quietly downhill to the status of farm labourers or at best small peasant farmers. My great-grandfather was one of these, in Uffington beneath the famous hill-figure, and my grandfather at the age of 10 was taken up to the last of the traditional festive 'scourings' in 1857 by Thomas Hughes of Kingston Lisle, best known as the author of *Tom Brown's schooldays*, who wrote up the event as *The scouring of the White Horse* (1859). Among the festivities were wrestling and back-sword play: these sports 'were kept up there perhaps as long as in any portion of Middle England' wrote the son of a rector of Childrey, a village a few miles from Uffington, who came there in 1882. 'The Childrey schoolmaster', he goes on, 'when he was a boy at Uffington, could throw all his schoolfellows' (Cornish 1939: 80). The schoolmaster was my grandfather, and my father was born in the village in 1874.

Like his brother and elder sister, he too, took to school-teaching, and when I was born in 1910 he was a master at Churcher's College, Petersfield, near the eastern border of Hampshire. My mother was a Phillips, originally from Brecon, whose parents died when she was a child, and now with only a brother and aunts in Newport and Cardiff. The ties with the Vale of White Horse were strong, and I spent much of my school holidays with my grandparents and aunts, my southern horizons bounded alternately by the West Sussex and Hampshire, and the Berkshire Downs. The school had been founded in the early eighteenth century for the sons of seamen, and was moved out of the town to its outskirts into new buildings of Victorian Gothic gloom in 1881, and became a normal unpretentious establishment of grammar-school type. Here my father continued to teach until his retirement, and here I entered at the age of 8 and left in 1927.

My schooldays were not unhappy (though I was delighted when they were over) but very unedifying. I suppose I was reasonably intelligent, but I was idle, wayward and capricious, exerting myself only on subjects that interested me, and acquiring a detestation of alternative activities such as compulsory games, sports and the OTC. As a result, on taking what was then known as the School

Certificate examination, I failed dismally, not once but twice, mathematics and science bringing me down each time. As a desperate measure I was then entered for the Higher Certificate, with English and French as my main, Latin and History my subsidiary subjects, and passed without difficulty. Unfortunately this did not qualify me for university entrance, dependent on the School Certificate. These unfortunate circumstances, for which I was entirely to blame, do not in retrospect seem to have caused any great distress to me, my parents, or my friends: entrance to university from the school was very rare, and my father himself held no degree. During my school years my education had been enormously enlarged by a remarkable group of men and women centred on the Petersfield Bookshop, a non-academic but highly intelligent company of journalists, writers, painters and craftsmen, from whom I learnt, with much else, something of writing to a set length and a deadline, and of book production from manuscript through proof. School had given me a good grounding in at least English, French, and Latin. Individual masters aroused interests outside the curriculum. One headmaster, a cleric as the foundation demanded, had a deep interest in Biblical textual criticism, and imparted its principles, rather incongruously, to the junior Scripture class, where I, perhaps alone, soon shared his enthusiasm. My senior French master later introduced me to Indo-European philology: one of his friends was Norman Jopson, later Professor of Comparative Philology in Cambridge, who often visited Petersfield, and between them they opened another exciting field of study to me. My History master, himself a landscape water-colourist of some talent, led me towards the graphic arts, and the history of art and architecture. All very useful to me later on, but not so immediately, to a boy of 17 who wanted a job in archaeology.

I must have been 14 years old when I decided on my future career. At least, in that year I laboriously wrote out in a school exercise book *The prehistoric remains at Petersfield*, complete with illustrations and a chronological table (taken from M. & C.H.B. Quennell's *Everyday life in the Old Stone Age*). It is of course an embarrassingly awful juvenile performance, even if the drawings of local surface finds of flint implements, on which it was based, are not too bad. In the previous year I had, greatly daring, sent some of these to Reginald Smith at the British Museum and received a courteous and helpful reply; my father too had encouraged me, giving me books including *The green roads of England* by Hippisley Cox (a London restaurateur and managing director of Romano's who did his fieldwork in a dog-cart and was a friend of Harold Peake, who once drove with him the length of the Berkshire Ridgeway). From then on I seemed to have assumed, without ever considering what immediate steps might be necessary to achieve the end, that I would inevitably be a professional archaeologist. But a fortunate introduction to real archaeology came a couple of years later. I had been looking at earthworks and picking up potsherds on the West Sussex downs, and in doing so stumbled on a Romano-British settlement site. The local vicar put a note about it in the parish magazine which was taken up by a Portsmouth newspaper and so came to the knowledge of O.G.S.

Crawford, then collecting material for the first Ordnance Survey *Map of Roman Britain*. He wrote to me, starting a correspondence which was soon followed by my visiting him at Southampton. From then on he became a friend of the family and my archaeological godfather. I soon became (like Charles Phillips and Christopher Hawkes) one of those he called his 'ferrets', to whom he would send maps on which to chase up and check antiquities, and by September 1927 I had my first contribution to ANTIQUITY published, in its first volume, on an Anglo-Saxon charter entry. From then on, my association with this journal has been continuous and delightful.

As a result of family visits to my grandparents I had come to know the museum at Reading, and its curator, W.A. Smallcombe: we used to stop off at Reading when driving from Petersfield. When I was about to leave school in 1927 he offered me a job in the museum 'at a nominal salary', which proved to be ten shillings (50p) a week. However, I was prepared to take anything that was going, and with my parents' agreement and financial help I was there by the autumn of that year. My duties were varied but only marginally archaeological: my main weekly task was to keep the live wild flower display stocked, replenished and labelled from the specimens brought in by volunteer week-end collectors, which I had to classify by sweating it out with Bentham and Hooker. I had taken an interest in the British flora as a schoolboy, and soon acquired a sound knowledge of elementary taxonomic botany. Archaeological salvation came with Harold Peake, whose house at Boxford was not far from Reading and who had befriended and encouraged Crawford in 1908, and now, twenty years later and prompted by Crawford, did the same for me. I found Peake, at that time President of the Royal Anthropological Institute, enchanting and stimulating, and visited him frequently. He could at times indulge in wild fantasies, but I usually spotted them for what they were, and above all he made me begin to think in terms of problems and internationally about archaeology, from Britain to Europe and beyond to the Near East. With H. J. Fleure of Aberystwyth he was newly embarked on those remarkable little books, *The corridors of time* (1927–36), now nearly forgotten, but in concept far ahead of their time. With John Linton Myres, who followed him in the RAI presidency, he saw the Institute, rather than the Society of Antiquaries, as the centre for a new archaeology facing interdisciplinary problems such as the origins of agriculture and metallurgy, and one sees how Gordon Childe's appointment as the Institute's librarian fitted in with this. It was all very exciting for me, and a welcome escape from the provincialities of Reading Museum.

Within a year, events decisive for my immediate future took place. Simultaneously with my discovery by Crawford, I had entered into correspondence with Dr Eliot Curwen and his son, also a doctor, Eliot Cecil, of Hove in Sussex. They had achieved in Sussex, and independently, the recognition of prehistoric field and enclosure systems on the Downs that Crawford had made in Wessex: both first published their results in 1923, representing new and high standards of archaeological fieldwork. By the 1920s too a further new development was taking place in British prehistory, the recognition of ditched enclosures of neolithic date, with Keiller excavating Windmill Hill from 1925 and Leeds at Abingdon in the next year. Air photography and fieldwork showed that within the hillfort of The Trundle in West Sussex there appeared another such enclosure, and this E.C. Curwen proposed to excavate in 1928, and invited me to join his small team. This was no small honour, as excavations were then not only very rare, but strictly private and personal affairs, and I enthusiastically accepted, and with my father also co-opted, camped and excavated on The Trundle for the two seasons of 1928 and 1930. In London, where, to anticipate, I was working from 1928, I had come to know Alexander Keiller, an amateur archaeologist of considerable private means inherited from the family firm manufacturing sweets and Keiller's Dundee Marmalade. At Crawford's instigation he had been excavating at Windmill Hill since 1925 and, like Wheeler, setting new standards of technical performance in the field. I visited the last season's excavation in 1929, and was impressed by the orderly lay-out of the cuttings. Technique at The Trundle in 1928 was rather primitive, with the turf roughly hacked off the approximate area of excavation, but in 1930 I laid out a formal rectilinear cutting in the Windmill Hill manner. Reginald Smith emerged from the British Museum to visit us – bowler hat, pince-nez glasses, dark suit with rose in button-hole – and sizing up the situation, commented briefly 'Very marmaladish'. For me The Trundle was decisive – I made the friendships with my fellow-diggers Charles Phillips and Grahame Clark that were to lead me into the new archaeology beginning in Cambridge, and the British Neolithic was thenceforward to hold me in thrall for decades to come.

My museum days came to an end in 1928 as the result of an archaeological row. The Royal Commission on Ancient Monuments for Wales and Monmouthshire had been pottering along ineffectively, run only by a Secretary and producing worthless inventories, for years, and the publication of its Pembrokeshire volume elicited a swingeing anonymous review in the first volume of ANTIQUITY over the initials 'O.E.' It was by R.E.M. Wheeler, and ended, 'Indeed with all restraint it may be urged that the Commission as at present constituted is a laughing-stock among professed archaeologists and is financially an unjust charge upon the State' (Wheeler 1927). The Secretary resigned, and W.J. Hemp, from the staff of the Ancient Monuments Inspectorate, was appointed in his place, accredited with one member of staff, a typist. Through Crawford, Hemp offered me this post, and in the winter of 1928 I joined the Commission office in London. I had at least a toe-hold in archaeology.

What, at this time, was the archaeology in which I was hoping to find myself a profession? As a protégé of Crawford and Peake I was unwittingly among the rebels rather than with the Establishment. 'In the mid-twenties of the present century', Wheeler later wrote (1958), 'the conventional centre of antiquarian studies was still dominated by the dilettante and the brass-rubber', and I quickly realized, at first with disappointment and soon with frustration, that this was where Hemp belonged and I did not. He took me to meetings of the Society of

Antiquaries and I was not impressed. Before 1929 the lay-out of the meeting-room was still that of 1874, when the Society moved into Burlington House, with central tables flanked by three rows of benches for Fellows. The seniors sat in the front benches, where they could chat, or look at *The Connoisseur* or *The Burlington Magazine* (or alas, the evening newspapers) before and not infrequently during a lecture they found dull. Slides were projected diagonally across the concourse, making for very awkward visibility for half the audience – but after all, you did not have to look if you were not interested, and many were not. But the library was magnificent, and I could use it as a member of the Royal Archaeological Institute, which I immediately joined. I was heavily blackballed when put up by Keiller for election to the Society in 1936 (largely owing to the unpopularity of my sponsor, I afterwards gathered), but got in next year.

Innovators looked to other institutions as a centre, as had Pitt-Rivers before them, Peake and Myres in particular turning to the Royal Anthropological Institute, and Section H (Anthropology) of the British Association for the Advancement of Science. Here, following Crawford's pioneer mapping of beakers and bronzes, Peake in 1913 set up a committee initiating the British Bronze Implement Catalogue, and I acted as Secretary to this for a time in the late 1920s. A comparable Megalithic Corpus (under Margaret Murray) was set up in 1919, and foundered; his Sumerian Copper Committee of 1924 used Cecil Desch's expertise in spectrographic analysis. These pioneer projects were in part the model for Alexander Keiller's and Charles Drew's stone implement petrological survey by the South-Western Museums Group, with which I worked from its inception in 1936. The pattern of archaeology in the 1920s was otherwise centred on museums (Reginald Smith in the British Museum before the arrival of those *enfants terribles* Kendrick and Hawkes; E. T. Leeds in the Ashmolean; R.E.M. Wheeler and Cyril Fox in the National Museum of Wales and Graham Callander in that of Scotland; H. St George Gray at Taunton and the Cunningtons at Devizes, for instance). From 1920 Crawford was Archaeology Officer in the Ordnance Survey, co-ordinating the work of the great amateurs in the field; the Curwens, Williams-Freeman, Heywood Sumner, Alexander Keiller and others. Academic prehistory hardly existed, with Miles Burkitt and J.M. de Navarro University Lecturers at Cambridge from 1926 and Gordon Childe taking the Abercromby Chair in Edinburgh in the next year. Much rested on the shoulders of those remarkable archaeologists who were amateurs only in that they did not hold professional appointments – scarcely any existed – and Derek Roe has recently paid graceful tribute to those in the palaeolithic field (Roe 1981), though it must be admitted that the wilder shores of lithic love were visited, in for instance some of the earlier papers of the Prehistoric Society of East Anglia.

My early and fortunate friendships with Hawkes and Kendrick in London, and Clark and Phillips in Cambridge, encouraged me and set me on a course of research. I had encountered the British Neolithic on The Trundle and before I left Reading I had the opportunity of publishing a fine pot from the chance find of a burial at Pangbourne. Among us juniors, Clark was grappling with the Mesolithic, Hawkes with the late Bronze and Iron Ages, so the Neolithic and earlier Bronze Age were a field open to me. I had started a corpus of British neolithic pottery after the first season at The Trundle, and continued to work on this. Wheeler had set Thalassa Cruso of the London Museum to do the same, but she withdrew in view of my having nearly finished mine, and he, then editing *The Archaeological Journal*, offered me publication if I produced a finished paper to a rather short deadline. This I did, encouraged by Gordon Childe, who wrote a companion study on the European background, so that the pair of papers on British neolithic pottery appeared together in 1931. In the meantime I was learning much from my association with the interdisciplinary studies then beginning in Cambridge between archaeology and the natural sciences, culminating in the formation of the Fenland Research Committee in 1932, of which I was made a member. I was not enjoying my work on the Welsh Ancient Monuments Commission, where I was now a junior investigator. I had taken an instant dislike to the landscape of North Wales – it was Mountain Gloom rather than Mountain Glory for me – and I have never liked the Highland Zone, though I had to be tactful about it when in Scotland. I found too that I was not temperamentally a field worker, and realised that, with no academic qualifications, my only hope of recognition would be through publications of adequate standards.

Chance intervened in 1933. I now knew Alexander Keiller well; his Windmill Hill material was available to students in his private museum in London, and he and others were realizing the need of a modern excavation of an 'unchambered' long barrow in Wessex. Crawford found financial backing, and Charles Drew, Curator of the Dorchester County Museum, was asked with me to dig one of the two long barrows on Thickthorn Down in Dorset. Keiller (also a friend of Drew) volunteered to join us and do the survey, a task he loved. I took my total annual leave of a month from the Commission, but as always, the work took longer than we had anticipated. Hemp visited the dig and I pleaded for a special extension of leave, which was refused out of hand, and he left. Keiller immediately asked me the verdict. He was furious, and said so, and then after a short silence offered me employment in a private capacity and a higher salary with him, to help with publication and further excavation. It was a difficult decision to make, and I consulted Crawford, who to my delight wrote 'I think you had certainly better accept Keiller's offer . . . one has to take risks now & then! . . . Keiller is erratic & at times infuriating, but he is a genuine enthusiast, & really loves archaeology . . . I have a feeling that you & K *will* work well together . . . K is open to ideas.' This entirely confirmed my own inclinations, and with no regret I left the Civil Service, where for five years I had endured Hemp's genteel antiquarianism in a deadening atmosphere of dim mediocrity, saved however by forming a friendship with Cyril Fox, one of the Commissioners, which enlivened and inspired me until his death in 1967. My architectural colleague on the

Commission, Leonard Monroe, sympathetic, humorous and a superb draughtsman, taught me much at the drawing-board and was a delightful colleague.

My next five years, as private archaeologist to the wealthy and eccentric Alexander Keiller, took me into an unfamiliar and sometimes extraordinary world. Crawford's estimate of him as 'erratic and at times infuriating' was true enough, but on the other hand he could be the most entertaining companion, with an alert intelligence, a remarkably wide range of knowledge, and financially able to act with complete independence of societies and institutions if he felt the need. I worked with him on the Avebury excavations from 1934, when he moved his establishment, with library and museum, to Avebury Manor. He certainly did not lack startling ideas, such as planning, with Hugo Eckener, its designer, to use the Graf Zeppelin dirigible for a grandiose archaeological air survey. 'It's so slow and so large,' he said to me, 'you could plot sites straight on to six-inch maps – and it's even got a *bar!*' He was the initiator of the stone implement petrological survey I have already mentioned and keenly interested in such interdisciplinary approaches to archaeology. At this time too the take-over of the Prehistoric Society of East Anglia was being engineered, as Charles Phillips has recalled in these pages. It was a deliberate infiltration of the Young Turks, headed by Grahame Clark – on the committee by 1932, editor by 1933, with W.F. Grimes and J. F. S. Stone newly on the committee, with Hawkes and myself soon to follow. We timed a critical meeting in Norwich in February 1935 so as to render it inconvenient for the opponents to dropping 'of East Anglia' from the Society's title to attend, and I drove from Avebury (rather fast, in Keiller's MG Midget) to cast my vote in favour. We had great good fortune with our first paper for the new *Proceedings of the Prehistoric Society* in 1935, on the Plumpton Plain (Sussex) Bronze Age settlements, by Curwen, Holleyman and Hawkes, as it had been turned down by the Society of Antiquaries as too technical. In 1935 I entered for the Diploma of the Institute of Archaeology of London University, founded through the efforts of Rik and Tessa Wheeler the year before, so that I was one of the first of its students. Wheeler did most of the lecturing, and I am one of the few who have heard him lecture on the lower Palaeolithic. After I had attended a couple of times he begged me not to appear again, but 'mug it up for yourself'. With the help of friends I did so, and obtained the Diploma in 1936.

As the Avebury excavations continued, and became to my mind more megalithic landscape gardening than research archaeology, I became increasingly bored and in need of some more congenial intellectual activity. The great prehistoric collections of Devizes Museum were near at hand, and I had become intrigued by the earlier bronze age grave-groups from Cunnington's and Hoare's excavations: perhaps a modest little paper on those containing the little knobbed pots called 'grape cups', less than a dozen in all, might be interesting to do? The result was rather more than that, and my paper on the

Early Bronze Age of Wessex of 1938, whatever its initial merits or defects, raised problems still topics of controversy today. While with Keiller I also did a rescue excavation of a long barrow at Holdenhurst near Bournemouth myself, and with him the remnants of another near Farnham in Surrey, and was becoming increasingly interested in these monuments. I was now married, and with my wife excavated at Ram's Hill on the Berkshire Downs a bronze age enclosure which Richard Bradley, following our trial trenches on an extended scale, was recently to show was a site of unique importance. We also did a rescue excavation on barrows on Crichel Down in Dorset, one of which contained a Beaker burial with a remarkable trepanned skull. My most valuable experience however was excavating at Little Woodbury in 1938–9 with Gerhard Bersu, from whom I learnt much. And under the threat of inevitable war, we were invited by Charles Phillips to work with him at Sutton Hoo in 1939, in the circumstances he has described. My memories of this extraordinary occasion are those of mixed feelings of inevitable excitement at the splendour of the finds, and a sense of frightened inadequacy in making the drawings to record the burial deposit, in which every feature was unique and startling, and where no precedent existed to guide us. We had to keep the sensational nature of our finds secret, carrying back the most valuable pieces to the pub in Woodbridge where we stayed, and locking them in a suitcase to await Kendrick's next visit to transfer them to the British Museum. Coming home one evening and making straight for the bar, I was met with the inevitable hearty greeting, 'How are the diggings, ole chap? Found any gold?' 'Yes, weighed down with it', I answered, covertly grasping in my pocket the box containing the great belt-buckle, over 400 grammes (16 ounces) of solid metal. 'Ha! Ha! Jolly good. Have a drink?' I accepted, knowing the truth would not be believed.

By the late 1930s British archaeology was taking on a shape still recognizable today. It had been the golden age of fieldwork on the Wessex and Sussex Downs, still substantially the close-cropped grasslands of sheep walks, and Ashbee (1972) has recently sketched this aspect of the archaeology of the period. The general pattern of our thinking over the whole field is perhaps best explicit in the Kendrick and Hawkes *Archaeology in England and Wales 1914–31* (1932), which opens 'We begin with "eoliths", and not very happily', and covers the field to 'that supreme English masterpiece, the Madonna of York Minster.' There were not many of us, and we had a lot to deal with, but we were doing our best to see our archaeology as a whole. We may appear to some today to have been sunk deep in the error of diffusionism and the heresies of invasion hypotheses. But such models of the past had one very valuable effect on our attitudes, in that we saw our insular archaeology as a part, if perhaps too derivative a part, of that of continental Europe and the Old World at large, and knowledge of the one was dependent on knowledge of the other. I saw that if I was to try to understand prehistoric Britain I must somehow make myself a European prehistorian as far and as soon as circumstances permitted, even if in 1939 they were hardly propitious. In that year, fired with enthusiasm by Grahame Clark's *Mesolithic settlement of Northern Europe* of 1936, I planned a book on the neolithic cultures of the British Isles combining all categories of evidence and what was known of the ecological background. When it was eventually published in 1954 I quoted in the preface from Sterne's *Tristram Shandy* on an author knowing 'no more than his heels what lets and confounded hinderances he is to meet with on his way'. Like everyone I met with these between 1939 and 1945.

On the outbreak of war I was living at Rockbourne near Salisbury, and joined the ranks of a locally formed light anti-aircraft battery stationed at Longford Castle under the command of Lord Radnor. When it was discovered that I could not only read and write, but type, I was made a clerk in the Battery Office, where, under the aegis of an agreeably eccentric and understanding Territorial Army sergeant-major, I found, once my not very demanding official duties of the day were duly performed, that I could continue to some extent to be an archaeologist. I wrote up the Crichel Down excavation report, and did a paper on the trepanned skull with its European counterparts. I also made an amateur foray into the sources of Geoffrey of Monmouth's twelfth-century *Historia Regum Britanniae*, later published in ANTIQUITY, so that the books on my office desk were not only *The King's Regulations* and the *Manual of Military Law*, but others, including on one occasion the massive volume of the *Monumenta Germaniae Historica* containing Mommsen's edition of Gildas and Nennius. A totally unexpected visit from the area Brigadier was announced – his foot was on the stair, concealment impossible – and I could do nothing but spring smartly to attention by the incriminating book, its title abbreviated to MON. GERM. HIST. XIII. The Brigadier gave it a fierce, inaccurate glance. 'Modern German history, eh! Glad you keep up with current affairs.' 'Yessir. Thank you sir.' It had been a near thing. Drinks all round from the Sergeant-Major in the canteen.

In 1941, through the good offices of Glyn Daniel, I found myself, with him and many other archaeologists, in the Central Air Photographic Interpretation Unit at Medmenham near Marlow; given (with Terence Powell) a direct commission, and to my horror, posted with two junior officers to start up an air photographic interpretation unit for the Far Eastern war in Singapore, in 1942. Fortunately for us, Singapore fell to the Japanese in February, by which time a delightfully leisurely air journey had brought us to Cairo. After some weeks of repeated but unanswered signals to the War Office I found myself allotted to India instead. I had spent my time quite profitably in Cairo, though the Museum of Antiquities was closed, but I met Archibald Cresswell, and learnt the rudiments of Islamic architectural history among the Cairene mosques. A similar delay in Karachi enabled me to visit Mohenjo-daro, but by April 1942 I was working with Glyn Daniel and Terence Powell in the Central Photographic Interpretation Section in Delhi, becoming a General Staff Officer in command of military air photography for South East Asia. By now

I had adjusted to my really very favourable war conditions during what I regarded (in Osbert Sitwell's phrase) as The Great Interruption, and had learnt how to continue being an archaeologist in the interstices of official duties, on my days off and in the evenings. Indian archaeology, of which, of course, I knew hardly more than was contained in Childe's *New light on the most ancient East* (1934), was too great a temptation to resist. Within a month in Delhi I found the Central Asian Museum housing all Aurel Stein's collections, and an excellent library, and had obtained permission to work on the reserve material, having written to Stein and received his blessing and encouragement. Within a year I was able to publish results in ANTIQUITY and, after Wheeler's arrival as Director General of Archaeology in April 1944, latterly in the journal he founded, *Ancient India*. When I returned to England in 1945 I had the material for a book, which was to be the *Prehistoric India* of 1950. The Oxford University Press asked me to write a little companion volume to Seton Lloyd's *Ruined cities of Iraq*, which I did, as *Some ancient cities of India* (1945).

Wheeler kept me closely in touch with his activities. He told me of his plans to follow up the finds of Roman coins in south India, and after his first visit, rang me up in Delhi to say he had something to show me. I went round to his office, where he sat with a tigerish grin on his face and a little pile of red sherds on the desk in front of him, which I saw and recognized as I came in the door, saying, 'Good heavens, Rik, you've found it. That's first-century Arretine.' 'Hooray! Of course it is. That's why I got you round – there are only two people in India who'd know what that was, and that's you and me.' Wheeler hyperbole of course, but the discovery in India of a Roman trading-post with imported Italian pottery was a real moment of drama he loved to remember, insisting on my re-enacting the scene with him in public nearly 40 years later, at the Southampton Hill-Fort Conference in his honour in 1971.

I found it fascinating to enter the totally new field of oriental archaeology, and despite the war help came from Childe, from Seton Lloyd in Baghdad and Henri Frankfort in Chicago. The new intellectual stimulus offset the dreariness of my military duties, which however I seem to have performed efficiently enough (they kept on promoting me) and which ensured my access to the source material in Delhi. Wheeler wanted to get me transferred from the army on to his staff, but I declined. I could not bear the thought of working with him, and I wanted to get back to England and find a job as soon as it became possible. In the event the Director of Military Intelligence in India was unwilling to lose me from his staff and vetoed the scheme. By May 1945 I had been sent back to England on indefinite leave pending release, with a remarkable episode behind me, and while I might be a Lieut-Colonel (which I regarded as a joke) I had neither a job nor any academic qualifications for one.

During the war my wife had come to know members of the Lane Poole family, including Austin, President of St John's College, Oxford, who suggested and facilitated my entry for a B.Litt. (with minimum period of residence) in the Modern History Faculty, with a thesis on William Stukeley, the eighteenth-century antiquary, and as a result I became a member of St John's as a research student in the autumn of 1945. I had already done some work on Keiller's Stukeley MSS, and used to hitch-hike to Oxford on my days off from the Medmenham air photo unit early in the war, to work on the Bodleian sources. Soon after I returned to England I ran into Gordon Childe at a London meeting, our first encounter since before the war. He asked me what I was doing, and I told him, 'Splendid! I want you to succeed me in Edinburgh. Good-bye!' He walked away leaving me incredulous and speechless. I returned to Oxford and Stukeley, dismissing the incident as fantasy, but later, in the winter, he wrote to say that the Edinburgh chair would not be advertised on his taking up the Directorship of the London Institute of Archaeology, and that he had submitted my name, together with those of Grahame Clark and others, with appropriate referees, as possible candidates. In the early summer of 1946, before I had submitted my thesis, I received a letter from the Secretary of the University of Edinburgh offering me the Abercromby Chair of Archaeology.

Of course, like everyone else, I expected Grahame Clark to be appointed. The University's decision to back such an outsider as me was extraordinary and in a way embarrassing, and it was clear that I would have to do everything I could to justify its choice. Two obvious tasks lay ahead. The first, within the University, was to build on the tradition of my predecessor by developing the Department of Archaeology into a centre of teaching and research on an international European basis. Constructing and teaching, single-handed, an appropriate course presented problems. Childe had devised an unworkable BSc, which I quickly converted into an Honours MA, to be taught over the two winter terms, as the chair was in fact only part-time, the summer free for travel and research. Childe explained to me that he began his course with the Scottish Iron Age (so that he could take students to see local hillforts) and proceeded to the palaeolithic, aiming then to cover British and European prehistory to the point where he began, but 'I never get there', he added wistfully, 'I never get there.' While I did not propose to adopt this eccentric scheme, I had no precedent to follow, having, of course, had no formal teaching in archaeology. I therefore decided to teach my students European prehistory as I would like to have been taught it myself, a process perhaps acceptable, but necessitating filling the alarming gaps in my own knowledge before instructing others even more ignorant. I gave five statutory lectures a week for two eight-week terms in my first academic year, writing notes daily until tea-time and delivering these as a lecture at the appointed hour of 5.0. In the meantime there were books to write or complete: the Oxford University Press had invited me to write a British prehistory for their Home University Library, and this appeared in 1949, and next year they published my William Stukeley, based on my B.Litt. thesis, and also in 1950 *Prehistoric India*, commissioned by Max Mallowan for the then new Pelican Archaeologies, appeared. Although *The neolithic cultures of the British Isles* was not published until 1954, it was finished by 1951. By now the new honours school of archaeology was beginning to attract the sort of students I had hoped for, and I had achieved a member of staff in the person of Richard Atkinson. The introduction of a dissertation as a part of the final honours examination enabled me to introduce students to research, and post-graduate research students followed. In this the whole-hearted cooperation of Robert Stevenson of the National Museum of Antiquities enabled us to work with freedom and encouragement on the collections in his care. As a result, a number of useful publications were produced, covering a wide range of Scottish archaeology. Side by side with these local studies I soon found students who could share my enthusiasm for working in the wider European field. In 1953 I was elected a Fellow of the British Academy, and of the Deutsches Archäologisches Institut.

My second task lay in excavation, partly a departmental need in that my students would need practical training. I was unprepared for the degree to which the active development of field archaeology in England up to the outbreak of war had been ignored in Scotland, where techniques of excavation, recording and publication were lamentably out-of-date. I was alarmed, but not despondent. Reform in fieldwork after the war came with the reorganization of the Scottish Ancient Monuments Commission: I was appointed a Commissioner and with Ian Richmond, and Kenneth Steer newly on the staff, was able to take part in an invigorating programme of modernization and consequent new discovery, with the active encouragement of the Secretary, Angus Graham. For excavation, my wife and I divided our forces, so that she embarked on a noteworthy programme of iron age excavations in the Borders in co-operation with the Commission, while I turned to the earlier monuments where my current interests lay. By sheer good luck my first Scottish site was the superb henge monument with secondary two-period barrow on Cairnpapple Hill, less than 20 miles from Edinburgh. Henge monuments had not then been heard of among Scottish archaeologists, and the unique nature of the site was unrecognized until I visited it within a few weeks of coming to Edinburgh. This I was able to excavate completely for the Ancient Monuments Department of the then Ministry of Works. Its publication, together with my wife's excavation of the multi-period hillfort of Hownham Rings in Roxburghshire, in the same volume of the *Proceedings of the Society of Antiquaries of Scotland* in 1950, with plans and sections in the modified 'Wheeler style' of draughtsmanship we had both adopted, was a manifesto of what current techniques could do in the north as well as the south of Britain. The principle established, a programme could be pursued, and I excavated with my students chambered tombs in Galloway and the Clava region, a stone circle in Perthshire, and finally, as an unexpected rescue operation, a turf-built long barrow with mortuary enclosure at Dalladies near Montrose. And with Richard Atkinson, there were the excavations at Stonehenge, and the long barrows of West Kennet and Wayland's Smithy.

In the meantime I was teaching myself European prehistory. I needed not only to read the literature, but to see material and landscape at first hand, and to meet my continental colleagues. A pleasant introduction to many of them came in 1949 with the organization of a week's Wessex Field School for young continental archaeologists for the British Council at Salisbury. The British Neolithic had led me first to France and Iberia, and I then moved to Scandinavia, the Netherlands, Germany and Central Europe, while the project sponsored by the Inter-University Council for Higher Education Overseas, for a survey of the monuments of prehistoric Malta under the direction of John Ward-Perkins and myself, took me to the Mediterranean and resulted in John Evans's classic corpus of 1971, as well as a joint Edinburgh–Cambridge student field class in the Lipari Islands in 1959. In 1960, with Nancy Sandars and the late John Cowen and Terence Powell, I made an adventurous study-tour of Hungary, Romania and Bulgaria; in 1966 Nancy, the Cowens and I had an equally exciting visit to the Caucasus, and two years later I made further visits to Poland, Moscow, Leningrad and Kiev with my former students Ruth Tringham and Bruce Chatwin. By the 1960s I felt I was getting a grasp of things, and my *Ancient Europe* (1965) fairly represents my teaching at Edinburgh at the time, and as the George Grant MacCurdy Lecturer in Harvard for a semester in 1961. The initial East European contacts have led to fruitful co-operation between these countries and younger British archaeologists, and in 1971 I went to Moscow on behalf of the British Academy to negotiate the first formal exchanges of visiting archaeologists with the USSR. At home my long-standing interest in La Tène craftsmanship, much stimulated by Fox in the immediately post war years, led to the organization with the British Council of an international exhibition of Early Celtic Art as part of the Edinburgh Festival of 1970, and later in the Hayward Gallery. A study of *The Druids* (1968) allowed me to link Celtic archaeology to the history of antiquarianism, which has for so long intrigued me. In 1977 I retired from the Abercromby Chair, and thanks to the good fortune of being bequeathed the house long lived in by my paternal aunts, have been able to return to the familiar countryside of the Vale of White Horse.

'Surely my starres impelled me to be an Antiquary, I have the strangest luck at it, that things drop into my mouth,' wrote John Aubrey to Anthony Wood (Hunter 1975: 74). I, too, have had the good luck to pursue archaeology over a fascinating period of its development. A country upbringing when agriculture was virtually unmechanized gave me a sympathetic understanding of pre-industrial technology: when George Sturt was writing his *Wheelwright's shop* of 1923 in Farnham, I, as a small boy, was watching traditional wagon-building as he described it in a village only 5 miles away. Archaeology for me has always been tangible and visible, and not an exercise in academic theory, and I have pursued it with unashamed enjoyment for the intellectual pleasure it has given me. Robert Braidwood in his Retrospect in these pages has perceptive comment on the 'new archaeology', which has for him, as it has for me, 'much of the eager, very earnest, quite humorless fervour of a new religious movement' (Braidwood 1981). Faced with this sort of thing there comes to my mind Max Beerbohm's drawing of Matthew Arnold, smiling quizzically at a very solemn small girl, his niece, later to be the formidable Mrs Humphry Ward. She asks him: 'Why, Uncle Matthew, oh why, will you not be always wholly serious?' *Touché*.

References

ASHBEE, P. 1972. Field archaeology: its origins and development, in P. J. Fowler (ed.), *Archaeology in the landscape* : 38–74. London: John Baker.

BRAIDWOOD, R.J. 1981. Archaeological retrospect 2, *Antiquity* 55: 19–26 [chapter 6 of this volume]

CORNISH, J.G. 1939. *Reminiscences of country life*. London: Country Life.

HUNTER, M. 1975. *John Aubrey and the world of learning*. London: Duckworth.

KENDRICK, T. D. and C.F.C. HAWKES. 1932. *Archaeology in England and Wales, 1914–31*. London: Methuen.

PHILLIPS, C.W. 1980. Archaeological retrospect 1, *Antiquity* 54: 110–17 [chapter 4 of this volume]

ROE, D. 1981. Amateurs and archaeologists: some early contributions to British palaeolithic studies, in J. D. Evans *et al.* (ed.), *Antiquity and man*: 214–20. London: Thames & Hudson.

WHEELER, R.E.M. 1927. Review by 'O.E.' of RCAM Wales, *Pembrokeshire inventory*, *Antiquity* 1: 245–7.

1958. Crawford and ANTIQUITY, *Antiquity* 32: 3–4.

3

Charles Phillips

Looking back over a concern with archaeology which has lasted for half a century I am grateful to have been present through a crucial period in its development.

There were few advantages in my earliest days. On my father's side I come from a line of farmers, land appraisers, bailiffs and the like which I can trace back in some detail for nearly three hundred years, living for the most part in Northwest Essex; on my mother's side my ancestors were North Wessex peasants and inn-keepers, with a probable admixture of Welsh cattle-drover blood at the end of the eighteenth century. Wantage and Abingdon were their local centres. All with the exception of one or two backsliders were strict Evangelicals, often wavering on the verge of Dissent, and none ever aspired to any higher standard of education than one who entered the Congregational ministry in 1827. Any known interest in learning or antiquity showed itself more among the Wessex peasants than the clod-hoppers of Essex. My maternal grandfather, who was a native of the Vale of White Horse, was personally known to me and was interested in the many relics of the past observable about him, an intelligent man but with little formal instruction.

I made a bad start by becoming an orphan at the age of five but from the beginning was interested in history and also endowed with a strong topographic sense derived from my father, which always led me to thorough exploration of my surroundings and a love of maps. A favourite amusement in my childhood was to draw elaborate maps of imaginary places. My formal education mainly took place at the Royal Masonic School, which in my time was just beginning to send a few pupils to the University if they could obtain awards.

My home life in the holidays from 1910 to 1917 was spent at Arundel in Sussex, where we lived in the shadow of the historic castle, but I doubt if I ever heard the word archaeology uttered during the whole of my schooldays. In 1917 and 1918 short periods at Plymouth and Great Yarmouth combined with the possession of a bicycle and one or two Ordnance Survey 1-inch maps began to fire my interest in the antiquities shown on them; I wondered at the many then enigmatic sites on Dartmoor and my first visit to the Roman coastal fort at Burgh Castle near Great Yarmouth marked a definite point of departure towards field archaeology.

I was fortunate in winning a History Exhibition to Selwyn College, Cambridge in 1919 and this set me on my way, but only on a long and oblique

progress towards what seemed an unattainable end. At that time the Archaeological and Anthropological Tripos was a new thing and largely directed to
preparing for entry to the Colonial Service. But any idea of abandoning the
Historical Tripos for this other study was frowned on by my tutor and for three
years my official studies were devoted to getting a good degree in History. My
ideas about my future were still vague and my first attempts to worm myself
into the group of habitués of the Downing Street Museum were not much
encouraged there.

Although it was soon my fixed determination to get into archaeology I have
never had any reason to regret the time spent on the study of history. Today's
growth of specialization in every aspect of archaeological work must often limit
perspective and prevent students from having a clear view of why they are
working in their particular niche. If some knowledge of history was always a
prerequisite before a career in archaeology it would be no bad thing.

I early resolved to spend all my spare time in a thorough exploration of the
country for 25 miles or more round Cambridge, to examine all the ancient
features shown on the Ordnance Survey maps, and travelled hundreds of miles
on my bicycle in the process. It was a pity that I did not know that Cyril Fox was
at Cambridge at that time bringing to completion his classic *Archaeology of the
Cambridge region* which was to be published in 1924. But I was an isolated figure
and did not make his acquaintance until years later.

When I had taken my degree a chance invitation to give some extra tuition to
push a backward pupil through his University examinations, accompanied by
the unexpected inheritance of a little money, gave me a new resolve. It was
obvious in 1925 that gainful employment in archaeology was very limited. I did
not want to work in a museum and an amateur must have financial
independence if he is to have any freedom of action. I therefore set up as a history
coach, and for the next ten years dealt with many pupils sent me by most of the
Colleges and also gave lecture courses for the Ordinary Degree. It was unheroic.
I had to work very hard but it was possible to save money and the lengthy
vacations could be employed in gaining experience in field archaeology.

But aside from my cycling explorations I did not get useful experience at
Cambridge and this came to me in the west of England.

My mother had now established herself at Bristol and in this way I met the
Bristol University Spelaeological Society. The prime purpose of this group was
cave exploration in the Mendips and elsewhere and its interests were wide.
There were important cave excavations in the Mendips and Wye Valley in
which I took part, and one section of the Society concentrated more on general
field reconnaissance and the excavation of surface features. The man who
introduced me to this group was John Davies, an invalid from the 1914–18 war,
who was a born field archaeologist and whose early death in 1930 was a great
loss as a mentor and friend.

The area of work was important and varied but it was the composition of the
Society which was particularly valuable. Most of the members were either

medical students or concerned with other scientific studies and they brought their training to bear on the work. Standards were high and everything would stand professional scrutiny, a valuable example to a beginner. While I was actively associated with the Society between 1925 and 1930 it contained at least six members, and possibly more, who were later to occupy professorial chairs, and today the Society continues to flourish.

It was in this period of the later twenties that I also made three other fortunate contacts which more than remedied my failure to get much out of the Cambridge situation.

The first was my meeting with O.G.S. Crawford when he visited the Bristol group in 1926. I had now got motor traction and one day was driving my Morgan three-wheeler up Burrington Combe in the Mendips. Near the bottom by Aveline's Hole I saw a man ahead of me pushing a heavily-laden bicycle. It was Crawford rigged for field work. I stopped and offered him a lift up the long hill. He accepted and at the top we drew up and had a long conversation. Here was real inspiration. He had now been Archaeology Officer at the Ordnance Survey since 1920 and we found we had much in common. This was the crucial moment in my career. Before we parted our future association was assured. We now corresponded frequently about field work and it was not long before he told me about the unrevised and neglected state of archaeology in Lincolnshire, where he suspected there to be much of importance, particularly on the Wolds. He suggested that I should examine this region, of which more later.

The second piece of good fortune was my introduction through Crawford to two doctors, the Curwens of Brighton, father and son, who had begun a systematic examination of the South Downs and sea plain in Sussex, with skilful excavation of the local hillforts and other prehistoric settlements. The younger Curwen was a pioneer in showing the true nature of the many signs of ancient agriculture still plentiful at this time. With him I took part in two excavations at the two-phase Trundle hillfort in 1929 and 1930, which gave me experience of expert work on the chalk and brought me into contact with the young Stuart Piggott whose star was soon to be in the ascendant.

The third fortunate meeting was at Cambridge with Grahame Clark, then a PhD candidate working at Peterhouse, and we were drawn together by a common dislike of the local archaeological situation, where the haphazard activities of the Downing Street Museum group of amateurs and the ineffective direction of the Department under Professor Minns were not following up with sufficient vigour the impetus given to local studies by the publication of Cyril Fox's book. Much of their work was done under the aegis of the Cambridge Antiquarian Society, but it was unsystematic and with the rashness of youth we were ready to challenge it.

Meanwhile from 1927 to 1931 I made expeditions into every part of Lincolnshire and examined the whole of this large county. I had to learn as I went along and I received the invaluable help of Mrs E.H. Rudkin, another worker with a great practical knowledge of the region: I also benefited from the knowledge of Mr Harold Dudley, the curator of the new museum at Scunthorpe, and, in the south of the county, Mr Harry Preston of Grantham had much to impart. As a result 14 long barrows were identified on the Wolds and a great amount of field archaeology ranging from the Mesolithic to the Middle Ages was noted and located on 6-inch maps supplied by Crawford. The combined result was published in two long articles in the *Archaeological Journal* (vols. 91 and 92, 106–87). These provided a basis for the great revival in Lincolnshire studies which has since taken place, mainly under the aegis of Mr Tom Baker and his assistants at the Lincoln County Museum.

During the late twenties Crawford's continuing demonstration of the use of air-photography as an aid to reconnaissance had drawn attention to an unexpected and extensive Romano-British occupation of much of the Fenland, which will be dealt with below. During this time I had become an unofficial helper in his work at the Ordnance Survey in the compilation of period maps and the long overdue revision of specific areas for new editions of maps in the 1-inch series. In this cause I also covered much of the Midlands and Southern Pennine area for the survey of megaliths, and did field work with Clark in connexion with a book he was writing on the mesolithic period in Britain. We spent a lot of time on the multi-period site at West Keal in the South Wolds of Lincolnshire.

My financial position having improved, I could now get some experience in the Highland Zone by carrying out excavations on megalithic and Dark Age sites in Anglesey in 1931–2, but I much wanted to throw more light on the relationship of the Lincolnshire long barrows to those in other regions. In 1933 and 1934 the complete excavation of a good example, Giants' Hills I at Skendleby in the South Wolds, was carried out with the help of Mr A.H.A. Hogg and others. This proved to be an important work and pointed the way to new ideas about the character of long barrows in general, which have developed since 1945.

But the early thirties saw other wider developments. The technique of pollen analysis had now reached Cambridge from Scandinavia and was being practised there under Sir Albert Seward and Harry Godwin. The Fenland area was a standing challenge for closer examination by scientists for a variety of reasons and, in particular, for archaeologists because of the sudden and unexplained Romano-British occupation of much of it for most of the first four centuries of the Christian era, after which it was largely abandoned once more. The independent work of Major Gordon Fowler of Ely had also recently shown how the earlier natural drainage regime of the Fens could be recognized in the ancient system of waterways revealed as wandering banks of raised silt left behind by the wastage of the peat which had grown up over them in post-Roman times.

To meet this challenge a pioneer co-operative group belonging to a variety of disciplines, known as the Fenland Research Committee, was set up under the leadership of Sir Albert Seward in 1932. This was to tackle the problems of the successive phases of the Fenland in post-Glacial times. I was Hon. Treasurer with a special interest in Romano-British affairs and Clark was prominent as an excavator and in particular as director of the Peacock's Farm excavation at Shippea Hill, which gave a view of the sequence of events in the south east part of the Fenland from mesolithic times to the present day. This was only one of a number of excavations and sondages directed to the same end. Palaeo-botanists, geologists, archaeologists and many other specialists concentrated their efforts to solve the problems presented by this highly individual area. At this time I visited Holland at the invitation of Professor van Giffen to study the *terpen* in the Groningen area, ancient settlement sites in an area having much in common with our Fenland.

Work with the Committee was good experience and lasted for seven years until the group was disbanded by the 1939 war; it ran parallel with another development in a more national field. In the early thirties there was only one body devoted entirely to prehistoric studies in Britain, the Prehistoric Society of East Anglia, whose membership was originally local to that region but was now expanding outside it. With little exception its work was directed to the study of palaeolithic man and liable to be the subject of controversy. Several of the members, including Grahame Clark, Christopher Hawkes and myself, believed that the Society should be enlarged to cover the whole country and all prehistoric archaeology, while the current President, Professor Gordon Childe, was less happy with the idea. A movement was begun and although there was some degree of resistance a referendum of the whole membership showed that there was overwhelming support for the change. So the Prehistoric Society came into being in 1935. I was Honorary Secretary from 1935 to 1946 and Clark was to be the editor of its increasingly important Proceedings for many years. A rapid increase in the membership and the continuing success of the Society have shown that the change was timely.

It was the intention of the Society to promote the complete excavation of a site of manageable size which, if chosen well, might yield a maximum dividend of new knowledge. A complete iron age farmstead showing good detail on an air-photograph had long been noted by Crawford at Little Woodbury, south of Salisbury, and to direct the full examination of this the distinguished German archaeologist Gerhard Bersu was brought in. In 1938 there were more than scientific motives behind bringing him from Germany, and over the period 1938 to 1945 in various places and contexts in Britain he had a healthy influence on excavating technique. I was one of those privileged to work with him in 1938 and should have continued in 1939 had nothing else supervened. While at this excavation we were visited by Mortimer Wheeler and also went over ourselves to see his classic work at Maiden Castle.

We were now coming to Hitler's war and for me the year 1939 was also to be memorable for another reason. In 1938 and 1939 the investigation of the group of burial mounds at Sutton Hoo close to Woodbridge in Suffolk was begun at the instance of its owner, Mrs E.M. Pretty. Work on several of the mounds in 1938 made it certain that it was an Anglo-Saxon cemetery of unusual importance, and one robbed boat burial found in that year showed its possibilities. In 1939 the excavation of the largest mound was begun by Mr Basil Brown and it soon was clear that this might cover an undisturbed ship burial. I visited the site at the invitation of Ipswich Museum which was then technically in charge, and saw the remarkable prospect which Mr Brown's cautious and skilful work had opened up. Before I left Sutton Hoo that day I saw to it that both the Office of Works and the British Museum had been alerted to the situation, but did not expect to have anything more to do with it because I was due to continue at the Prehistoric Society excavation already mentioned above.

But I had only been at Salisbury for a few days when I was asked by the Office of Works to direct the completion of the work at Sutton Hoo, something entirely unexpected. I accepted and the sequel is widely known. Working between July 10th and August 25th, and aided by a team of experts, a royal East Anglian ship burial of the first importance and richness was found, recorded and removed to the British Museum; the vessel in which it had been placed was also cleared and studied as completely as time permitted.

This was an anxious time for me because the work had to be carried out with all possible care and speed in the open air in the shadow of impending war. With great generosity Mrs Pretty presented the finds to the nation and a new dimension was added to Anglo-Saxon studies by this remarkable assemblage. I wrote the preliminary report on the excavation and read it to the Society of Antiquaries in April, 1940, after the war had broken out. From that point the study of the find and its implications was the responsibility of the British Museum.

In the war I served in the Royal Air Force and was one of the large group, including many archaeologists, which worked at the Central Air photographic Interpretation Unit at Medmenham and later in 1944–45 was at the Directorate of Military Survey, which contained a large element of Ordnance Survey staff.

Already by 1936 I had given up most of my teaching work at Cambridge and had now been Librarian and a Fellow of Selwyn for a number of years. After my demobilisation I returned there where, as a married man with a family, I had to consider my future and was already forty-four years of age. It was now that unexpected events placed me in the post of Archaeology Officer to the Ordnance Survey.

As we have seen earlier O.G.S. Crawford had held this post since 1920. His relationship with the Survey, which was effectively ended when its headquarters at Southampton was devastated by an air raid in November 1940, had been complicated, in fact a love-hate affair. It had given him a great opportunity to put archaeology in the Survey on a better course, but this had to be done, initially at least, in an atmosphere of suspicion of what he was about and in a time when drastic post-1922 economies restricted the activity of the Department. His own prickly temperament contributed to this and much of his ability to carry out a wide programme of field investigation and the production of period maps came from an early recognition that, within fairly wide limits, it was most profitable for all concerned to let him have his head. He made remarkably good use of this freedom. It was sad that the 1939 war closed down his painfully built up little Branch, which never contained more than a handful of people, just as the Survey was entering on a new phase of activity with more resources. Disaster struck at Southampton in 1940 and he spent the last five years to his retirement in 1945 on other work. But the records he built up largely survived the war through his own prescience, and his world-wide reputation as a force in archaeology did not depend on his relations with the Ordnance Survey.

As Crawford's Assistant since 1936 Mr W. F. Grimes was his natural successor, but his early removal to be Keeper of the London Museum opened the way for me. I saw a big opportunity for useful work on a national scale, applied for the post and was working in it at Chessington by January, 1947. My days as an amateur were over. As I regard my period at the Ordnance Survey as my real life's work towards which I had been moving over the previous twenty years my relations with this body and some ideas about State archaeology in Britain must dominate the rest of this account.

We must first consider the past record of the Survey in its dealings with archaeology. Between 1791 and 1824 there was no emphasis on the supply of antiquities for inclusion on the original 1-inch map series. Many naturally found places on the maps as obvious physical features, and in exceptional cases the work of leading antiquaries of the time was included in some quantity, as with Sheet XIV where the influence of Sir Richard Colt Hoare and William Cunnington's field work in the Salisbury Plain area appears strongly, but antiquities had no systematic treatment in the series as a whole.

When the 6-inch scale survey of Ireland was carried out between 1824 and 1846 new problems arose. The Director, Thomas Colby, was a man of wide ideas who believed that more purposes than the production of maps might be achieved and statistical, geological and other studies might usefully be added to the work while it was in progress. Colby's ideas proved to be unacceptable, if only on the score of cost, but to deal with the high incidence of place name problems and surveyable archaeological features which could not be overlooked on a 6-inch survey, a special Topographical Section was set up, largely on the initiative of Thomas Larcom who was in charge in Ireland. This employed experts in Irish language, history and local lore who, in the persons of John O'Donovan, Eugene O'Curry and Thomas Petrie were fully professional. However much it may have been disliked by the Treasury and dissolved before the survey was completed in 1846, this Section provided the first model of how to study a country's antiquities for cartographic and wider scientific purposes, and its records, now in the custody of the Royal Academy in Dublin, have proved to be invaluable.

After 1855 there followed the general survey of Great Britain at the 25-inch scale which was bound to involve much antiquity detail and this was completed by 1894. During the whole of this great work, to begin with under the direction of Sir Henry James, the Survey was not indifferent to the mapping of many surveyable antiquities which were met with all over the country. The help of the growing body of local archaeological societies was welcomed and broadly sufficient instructions were issued for the treatment of the features encountered, but all through these 40 years, with only one or two known exceptions, there was no person in the field or office staffs who had a real interest in the subject. Features considered or certainly known to be antiquities were accurately surveyed but inaccurate descriptions abounded, much obvious material was overlooked and hoary errors from sources long known to be suspect were allowed to remain on edition after edition as late as 1920. Some of this was unavoidable owing to the current state of knowledge, but more professional treatment would have produced better results. After 1880 archaeology was making rapid advances. There was growing protest against the weakness of Survey practice with antiquities, and the criticism became unanswerable as the twentieth century began. When Sir Charles Close became Director-General in 1912 it was the first time that the Survey was under the control of a man with a real knowledge of the subject, and he was able to remove this reproach by appointing Crawford as the first Archaeology Officer.

In 1910 W.H. Hudson in his book *A Shepherd's Life* wrote the following passage with special reference to the downlands of Southern England, but broadly applicable to the country as a whole:

One must lament the destruction of the ancient earthworks, especially of the barrows, which is going on all over the Downs, most rapidly where the ground is broken up by the plough. One wonders if the ever-increasing curiosity of our day with regard to the history of the human race in the land continues to grow, what our descendants in the next half of the century, to go no farther, will say of us and our incredible carelessness in the matter! So small a matter to us, but one which will, perhaps, be immensely important to them! It is perhaps better for our peace that we do not know; it would not be pleasant to have our children's and children's children's contemptuous expressions sounding in our prophetic ears. . . . Still one cannot but experience a shock on seeing the plough driven through an ancient smooth turf, curiously marked with barrows, lynchets and other mysterious mounds and depressions where sheep have been pastured for a thousand years, without obscuring these chance hieroglyphs scored by man on the surface of the hills.

When Hudson wrote this passage the country was nearing the disaster of 1914 when the wholesale destruction of landscapes still easily detectable on the surface was to begin and continue through a second war into our age of advanced technology; today most of the traces of an abandoned medieval village can be levelled by a bull-dozer in the course of a day; ploughing up marginal lands to get government grants and other state-directed activities like the Forestry Commission have carried destruction into areas still full of evidence of man's past.

But even before 1910 there had been stirrings of conscience and for the first time since the days of John Leland the State was to take some notice of our archaeological heritage. An Act for the scheduling and protection of ancient monuments was passed in 1882, and early in this century three Royal Commissions were set up with the duty of preparing full reports on the antiquities of all kinds still surviving in England, Scotland and Wales. But the Act, although it made a beginning, was unable in practice to secure a successful prosecution for damage to an important site for many years to come, and the resources made available to the Commissions were insufficient for the huge task before them.

Some better co-ordinated system might have been achieved at this stage. Archaeology, topography and cartography ought to be firm allies, for they are all concerned with the study and record of the varying imprint of man's use of the earth's surface. It may be that the criticism of the Survey's treatment of antiquities had some influence on the way that State archaeology began to develop, but there seems to be no sign that in its early planning any attention was paid to the Survey as something with which it might be linked. The anomalous character of the Survey as a body which was still under military direction, though answerable since 1870 to the Board of Agriculture and its successors, may also have had its effect. Its history was probably little known and the successful experiment made during the Irish survey was forgotten, but it is surprising that no one ever seems to have considered that it might become the nucleus of a larger organization which, among other matters involving topographic studies, could also carry out the scheduling and defence of monuments and perform the more detailed local investigations which fell to the Royal Commissions. No doubt there would have been opposition from the Ordnance Survey and the War Office, but there was no obvious reason why the training of soldiers in survey and the production and revision of the country's map systems could not have continued within a larger body, some of whose sections dealt with various aspects of antiquity survey and record.

But the chance to rationalize all this work in one body passed, and in the years which followed the different elements of State archaeology got themselves into entrenched positions with no real co-operation which, as the archaeological work of the Ordnance Survey developed rapidly after the 1939–45 war, became clearly unco-ordinated and provoked enquiries and demands for reform in the sixties. In the course of these the Ordnance Survey was rapped over the knuckles and told to be 'less intensive' on this side. Since then there have been some efforts to increase the country's archaeological potential in general, but we still do not have a tightly co-ordinated state system which provides good cover for the whole country all the time. The Ordnance Survey, now recently fully civilianized, continues its overall cover of the country for its own purposes, but seems about to abandon any concern with archaeology beyond the long established practice of showing archaeological features on its maps.

Having said this I will now describe the post-1947 progress of archaeology in the Ordnance Survey till my retirement in 1965. One of the less expected results to follow the war was a remarkable upsurge of public interest in the subject. This owed much to the BBC's *Animal, Vegetable, Mineral?* programme compèred by Glyn Daniel and assisted by other distinguished archaeologists including Sir Mortimer Wheeler. These coincided with the opportunity given by war damage in many towns to examine their earlier phases by excavation before rebuilding. Volunteers flocked to help at many of these sites and archaeology became news.

After the war the Ordnance Survey had two main tasks before it, which arose from recommendations made by the Davidson Committee which had rescued it from its run-down condition in 1935. These were postponed by the outbreak of war but taken up again in 1945. One was a new survey of all cities, towns and built-up areas at the scale of 50 inches to the mile; the other was the complete revision of the 25-inch maps of the country, with the exception of a few mountainous areas where the 6-inch scale would continue to suffice. In the course of this work, estimated to be completed in the early eighties, a new system of revision was to be set up which would ensure the continuous presence of revising staff in all parts of the country.

The expansion of many activities which might be disastrous to archaeological sites which followed 1945 made it vital that the Ordnance Survey, as the only body which had an archaeological interest and also an obligation to revise the whole country before the end of the century, should be equipped to survey and record in essentials what had survived war-time pressures and was liable to early destruction. The use of earth-moving machinery, ploughing of marginal lands, Forestry Commission planting, open-cast mining and the continual spread of housing, new roads and much else would all add their quota of loss as the revision proceeded.

The work of the other State archaeological bodies was, by their constitution, inadequate to supply this need over more than a small part of the country within this period. The Ordnance Survey with its duty to cover the whole country could at least recognize what had survived, survey it, place it on the maps where appropriate, and make a fair record for the future.

It is not necessary to detail all the problems met with in reviving the archaeology side at Chessington, virtually defunct except for Crawford's pre-war records which had been safely in West Wales in the war period. The only one of his small staff to return was the Assistant Archaeology Officer, Mr W.F. Grimes, who was Crawford's successor, but he was now leaving to be Keeper of the London Museum; a new beginning had to be made. Staff must be recruited and this exclusively from within the Survey staff which was not likely to contain many people ready or competent to work in archaeology. But, in fact, I was able to gather a small nucleus of able people, mainly from the field side. Based on this the building-up process was to continue till 1952 and it was sometimes hard to convince those in power that it was necessary.

The essential point was that the work was now to cover the whole country and continue. A staff had to be created trained to deal with the many field problems met with in a wide variety of backgrounds, to see the results properly placed on the new maps and also to begin an on-going record of all known archaeological occurrences on a topographic basis using the new National Grid system for terms of reference. Each of the six survey Regions was to be worked by a field section briefed from every available source of information, including air photography; here a liaison with the Cambridge Committee on Air-photography, just beginning its brilliant explorations under J.K.S. St Joseph, led us to the identification and survey of many new features of all periods.

At Chessington a library was built up for the use of the Division. The new title showed archaeology's improved status in Survey affairs. No efforts were spared to keep the field sections fully briefed about the expected content of the areas in which they were working. It was important that our work should be done in advance of that of the general revision so that our results could be incorporated in the final result. By 1952 field, recording and office duties were going well and the expertise of the field sections was developing fast. Mr A.L.F. Rivet joined the staff as Assistant Archaeology Officer and did notable work with period maps. Their compilation was resumed, new editions of earlier ones were published and the list of new productions in this range grew. In due course a Branch Office under his direction was opened in Edinburgh to deal with the special problems of Scotland.

It must not be supposed that the progress of the Division was an unbroken success. The general revision had begun by the close of 1945 and I did not begin work till 1947. It took two years to gather and train a good nucleus for the later staff of some 65, and with allowance for working out the best procedures it was 1950 before we could make an effective contribution. By that time the general revision had moved on and there was a backlog of newly revised areas which had not been examined for archaeology. Some of the less important areas had to be bypassed for later treatment and East Anglia suffered in this way. In most places we kept ahead of the general revision but I do not know how far these deficiencies were made up after my retirement.

There were always difficulties in getting suitable staff when our field of choice was confined to the Survey, and it was also unfortunate that most of the staff were of much the same age and promotion prospects were bleak in the Division. Family responsibilities grew and it was inevitable that by the early sixties some of the best men, as good surveyors, were already seeking and getting promotion in other parts of the Survey; their specialized knowledge of the Division's work was wasted.

I have no complaint to make about those in control in my time. The building up of the Division cost some battles, but we met with much in help and understanding. One of the weaknesses of the system which has now passed away with the civilianization of the Department was that those in the higher control posts were often military men who were doing terms of duty and as soon as and even before they became attuned to the way the Division was working they were liable to return to military duties. This affected all parts of the Survey. Most of our superiors were helpful or Division staff would not have risen to 65, though even that number was only just sufficient to do the work and amounted to about one-sixtieth of the entire Survey staff.

I am not fully informed about all that has passed in the years since my retirement. The Survey has returned to its old home at Southampton, and my only continuing contact has been through the compilation of a last period map *Britain before the Norman Conquest* and writing contributions to the Official History. Civilian control is now complete and not long ago we learned that the post of Archaeology Officer had been abolished.

For the second time in half a century the whole of the Ordnance Survey's affairs and organization have been examined by a Committee, and its report was published in the autumn of 1979. Since it is plain that for some time past the Survey has been uneasy about its archaeological side perhaps we may be thankful that, while the disbandment of the Division is recommended, it is suggested that the skills of what remains of its staff should not be wasted but divided among the three Royal Commissions, which should also share the management of the large non-intensive record which has been built up since 1952.

It remains to be seen what practical results will emerge from this. How will information about new features and sites for inclusion on maps of appropriate scale be sent to the Survey with expectation of action when it seems that already some quite important items are being dropped from new editions? The Royal Commissions are active and admirable bodies, but even with some accession of staff it is difficult to see how they can provide that constant surveillance of developing archaeological topography over the whole of Britain which was supplied when the doomed Division was at its best.

I have said a great deal about the Ordnance in one way and another for most of forty years. I have lectured about its archaeological work in most parts of the country and I know that there is great pride in our map systems and some dismay that they may be entering a period of decline. The effort which was made in the Ordnance Survey after 1947 is not all waste and it is a comforting thought that devoted amateurs have a continuing record of achievement; they are now operating by thousands compared with those who were active at the time I met Crawford at the bottom of Burrington Combe.

4

Christopher Hawkes

1905–1920

My father's forebears were ironmasters in Birmingham. Yet neither he (born 1877) nor my uncle (born 1870), let alone five aunts, knew more than the name of their firm, The Eagle Iron Foundry. When their mother died and the family moved to Beckenham, all were children. A remote cousin Arthur, Borough Librarian of Wigan, genealogist, and thence FSA, wrote when I became that (1932) to tell me that Hawkeses were Warwickshire under Charles II already, when a branch went to Ireland. But he said nothing of William Hawkes, who in 1824 (June), with a young Mr M.H. Bloxam of Rugby, went to Oldbury, in the country near Atherstone, and opened a barrow. Bloxam stated, naming him and the firm, that he was leader of the dig, when publishing it in Charles Roach Smith's *Collectanea Antiqua*, vol. I part 3 (issued 1843, then in whole vol. of 1848), 33, with Pl. xiv, engraving of the finds. (My knowing this is entirely due to Sonia Hawkes's finding it, in her luckily-obtained *Collectanea* a few years ago.) His publication cited in *VCH Warwickshire* and in Gerloff, 1975 (172 and Pl. 27 no. 332) was thus his second, and the first needs adding to the barrow's bibliography.

The finds (apart from Anglian intrusions) were urns, other bronze-age pots and a tanged bronze knife-dagger (332 in Gerloff). Bloxam, keeping all for his collection, now in Warwick Museum, became a blameless county antiquary; William Hawkes never. And the labour champion G.J. Holyoake, employed at this foundry throughout the 1830s, recalled (his 1892, 19–25: I owe this with thanks to Paul Morgan, Bodleian Library) that as its master he was brutal, a tyrant, the terror of his workmen – and an ugly-faced red-head. The description of Timothy his brother, joint master, reminds me of a miniature I have, *c.* 1870, of my grandfather Charles Samuel (died '95). But there are other researches on the family, as I know from my son; what I here must explain is its connexion with my own archaeology. Charles Samuel and the rest had a violent quarrel, in his youth (*c.* 1850); this and his first wife's death, as he told his sons, drove him off to South America, into engineering business (Shaw & Hawkes), never returning nor re-marrying till late in the 1860s. But his Spanish jokes and stories left my father with a lifelong feeling for all Spanish lands; and thus, sailing once to the Canaries, he happened on my mother – who herself was half Spanish.

Her forebears in England were Kentish Cobbs – family researched by an older cousin Alfred – who from farming (as already under Edward II) turned in the course of the eighteenth century to brewing. This at Margate (with the Fleet in the Downs) did so well that her grandfather could go to be a doctor, and his eldest and youngest sons both into the wine trade; the Spanish marriage of the youngest, Charles, came in 1873. Two years after, having borne my mother, Eleanor, the young wife died giving birth to my Aunt Victoria. Charles was left in great grief; but while in London rising to management with Cockburns, shipping port, he re-married and flourished, till an accident killed him in 1895. Both the half-Spanish daughters, independent after that, took to travelling, together or apart; at first with their girlhood teacher of French, Mlle Danton – as on Eleanor's voyage to the Canaries, resulting in her marriage (1904). Learning all this, I felt a boyish curiosity for Spanish, French and all such foreign countries: copying maps from the atlas, and never made shy by foreign languages. Through the same Mlle Danton I had French along with English.

Yet though we twice, when I was small, went to sea-side Normandy, and even once to Paris and to Switzerland, it was southern England's scenes, and reading Kipling on its past, that led me to history – also my London day-school teachers. I was entranced when those ladies, skirts long, belts tight and collars high, taught the Conquest with the Bayeux Tapestry to make it come alive. History had been my father's Cambridge subject (under Lord Acton); once at Canterbury he showed me (at six) how round 'Norman' arches passed to pointed; my drawing such, and Roman ones, with proper-dressed people and with horses, was guided by his knowledge and his own far greater skill: he had been, when up at Trinity ('94–'97), the lively artist 'C.P.H.' on the *Granta*. But also, since his out-of-door diversion was the Beagles, the friends who in vacation took him with the pack to their county, Northumberland, had him afterwards joining the Special Reserve, Northumberland Fusiliers. Thus his call-up in August 1914, and our soon going north to be with him, introduced me to the English North-East – and to its wealth in archaeology.

Near us were the ancient churches, Monkwearmouth and Jarrow; so was Durham Cathedral. Among my visits to these and to others, with my mother, was a Durham one in 1916. Our cathedral verger and his party, all women but for me, were in the Galilee Chapel at the tomb of the Venerable Bede. Then the door was slowly opened and there entered a white-bearded cleric, in black cap and cassock. With the verger hissing 'Hush! Canon Greenwell!' he shuffled to the tomb; turned his eye on me, the only boy present, and addressed me a harangue, on Bede the monk of Jarrow and father of English history. That Canon Greenwell was born under George III, and would die in two years at 98, I could not know; nor how renowned were his excavations, his *British barrows* (1877), and their spoils and his further implement collection; nor that a dozen years on I was to meet them in the British Museum. Other things were more exciting. On Newcastle Town Moor I could ride a horse, and a bicycle everywhere. Along a stretch of Hadrian's Wall, with a stop for climbing into Brunton turret, at the Chesters fort and at partly-excavated Corbridge, I could get a first sight of the reality of Roman antiquities. And in 1919 when we were moved to Salisbury Plain, came prehistory. I at last could *see* barrows; tread the sward among the stones of Stonehenge; pass from Britons to Normans at Old Sarum – St John Hope's excavations being still barely five years ended; discover Salisbury's cathedral; and meet in the Museum Frank Stevens, the genial curator. Thus Wessex enters the tale; there too I was a scholar now at Winchester (scholars' fees were then £7 a term . . .). With my second summer term, the tale moves on.

1920–1930

Just as previous family events, and then the War, gave me chances that good fortune had prepared me for, so a chance came in 1920 not from my conforming to the habits of the school, but from its library's possession of the book in which I found the opportunity. It was Williams-Freeman's Hampshire *Field archaeology* (1915). For country bicycling, on any free summer afternoons, all the Hampshire downland was open; amongst its ancient features were Roman roads, and the book had notes on some by an O. G. S. Crawford, of East Woodhay. So I tried him with a letter, and was thrilled to get a friendly reply, written while he was excavating barrows up at Roundwood, from his tent (see his 1922a: 189–209; and 1955: 152–3). Pen-friendship ripened; by October, he was starting at Southampton as the Ordnance Survey's Archaeology Officer, and in summers soon afterwards was lending me 6–inch maps, for checking antiquities wherever my bicycle could reach them (compare his 1955: 151–2, 154). Then he had me write an article – my first – on Hampshire trackways. And in 1925, when it appeared, and I was at Oxford (a New College scholar), those memories had their place alongside of my other, in-school recollections of Winchester. Of these I will only say that senior classicists were taught Athenian monuments, and then the Roman Forum's; that a whole year of the course in natural science was geology; and that I loved the Archaeological Society no less for its objectives' being chiefly architectural, while its mentor Cyril Robinson, a man of many parts, gave the friendliest recognition to my fieldwork. And that, I resolved, must next take me on to excavation.

The Winchester St Catharine's Hill had its chapel (too little noticed now by medievalists) found and excavated, August 1925/6, by volunteers – of whom three, Nowell Myres, Charles Stevens and myself, undertook to dig parts of its Iron Age hillfort, in the next two Augusts: invited by the Hampshire Field Club, with a grant, which subscribers augmented, for expenses and labour. To our report (1930a), published by the Club, I added Iron Age excursuses and also a medieval; our hillfort findings I have lately re-assessed (1976d). But I had Roman work besides: from Oxford (where I later had tutoring from R.G. Collingwood), Miss M.V. Taylor's commendation brought me briefly, in 1925 along with Myres, to the Mortimer Wheelers' fort near Brecon on the Usk;

through July '26 to Donald Atkinson's Wroxeter forum; and in September to sole charge at Alchester (report, my 1927). I was on foot with a Cambridge friend in mainland Greece, next spring; that summer, with another, walked the length of Hadrian's Wall; and wrote for ANTIQUITY 1929 on Masada (then in British-administered Palestine) and its Roman siege of AD 73, from air-photographs through Crawford, his bibliography, and Josephus's description. Thus when at Sheepen, outside Colchester, Iron Age and Roman appeared together, and the Antiquaries' president Peers, Chief Inspector, planned digging there for 1930, I was proud to be put in charge (Myres relieving me awhile) along with Colchester Museum's Rex Hull, that year and for the next two, Hull then continuing alone until 1939. Colchester was Camulodunum; our report, published 1947, bore its name. J P. Bushe-Fox was our visiting Director – in 1931 he and I were nearly killed in the fall of a trench. From that, Stanley Casson spun his thriller, *Murder by burial* – yet Bushe-Fox had merely had my trench's timbers taken out to let him look at it. But I will pause here at 1930 and the two years previous. From September '28 I was an Assistant at the British Museum.

1930–1940

Two years there made me a 2nd-class Assistant Keeper; next above, lst-class, was Thomas Kendrick; we were friends from the beginning. Pay was little, but my father took comfort from his old Dulwich schoolmate T.A. Joyce, the Museum's great Americanist. The British and Medieval Antiquities Depart-ment, which Crawford had urged on me (his 1955: 173: what other jobs existed?), had at first no vacancy; only luck, bringing O.M. Dalton its Keeper to retire unexpectedly, created one. Publicly announced, but drawing just three applicants, from Pembrokeshire A.G.O. Mathias, Basil Gray and me from New College, its exam. was four non-archaeology papers and an interview; on the board was the new Keeper, Reginald Smith. Entering the Department, I was set to two catalogues: one was of mainly eighteenth/ nineteenth century medallic miscellanea (1930e). The other – Allen Sturge's collection – was of flints, and for its British Isles volume (1931g) I classified and counted some 86,425.

Stone Ages, Palaeolithic especially, were new to me. Yet remembering school geology my interest grew: six years on (for 1938a) I did the Swanscombe skull-related hand-axes. But 1930–1 were great Iron Age years: for St Catharine's, I had treated British-Continental links; and after 'Hill Forts' in ANTIQUITY, with British A-B-C, came 'The Belgae of Gaul and Britain' with Gerald Dunning. These works were acclaimed, but the 'Belgae' had mistakes, as in bringing Cassivellaunus and Catuvellauni to Hertfordshire straight from the Marine's Catalauni, among Belgic invaders of '75 BC'. And whereas the A-B-C revised for 1959 and '61 was shot at, that error in the 'Belgae' survived till I corrected it myself: 1965, and more corrections by myself since then. It was the

early 1930s too when excavators, first the Sussex Curwens, started bringing me
their pottery for report, Bronze or Iron Age or Roman; the Museum did many
such jobs for correspondents and visitors. But my Late Bronze Age, as in 1933d,
still credited Crawford's 1922b, with Deverel-Rimbury invasion eighth century
BC. Visitors ranged from humble folk to Adolf Mahr from Dublin, Cyril Fox
from Cardiff and from Edinburgh Gordon Childe; from Germany came
Jacobsthal, Unverzagt and Gerhard Bersu.

Such contacts with the Continent increased when Professor Myres at Oxford,
Nowell's father and later Sir John, succeeded in his drive to found two
international congresses; the Pre- and Proto-historic one, preceding the
Anthropological, was for August 1932 in London. Ralegh Radford was
secretary for this; and when countries picked permanent national secretaries, the
two for Great Britain were Gordon Childe and myself. The Secretary-General
was Myres, the President was Peers. We all went to Paris for the pre-congress
Council, at the Institut de Paléontologie Humaine under Marcellin Boule. For
Peers, presiding inexperienced with foreigners, Boule made trouble: with the
Germans, then the Italian, whom he charged with favouring a friend (he
believed) of Mussolini. Ugo Rellini replied *'En Italie tout le monde est ami de
Mussolini'*. *'Tous les autres sont en prison!'* shouted Boule – but the door flew open
suddenly: for a late-comer, rosy-cheeked and sky-blue-suited, don Pedro Bosch
Gimpera. His charm brought immediate peace; every problem could be solved.
At the Congress, in the Strand at King's College, the Palaeolithic section's
chairman was Smith. He gave an opening address of nine words: 'No Smoking.
Défense de fumer. Man raucht nicht hier.' He knew the Abbé Breuil had smoked in
the British Museum.

I was charged with the book-exhibition, 'no sales across the counter'. Flinders
Petrie left his pile of books for Lady P. to sell; she sold them for cash down,
ruthlessly. I had long known them both (and Margaret Murray) through my
aunt Victoria, a fan of theirs and lover of their ancient Egypt; she preferred
archaeology in countries eastward of home. Being out of my reach, I had to
value them most, following Childe, for diffusions into Europe; but I was glad to
be re-awakened, by Bosch and soon Pericot, to Spain – and to Germany by
Bersu. He had invited a review of recent English work in prehistory, for his
Römisch-Germanische Kommission (1932b), from Kendrick, who brought me
in for the Late Bronze and Iron Age; kept in English, with Roman and Saxon
chapters added, this was our book 1932a.

Prior to Germany indeed in my interest was France, pre-Roman and Roman.
I had lately been at Arles and at Nîmes (where old deaf Espérandieu had asked
'Que voulez-vous de moi' and put my mouth into his ear), and then at
Saint-Germain. Older still, the Museum's Salomon Reinach, champion of
Glozel, which Crawford was denouncing as a fake site, struck me once again
dumb: *'Eh bien, jeune homme, êtes-vous Glozélien? Ou non? Connaissez-vous Artur
Evans?'* (Sir Arthur had switched to Crawford.) *'Il m'a trahi!'* Only my welcome

from the younger keeper Lantier consoled me. At Épernay the curator Abbé Favret, supposing me a British Museum grandee, had mounted a mayoral reception; how he laughed when at the station, from a third-class compartment, the real Hawkes descended! But *'on s'arrangera'*. Reception, speeches, and tour of the collections, went as planned, and we ended with champagne after visiting the tunnels where they make it. I had kindness at Strasbourg too, from the paternal Robert Forrer. But in spring 1933, Bersu in Germany was a kind host and organizer also. His route for me started in the Netherlands at Groningen, in a German party headed by his old chief Schuchardt; van Giffen showed his Ezinge *terp*, newly dug; Ernst Sprockhoff made me a lifelong friend. For Camulodunum comparisons, the route was next to Haltern, then to Dortmund and Münster museums; Hull joined me at Cologne, for Mainz with Gustav Behrens, and soon again at Trier after other such visits. Out of Belgium next and France, I re-joined the Bersu couple then in Switzerland, at Vindonissa (now with my fiancée who was travelling Neolithic).

These journeys, so rapid and cost-cutting (never any grant), nonetheless gave a first-hand knowledge of material, and welcome individual acquaintances; back in the Museum, they aided re-assessing our Department's collections from the Continent. Soon after, I ran into trouble through impertinence to Smith; it passed, but I was told to take a rest, and being married now, Jacquetta sustained me. We went on excavations both in 1934, with Olwen Brogan at Gergovia (see my 1971b: 5) before excursion farther south, and in '35 in Hampshire for the Field Club at Buckland Rings, Lymington. We dug for it again in '38 at Quarley Hill; in '39 at Bury Hill (Clatford) with a trial cut at Balksbury; in 1956b I re-assessed the reports, along with other ones. But 1936 had had the Prehistoric Congress in Oslo. Besides the Bygdøy Viking Ships we had the Congress Ball, led off for Austria, with the president Brøgger's wife, by the red-bearded Oswald Menghin, his coat-tails whirling to the strains of 'Congress Dances'. Yet Norway's massed students singing *'Gaudeamus igitur, iuvenes dum sumus'* had a sadness, for war already loomed, with the outbreak in Spain, and besides Mussolini now there was Hitler. Bersu was ousted from his Kommission (and our Council) to a lowlier post in Berlin, where he and Maria entertained us, after Norway and Sweden, on our way through to Hannover, Netherlands and so back home. Soon I watched them digging Little Woodbury, whence war let them first (through Childe) stay in Scotland, but in summer 1940 interned them in the Isle of Man. Annually, after the Bersu-sponsored 1932b, we had reviewed the periodical publishings in British prehistory (1933h; 1934h; 1935l; 1936g); and in the war came our Penguin book *Prehistoric Britain* (1943a). And from the Congress year to the war, along with reports on my excavations and 'The Double Axe' for Myres (1940d), and a Museum re-display of Continental Stone to Bronze Age (A.K. 1st class under Kendrick now as Keeper), I did the periods to 1400 BC as *The Prehistoric foundations of Europe*.

1940–1950

Nearly everything surveyed there, and afterwards concertedly for Britain in 1948b, came from studies and excavations too small by the standards of today. Few were the works giving thorough distribution–lists, fewer the excavations on at all a large scale. Laboratory processing of finds still had not advanced far; chronology had to extrapolate from lands with protohistory and history. So in the war years many, whether in uniform or out of it (as was I in the Ministry of Aircraft Production), felt the need of fresh starts, from new assessments; conferences were held, in Oxford, in London twice, and next in Cambridge; the Oxford one led, through Miss Taylor and supporters (Nowell Myres and me), to creating the CBA. Of recent work, ANTIQUITY gave a whole number to Sutton Hoo. I had prevailed on Bushe-Fox, now Chief Inspector, to consign the dig to Phillips, summer 1939, but soon was storing British Museum treasures in the London Underground. Besides putting many lesser things in print while war allowed, I had *Foundations* out in April 1940. I believe it helped me (1948) into the British Academy, and in 1946 back to Oxford for the Chair, brand new, of European Archaeology. My Inaugural Lecture was 1948a. I joined in the fresh starts and new assessments: partly at home, for the Archaeological Institute in Lincolnshire and at Salisbury, reviewing Pitt-Rivers's Cranborne Chase excavations (1948e, helped by the Piggotts; I was editor now of its *Journal*), and partly abroad. In Belgium at a Mariemont conference and the Brussels Anthropological Congress, I could find foreign friendships new and old. My renewal with Pericot had come through the summer-school and opening of the museum at Ampurias, 1947; at the *fiesta maior* of La Escala we all danced in the *sardanas*.

I had come there from our first family holiday abroad, in Dordogne; its high spot was the visit to the painted cave of Lascaux, conducted by Ravidat, its discoverer, specially for us, by the light (no electric yet) of hand–held acetylene lamps. From its first publication, with Windels's photographs and text by Annette Laming, I did the English translation (adding preface): my 1949. But the great year was 1950, which brought me to Italy. My Prehistoric Society lecture (twinned with Childe's) on the Final Bronze Age (1948c; d was Spanish, translated from French), was in April re-cast for the Mediterranean Congress in Florence. The dates were too low, and von Merhart repeated his rebuttal (echoed meantime to me in Munich by Werner and Milojčić), in a noble oration, that August, to the Congress at Zürich (his 1953): Emil Vogt, its president, wrote the like (his 1950). Yet the Congress was delightful throughout, and so were its excursions: at Sion in the Valais, Märta Strömberg of Lund was my partner in an exhibition tango. Van Giffen said, 'I did not know you were such a man.'

1950–1960

Barcelona had a Balearic summer-school impending; I was awaited from Switzerland, at Ampurias, by wife and son. His falling briefly ill, and crowds and noise, spoilt the visit; but after Pericot had taken us to Bagur, his country home, we were ready to join the party for Mallorca. We called on the Robert Graveses, who kept the family on while I completed the tour of talayots, tombs and caves; we all took motor-boat next for Menorca, thence Ibiza, then from Barcelona home. But I had shirked inoculation, and was scarcely back at Oxford in my Keble college rooms, when I was more than briefly ill, and two months in the isolation hospital. These gave, while I recovered, opportunity to meditate on what I ought to do in the University. It prescribed me no aims, but was leaving me to make them what I could.

February had brought me already one great proposition: by Lord Cherwell, 'the Prof.' of Experimental Philosophy (physics), for a Physics Laboratory to serve archaeology by research. To my doubts whether any good physicist would opt to direct it, his reply was to introduce me (at high table dinner in Christ Church) to E.T. Hall. Little later, Teddy Hall – a lively New College character – with his doctorate won for optical spectrometry, was ready; and in 1953, with Maurice Bowra as Vice-Chancellor, the Laboratory was approved – on one condition: a grant must first be offered by a non-science body, to guarantee our aims as archaeological. Opponents seemed to fancy that I never could get one. But I had just been made the first MacCurdy Lecturer at Harvard; in a symposium there mounted by the Wenner-Gren Foundation, I gave a 'Theory and Method' lecture (for printing 1954); and its Director Paul Fejos, that winter in New York, was happy to fix me the grant, which Oxford accepted. From the Lab's tiny premises of 1955, with Teddy joined soon by Martin Aitken, and with its journal *Archaeometry* (my name), it has achieved world status – with further successes right ahead. But the Oxford of the '50s needed some for archaeology itself. My Presidential Address to the Prehistoric Society – getting applause, but not everywhere approval (1951a) and 'Bronze-Workers' (b, British Iron Age) for Crawford, cut no ice in it. My hand must be turned to academic politics.

To abridge a long tale (omitting friendly helpers' names), I first gained an Assistant, Margaret Smith, and somewhat later a Diploma-course. Unlike the prehistoric part of that in Anthropology (on which after seven years I was given the help of Baden-Powell), this course was European, Neolithic to early Post-Roman. Then came rooms and a secretary, for me and Ian Richmond (Roman Empire archaeology), adjoining the Ashmolean Museum, which was charged with our finances. Its high administration never had smiled on such professors. In 1961–2 came our Institute, free of it.

Meantime my resumed late bronze age essays (1952a, and 1953a with Willem Glasbergen) took a firmer base for Britain in the *Inventaria Archaeo-*

logica, of which Margaret Smith, taking over, did numerous sets; in 1955–6, with a Leverhulme Travelling Fellowship, we each went to the Heuneburg excavation, then to Switzerland, Austria and Bavaria, prefaced by a December stay with Sprockhoff, up at Kiel; he took us visiting. At the Fehmarn neolithic long mound with small slab-cist exposed, he lay down in it crouched: no room for collective interments! The excursion, typical Sprockhoff, had been just to show that – but how rightly. We marched, through oncoming snowfall, back to the car. After Colchester diggings, later '56/7, we wrote on buckets and cauldrons, Late Bronze and Hallstatt: 1957d, built on E.T. Leeds's survey, and raising his dates for them – our own need raising now. Greatest novelty was Margaret's demonstration, matching Isobel Smith's and Jay Butler's from a different angle, that the southern English bronzes found with Deverel-Rimbury pottery had to start it not in the eighth century (Crawford 1922b) but at least two hundred years before 1000 BC (her 1959). As had our 1957, this affected also Ireland: first with the Prehistoric Society, 1951, and lastly in Dublin with the British Association, (Section H presidential: 1957c).

1960–1971/2

Radiocarbon dating was then coming on, but its tree-ring calibration and all dendrochronology, for most of us, were hardly on the horizon. By many, they were sharply contested, some even discounting them a dozen years after. As for me, I have eagerly followed their gradual improvements. But all the prior doings of the 1950s, today, seem remote. Among them had been the Congresses of '54 and '58, Madrid and Hamburg; four years on, at that in Rome, my subject was optical spectrometry (1962a). The turn of 1958/9 was more momentous. The London Iron Age Conference, early December (with my revised A-B-C: 1959b and '61b), had after eight weeks taken me and Sonia Chadwick into marriage. For us both (since '53 I had been single) it began a new era. Soon in the Netherlands briefly, then to Portugal for excavation in Iron-Age *castros* (1984a: begun in spring '58 at Sabroso), we were ready, first for a longer Continental trip in '60, and next for resuming Sonia's Wiltshire excavation, early Iron-Age, on Longbridge Deverill Cow Down. Other subjects then absorbed her, while mine had been Archaic Etruria (1959a), moving now to Mrs Elsie Clifford's *Bagendon* (1961d and e), then to Bronze Age gold (1961c and g, and 1963a with Rainbird Clarke). We had moved house to Dorchester-on-Thames; I was president of the Hampshire Field Club and soon of the CBA; 1964a, my Address to it, lamented lack of money. At the Institute in Oxford I was settling down to teaching (Jeffrey May and David Ridgway first of all); but a visit there from Munich by the magistral Joachim Werner gave my thoughts a new turn: to Sutton Hoo.

Concerned only briefly with the burial in 1939, but more conversant now with Anglo-Saxon studies, through Sonia's, I repeated Werner's pleading for its full publication (his 1964: 215), yet welcomed the delay because of recent up-dating of the coins: Lafaurie 1960, my '64b. I am told that the official fresh start may have answered my voice in that ANTIQUITY contribution – absent, however, from the official publication's 26-page-long bibliography. Anyhow I was busier with Celts, invasions, and Belgae (1965a-b; 1966a; 1968), Atlantic voyages and Portuguese gold collars (1969b; 1970), hillforts and their defences (1971b), and the North-Italian origin of Germanic and Scandinavian rune-script (1971a). In Oxford – where we found our present home – besides the teaching, there were fears for the Institute's premises as late as my retirement. My final 18 months brought our stay in Budapest, for the British Academy (whence 1974a); then the Rennes Celtic Congress (whence '73a), the Celtic Art symposium at Oxford ('76a), one in N Italy ('74b), and my essay 'Europe and England: fact and fog' (1972a).

1971/2–1981/2

Retired on 30 September '72, friends' kindness in my 65th year having given me a Festschrift (their *ECLP*), which more of them followed for my 70th by a birthday party, I was grateful for all, and to Fortune, but had much to do still. From November '74 through '75 it was lectures: Belfast, the Oliver Davies (1975, mainly microliths and megaliths); Rome, for the Lincei (1978b with c, on British Celts – out of Western-Central Europe, never Northern); Oxford, the Sir John Myres Memorial, on Greeks exploring Europe, mainly Pytheas (1977a); and London, the Mortimer Wheeler, on Britain and Caesar (1978a). Re-examining the classical texts shed light (as in 1980a, and Mays 1981) upon our Iron Age; Caesar and his sources too on Belgae – though invaders wouldn't ever swamp natives (1968, 1980b): new masters' ascendancy would renovate society and economy, whence my (1973a) 'Cumulative Celticity'. In 1973b, I supported my Austrian friend Dr Haberl, on (again with ancient sources) her Late and Post-Roman land of Noricum; the natives there outlived the upper class's retreat to Italy, and received some Germans from Bavaria not until later.

The archaeology of settlements, Iron Age and Bronze Age, now flourishing, can accommodate 'historical' modes of thought; so may earlier Bronze prehistory, with burials illumined likewise with help of science and statistics. The passage to it from native Neolithic here is critical: while natives' power is static, metal industry's weapons are dynamic. In 1974b and 1977b, I upheld and then advanced beyond Sabine Gerloff ('75) on the 'Wessex' and Armorican Early Bronze Age. For relations oversea there can of course be various models: a religious one is offered in my 1981 on sun-discs. Soon I hope to re-consider cauldrons, in their dating and their class and ceremonial significance. (And see Gerloff 1981 on British Late Bronze Age chronology.) For religion, funeral-rite, equipment, class structure and dynamics of mobility, our prehistory has been lacking one dimension, the Indo-European. Edinburgh, Sheffield, Oxford, Heinrich Wagner's Belfast, all pipe, but who dances? Who in these islands will listen to Marija Gimbutas, professor at Los Angeles, or read, or would write for, what she did so much to found (in 1973), *The Journal of Indo-European Studies*? Philologists; some prehistorians of other lands; of ours, hardly any. Will a coming generation close the gap? Meanwhile, besides reviews, I work on brooches (1979a, 1982a, and for a Corpus 1987a). Excavation-reports also: Portugal (with 1984a); contributing for Sonia on Longbridge Deverill; and for Philip Crummy, on Camulodunum again.

Some further thoughts

Telling my tale at speed may have made it too breathless – omitting e.g. my teaching at Munich, '74. But Glyn Daniel as Editor wanted me to add more thoughts. To my preface of social history I needn't return – except for this, that I've owed a great deal to the fortune that drew me to languages. They widen reading, and even if not well spoken, make people everywhere easier to get on with. Also to sort them mentally as dull or charming, fools or wise. Names in one's working bibliography then come alive, and judging which to trust more than others isn't limited to English ones. To start with little 'teach-yourself' books isn't hard. How many of us try them? And my experience also recommends to archaeologists their doing more periods than one. Museum folk and workers in Units must do it for their regions; academics, less regionally pent, can have a tendency to pen themselves in chronologically, so that one-period teaching – and researching, if they do it – can eventually seem their ideal. Yet work in any period will gain from acquaintance with the periods next before and after. And most undergraduates must anyhow be marched through a lot of them.

  Why was the course I started at Oxford post-graduate only, for Diploma? I have mentioned my teaching for the one that existed already, in prehistory with others' anthropology, physical and social; the examiners had to mark papers in all three subjects. What didn't exist was a course under different control, in later-prehistoric and the fringes of historical archaeology. Balance called for this beside the other, and confining it to Europe would prevent diffuseness. It had a general paper, Late Neolithic to early Post-Roman (touching Roman fringes only), and stiffer special period and region ones; people chose their options for these, and at first I taught for everything. The graduates it took were from any undergraduate subject, and people doing well in it could then be admitted for a thesis. I aimed at producing young teachers or other professionals; and a number now are in post, in museums or as lecturers – or indeed as professors. A first-degree course would be our next stage ahead; but I didn't expect it soon, and the Institute is much too small for it.

Let me turn to archaeology's more philosophical emanations. They seldom start very far back in its accumulating literature. Growing up with the subject since the '20s may be thought to have biased me, but although there was formerly far less literature than now, has it all become useless? How much pre-Binford, pre-David Clarke, pre-Renfrew, is used unless for contrast with modern enlightenment? New discoveries and methods must of course give rise to new thought. Yet the first two-thirds of this century already had its novelties; and if appearing now dwarfed by what has followed, they were big enough to make a crescendo of advance, so that modern ones differ in degree from them rather than in kind. The three modern writers I have named can all be read as meaning this; the Editor too, as historian of archaeology.

The philosopher R.G. Collingwood (see van der Dussen on him, 1981) at Oxford taught me archaeology for Roman Britain. His kindness as a tutor only froze to icy wrath when an essay of mine repeated a lecture of his own. 'That lecture should have made you do some *thinking for yourself*! You've no business to come here and read me a copy of *mine*.' His voice was shrill with anger. What I'd taken from him showed that Roman Britain's rural peasants were its link of continuity with prehistory; I ought to have added most of the masters in the villas, as stemming from iron-age masters. Approaching class society and economy as I did, from Plato and Aristotle, Hobbes and Locke and Rousseau, I saw Crawford's field implying them; but Collingwood's meant inferring them, with a stricter regard for degree in the quality of evidence. The four-tier scale of archaeology's capacity for inference, in my 'Theory and Method' at Harvard (issued '54) – easiest from things to their uses, and thence to economics, harder to social forms and hardest to religious – entered soon into a talk with the veteran Alfred L. Kroeber, looking over the bay from a seat on his campus at Berkeley. Prehistory and anthropology: can we view them as one great 'process', or do 'human wills sometimes get the better of circumstance' (a dictum of Myres) as seen in history? Like skinning onions, the enquiry has to start from the actually visible; 'process' may be the heart, but finding any must go skin by skin. My skins come in tiers of cognition. I had a four-tier scale for them already in my address to the Prehistoric Society (1951a): its tiers were degrees in availability of evidence from history – hence some prehistorians' disapproval. Anthropology's relevance for us seems to me to be inversely proportional to history's – and further to that, see above on the Indo-Europeans. But the primacy, in all our thinking, must be held by *things*. (Biological, geological, and features in the ground, as well as artifacts: they all mean people.)

Beakers are things. David Clarke, who inspired my 1973 on social class, and on the dubiousness of 'cultures', wouldn't ever tell me why he thought Beakers were at last given up. For answer, find the drinking-vessels that were used in the next period after! But I've preached already on that; and altogether, I think, quite enough. As for models, they're theories for explaining the *systems* which ought to be formed by *things*. The more we learn of things, and see them in their systems, the better for archaeology – and philosophy.

Postscript, 1987

Here ended the article of 1982 (re-printed now with few adjustments). A new example of things as archaeology's natural base, the early portion of the Corpus of Brooches in Britain, presents these grouped in the system formed by the late Rex Hull, its creator – brought as his successor by me to take account of an expanded content, 1987a; 1981a and 1983a are examples too, though essentially each deals only with a single thing, of the Bronze Age: one a cup and one a sun-disc. And of reasoning from things more explicitly to people, an example is 1982a on the Iron-Age brooches of Ireland; another, 1983e, reasons to people entering Britain (few in numbers again) out of Belgium: from pot-forms, Late Bronze (though never with Urnfields), afterwards Hallstatt, few but preceded by wide-scattered swords for mounted warriors (Cowen 1967, but treated after Marien 1958). Both, in their reasoning, resemble my 1968 'New Thoughts on the Belgae' (lying also behind 1984b and my couple of 1982 reviews): essential to the case for any movement of people is moderation, and it naturally leaves untouched the proper evidence for trade. For the trade in our Iron-Age tin, where this is primarily Greek-textual (Diodorus), I have shown in the course of 1984c how mistranslations have twice led to popular errors, but I want to conclude by turning away from detail: to a broader viewing of Europe's later prehistory, with a reminder to its archaeologists of the refusal, by almost all of them, to face any question of language. (See above under 1971/2–1981/2, near the end.) The Celtic especially, as I already was protesting in my 1966a (near the end of that); while 1973a (British 'Cumulative Celticity') was archaeologically based, its linguistic corollaries have lately once again been needling my mind. Hence, to archaeologists and linguists both, at the end of 1984d, my unison call with Martyn Jope for a narrowing of the gap that still divides them; and further, from particular starting-points, my own attempt at this, now printed in the USA, 1987b. But there I must stop.

Works by various authors mentioned in the text

CRAWFORD, O.G.S. 1922a. Excavations at Roundwood during 1920, *Proceedings of the Hampshire Field Club* 9: 189–209.
1922b. A prehistoric invasion of Britain, *Antiquaries Journal* 11: 27–35.
1955. *Said and done, the autobiography of an archaeologist*. London: Phoenix House.
DUSSEN, W.U. VAN DER. 1981. *History as a science: the philosophy of R.G. Collingwood*. The Hague.
ECLP. 1971. See introductory paragraph to Works by the author below.

GERLOFF, S. 1975. *The Early Bronze daggers in Great Britain and a reconsideration of the Wessex Culture*. Prähistorische Bronzefunde VI.2. Munich: C.H. Beck.
1981. Westeuropäische Griffzungenschwerter in Berlin: Zu chronologischen Problemen der britischen Spätbronzezeit, *Acta Praehistorica et Archaeologica* (Berlin), 11/12: 183–217.
GREENWELL, W. 1877. *British barrows*. Oxford.
HOLYOAKE, G.U. 1892. *Sixty years of an agitator's life* 1. London.
LAFAUHIE, U. 1960. Le Trésor d'Escharen

(Pays-Bas), *Revue numismatique* 6 (sér. II): 153–210.

MARIEN, M.-E. 1958. *Trouvailles du champ d'urnes et des tombelles hallstattiennes de Court-Saint-Étienne.* Brussels.

MAYS, M. 1981. Strabo IV. 4, 1: a reference to Hengistbury Head?, *Antiquity* 55: 55–7.

MERHAHT, G. VON. 1953. On Late Bronze and Early Iron age chronology and sheet-bronze vessels, in *Congr. Internat. Sci. Pré- et Protohist. III, Zürich 1950, Actes*: 212–16.

SMITH, M.A. 1959. Some Somerset hoards . . . *Proceedings of the Prehistoric Society* 25: 144–87; and thereto, wed as Margaret Brown, her spectometric sequel (188–208) with Audrey Blin-Stoyle.

VOGT, E. 1950. On the Swiss Late Bronze Age, in *Jahrb. der Schweiz. Gesellsch. f. Urgeschichte* 40.

WERNER, J. 1964. Frankish Royal tombs in the Cathedrals of Cologne and Saint-Denis, *Antiquity* 38: 201–16 (on Sutton Hoo, 215).

WILLIAMS-FREEMAN, J.P. 1915. *Field archaeology as illustrated by Hampshire.* London.

Works by the author

These have named him variously as HAWKES, C.F.C., or HAWKES, CHRISTOPHER.

In the volume marking my 65th birthday, *The European Community in Later Prehistory*, J. Boardman, M.A. Brown and T.G.E. Powell (ed.) (=*ECLP*, publ. 1971), Mrs Margaret (M.A.) Brown listed (271–87) my archaeological writings 1925–70. In quoting any here, when their year had more than one, I have added to her list, marking their position in her order, serial letters (a, b, c, etc.) in the usual manner. (1934h, accidentally omitted, is *Archaeological Journal* 90: 275–97.) Those for 1970–81, reproduced from *Antiquity* 61: 101, were compiled by me, as now have been the rest.

1970. The Sintra gold collar, in G. Sieveking (ed.), *Prehistoric and Roman studies* (= *British Museum Quarterly* 35 (1971)): 38–50.

1971a. Runes and the Caput Adriae, in V. Mirosavljevič *et al.* (ed.), *Adriatica Praehistorica et Antiqua : Mélanges Grga Novak*: 399–407.

1971b. Fence, wall and dump, from Troy to Hod, in M. Jesson & D. Hill (eds.), *The Iron Age and its hill forts*: 5–18.

1971c. North-Western Castros, excavation, archaeology, and history, *Actas do II Congresso Nacional de Arqueologia, Coimbra 1970*: 283–6.

1972a. Europe and England: fact and fog, *Helinium* 12: 105–16.

1972b. Review of Colin Renfrew, *The emergence of civilisation: the Cyclades and the Aegean in the third millennium BC* (1971), *Times Higher Education Supplement* (October).

1973a. Cumulative Celticity in pre-Roman Britain, *Études Celtiques* 13(2): 590–611.

1973b. Edited. *Greeks, Celts and Romans: studies in venture and resistance* (with S. Hawkes) (foreword, four commentaries and collaboration with J. Haberl): 97–149. London: Dent.

1973c. Rescuing archaeology, *Rescue News* 5: 2–3.

1973d. Innocence retrieval in archaeology, *Antiquity* 47: 176–8.

1974a. Bronze Age Hungary, a review of recent work, *Proceedings of the Prehistoric Society* 40: 113–17.

1974b. Zur Stellung und Zeitstellung der Wessex Kultur Südenglands, in *Atti del Simposio sulla Antica Età del Bronzo*, 1972: 291–5.

1974c. Double axe testimonies, *Antiquity* 48: 206–12.

1974d. Review of H. Hencken, *The earliest European helmets*, *American Journal of Archaeology* 78: 92–3.

1974e. Review of K. Spindler, *Magdalenenberg I, II*, *Antiquies Journal* 44: 98–l00.

1975. Archaeology and ancient ideas of a plenteous West, *Ulster Journal of Archaeology* 38: 1–11.

1976a. Celts and cultures, in C.F.C. Hawkes & P.-M. Duval (eds.), *Celtic art in ancient Europe* : 1–27; also 164–5; 281–2.

1976b. Insular Hallstatt and Early La Tène in Britain, *IX Congr. Internat. Sci. Pré- et Protohist., Nice, Colloque XXIX, No. 4* (prétirage).

1976c. Review of R. L. S. Bruce-Mitford, *Aspects of Anglo-Saxon archaeology*, *Antiquaries Journal* 66(1): 104–5.

1976d. St Catharine's Hill, Winchester: the report of 1930 re-assessed, in D.W. Harding (ed.), *Hillforts*: 59–74.

1976e. Review of J. V. S. Megaw (ed.), *To illustrate the monuments*, *Times Literary Supplement* (October).

1976f. Review of M.-R. Sauter, *Switzerland, from earliest times to the Roman Conquest*, *Times Literary Supplement* (October).

1976g. North Germany, Britain and the Fengate Pin, *Antiquaries Journal* 66(2): 234–5.

1977a. *Pytheas – Europe and the Greek explorers.* Oxford: Blackwell.

1977b. Zur Wessex-Kultur, *Jahresbericht d. Inst. f. Vorgeschichte d. Univ. Frankfurt A.M. 1977* (issued 1978):193–9.

1977c. Review of M. Herity & G. Eogan, Ireland in prehistory, *Ulster Journal of Archaeology* 40: 92–6.

1978a. Britain and Julius Caesar, *Proceedings of the British Academy* 63: 25–92.

1978b, c. I Celti nella Protostoria Britannica (trans. Francesca Ridgway), in *I Celti . . . nella Britannia*, abridged, 1–12, as The Celts in British prehistory; also as 1978c in *Irish Archaeological Research Forum* 4(2): 1–6, with 'Some further thoughts', 39.

1979a. Contributions to Dr Grace Simpson, *Antiquaries Journal* 59: 319–42, on penannular brooches in Portugal and Spain (320–22).

1979b. Review of G. Webster, *Boudica*, *Antiquaries Journal* 59: 1–i, 450–1.

1980a. Caesar's Britain: an oppidum for Cassivellaunus, *Antiquity* 44: 138–9.

1980b. From Caesar and the century before him, to the Essex of Claudius, in D.G. Buckley (ed.), *Archaeology in Essex to AD 1950*: 55–8.

1980c. Review of K. Spindler, *Magdalenenberg* III, IV, V (as 1974e: 1973, 1976, 1977), and with E. Hollstein on its dendrochronology, W. Kimmig (ed.), *Antiquaries Journal* 60: 16–18.

1980d. Review of Bruce G. Trigger, *Gordon Childe*, *Times Literary Supplement* (28 November).

1981a. The Lansdown sun-disc, in H. Lorenz (ed.), *Studien zur Bronzezeit: Festschrift Prof. W. A. von Brunn*: 119–30.

1981b. Reply by The Gold Medallist, *Antiquaries Journal* 61: 9.

1981c. Alcoholic food-vessels? *Current Archaeology* 79: 255.

1982a. The wearing of the brooch: early iron age dress among the Irish, in B.G. Scott (ed.), *Studies in early Ireland*: 50–70.

1982b. Archaeological Retrospect 3, *Antiquity* 66: 93–101.

1982c. Review of Barry Cunliffe (ed.), *Coinage and society in Britain and Gaul: some current problems*, *Antiquaries Journal* 62(1): 151–2.

1982d. Review of Clive Partridge, *Skeleton Green: a Late Iron Age and Romano-British site*, *Antiquaries Journal* 62(2): 411–12.

1983a. The Gold Cup from Rillaton in Cornwall, *Antiquity* 67: 124–6.

1983b. Review of Colin Renfrew, *Towards an archaeology of mind*, *Antiquity* 57: 147–8.

1983c. Review of W.J. van der Dussen, *History as a science: the philosophy of R.G. Collingwood*, *Antiquity* 57: 150–1.

1983d. Review of Grahame Clark, *The identity of man*, *Antiquity* 67: 232–3.

1983e (issued 1984). Belgium and Britain in the Urnfield and Hallstatt Periods, *Bulletin des Musées Royaux d'Art et d'Histoire, Parc du Cinquantenaire, Bruxelles* 54.1: 25–35.

1984a. The Castro Culture of the Peninsular North-West: fact and inference, in T. Blagg, R. Jones & S. Keay (eds.), *Papers in Iberian archaeology*: 187–203.

1984b (dated 1982). Colchester before the Romans, or Who were our Belgae? A lecture of 1950 re-assessed, *Essex Archaeology and History* 14: 3–14.

1984c. Ictis disentangled, and the British tin trade, *Oxford Journal of Archaeology* 3: 211–33.

1984d. Celtic studies, Oxford, July 1983 (with E.M. Jope), *Antiquity* 68: 90–4.

1984e. The bronze dagger, form and comparisons, pp. 13–18 of A.D. Jackson, The excavation of a Bronze Age barrow at Earls Barton, Northants., *Northamptonshire Archaeology* 19: 3–30.

1984f. Review of Sigfried J. De Laet, *La Belgique d'avant les Romains*, *Antiquaries Journal* 64(2): 434–5.

1985a. Review of Sarah Macready and F.H. Thompson (eds.), *Cross-channel trade between Gaul and Britain in the Early Iron Age*, *Antiquity* 59: 73–4.

1985b. English translation (1983, with Sonia Hawkes) of Joachim Werner, *Germania* 60 (1982): 193–209, as *The Sutton Hoo Ship-Burial, Research and publication between 1939 and 1980*, privately printed at Oxford.

1986a. Irish archaeology and history, with the Greek and Roman record (author's abstract), in E. E. Evans, J. G. Griffith and M. Jope (eds.), *Proc. VII Internat. Congress of Celtic Studies, Oxford, July 1983*: 278.

1986b. The Research Laboratory: its beginning, *Archaeometry* 28.2: 131–2.

1986c. Memoir of Sir Thomas Kendrick, *Dictionary of National Biography Supplement 1950–1970*.

1986d. Archaeology in Britain since 1945, reviewing the book so named, *Antiquity* 60: 175–8.

1987a, with M.R. Hull, as co-author after his death, of his *Corpus of ancient brooches in Britain: Pre-Roman bow brooches*. Oxford: British Archaeological Reports.

1987b. Archaeologists and Indo-Europeanists: can they mate? Hindrances and hopes, in Susan N. Skomal & Edgar C. Polomé (eds.), *Proto-Indo-European: the archaeology of a linguistic problem*: 203–15.

1988, in the present volume. 1982b in revised form, with bibliography completed.

In preparation. *Camulodunum 2* (sequel to 1947a) (with Philip Crummy).

5

Seton Lloyd

Almost half-a-century ago, I was once referred to by Sidney Smith as someone who had entered archaeology 'by the back door'. In those days there was no well-defined 'front door', though Smith and others were doing their best to create one; and, since I was myself then already well established in a more conventional profession, the implied reproof was perhaps justifiable. In truth, the potential advantages of an architectural training to a field archaeologist were not at that time fully understood, and one purpose of the present writing is to make their significance more apparent.

My own architectural training was a more than ordinarily lengthy affair. When I qualified in 1927, my record of 'Practical Experience' much exceeded the period canonically required. (It included a 12-months spell in the Gray's Inn office of Mrs Gillian Harrison, the first woman architect ever to be awarded a Fellowship of the Royal Institute.) Later in the same year I had the good fortune to be accepted as a junior assistant to Sir Edwin Lutyens, and those which followed were of a sort that one does not easily forget. I recently enjoyed reading Mary Lutyens's study of her father's life and character; but it did at times remind me of the well-known comment by a child on an instructive birthday present. 'This book', she said, 'tells me more about penguins than I care to know.' My own memory is a more day-to-day affair: a picture closely resembling Bernard Partridge's caricature in a contemporary issue of *Punch* (20/7/1927). Here 'Lut' is seen at work in his office overlooking Queen Anne's Gate: a bare room, roughly stripped of all distracting decoration (ornamented at one time only by a painting in oils of Miss Gertrude Jekyll's gardening boots), and he is surrounded by small pipes, ready-filled with tobacco, among a litter of sheets from the special sketching blocks always referred to by him as 'virgins'. And one remembers *Punch's* caption to the picture: a 'jingle' commonly supposed in the office to have been written by himself:

Dead clay and stone leap up at his reveille
To instant life; as by a magic spell he
Inside that massive brain can mould (like jelly)
A royal Doll's House or a second Delhi.

In my time these two miracles were already ancient history, and I had to content myself with work, e.g. on the design for an Ambassador's study in the then new

British Embassy at Washington, seated at (or on) a table ten feet square which had once carried the full-size details of the Cenotaph. After two years in this stimulating atmosphere, I managed to initiate a small practice of my own, using a room off Piccadilly, once occupied by Fanny Burney.

My transition in 1929 from 11 Bolton Street to the Egypt Exploration Society's excavating camp at Tell-el-Amarna was originally in the nature of an accident. To the Director, Henri Frankfort, who was about to begin a new season's work, my arrival must even have been something of a shock, since it was in fact my partner (the late E.B. O'Rorke RA) whom he had interviewed a month earlier and engaged as architect/surveyor. Last minute developments had necessitated an exchange of rôles, and O'Rorke had remained in London to supervise our first major commission. Frankfort accepted the *fait accompli* with characteristic good grace and, in the months that followed, a close friendship developed between us. If the impulse which led me to this sudden decision can now be seen to have had roots in earlier times, they may most easily be revealed biographically.

My father's family is irrevocably categorized as 'Middle Class' in a book by Lewis & Maude (1949: 50), where it is grouped with others such as Gurneys, Frys and Barclays over the following, partly facetious comment: 'The influence of the middle class banking Quakers of the eighteenth and nineteenth centuries was both great and good, as was only to be expected when "the silence in Meeting was such that the drop of an eighth in Consols was clearly audible".' One remembers that, to maintain this traditional decorum, bankers' wives were as a rule discreetly chosen from within the Society of Friends. (A deviation was almost created in the late eighteenth century by one Charles Lloyd, who, 'finding it impossible to remain insensible to the charms of Sophia, daughter of Samuel Pemberton of Birmingham, went so far as to make her an offer in a letter, but, thinking it premature, he hired a postchaise, overtook the mail and got it back again' [Sayers 1957: 25]). My Lloyd grandfather needed to look no further than his Howard cousins, to find a wife whose father and grandfather were both Fellows of the Royal Society. My grandparents have some relevance in the present context because as a schoolboy I was frequently ill, and spent many months with them in their strikingly beautiful home, Grafton Manor near Bromsgrove. Much of the Tudor building had survived, including a sandstone porch in precociously classical style, bearing the arms of Queen Elizabeth I and the date 1567. The Estate Book of the original owner, with his steward's accounts for the years 1567–9, has somehow survived and was published early in the present century by the late John Humphreys FSA (Humphreys 1918). I was given an offprint of this document by my grandmother, and was deeply impressed by her explanation of the letters after his name. The possibility of one day becoming an 'Antiquary' greatly intrigued me and, as a second year architectural student, I was inspired to make measured drawings and a structural analysis of Grafton Manor. Other similar studies followed, but less expected developments were to take place before my election, 40 years later, to a brief Vice-Presidency of the Society.

Tell-el-Amarna was not a site where one could learn much about excavating technique. The building remains were unstratified and, on this occasion, the discovery, barely a foot beneath the surface, of a jar containing 21 bars of gold gave a false impression of archaeological routine (Pendlebury and Frankfort 1933: 61). In a report on this discovery the writer observes: 'A chip had been made in the jar-lid by the tethering-stake of a local worthy. His feelings on hearing what he had missed are recorded but inconvenient to print.' But I did become fascinated by the sophisticated architecture of palatial buildings in the Northern Suburb. I made plans and reconstructions, using the style of draughtsmanship currently taught at the Architectural Association from which I had recently graduated, and these pleased Frankfort. Later in the season, when James Henry Breasted brought his patron, J. D. Rockefeller Jr, to visit the excavation, I was commissioned to make an elaborate scale-model for the newly-founded Oriental Institute of Chicago University (Lloyd 1933: 1–7). It was then also that Frankfort was asked to take charge of the same Institute's projected 'Iraq Expedition', and it was agreed that I should accompany him as senior architect. In subsequent seasons at Amarna, I was replaced successively by two fellow graduates of the 'AA': Ralph Lavers and Hilary Waddington.

My first seasons in Iraq – at Khorsabad and Tell Asmar – were mainly occupied in learning, and then teaching, the technique of wall-tracing in mud-brick buildings, frequently demolished and rebuilt in antiquity. The few surviving *usta* workmen from Koldewey's excavations at Babylon were now too old to be much help, and a younger team of wall-tracers had to be assembled. About this type of excavation so much has already been written by myself and others (e.g. Lloyd: 1963), that any problems which remain can safely be left in the hands of those still active in the same field. But it is worth emphasizing that, once perfected, the procedures involved can now be carried to a peak of fine craftsmanship. Selected at random from my own experience in this respect is an episode during the excavation of a neolithic village with houses built of *pisé* clay (*tauf*). On a certain occasion, two of my most skilled *ustas*, both tracing the same telltale facing of plaster which indicated the presence of a wall, could suddenly be seen unconsciously approaching each other from opposite directions. But from their relative positions it became clear that one or other of them was cutting away the wall itself to expose the reverse side of the plaster. A pause ensued during which bets were laid as to which of them was right; and then (to avoid a blood-feud), both were transferred elsewhere.

Occurrences of this sort are of course no more than items in the complicated duties of an excavator himself. Visiting in turn each centre of activity; called upon by individual pickmen to solve the enigma of some disintegrating structure; standing aside in a mental attempt to interpret the logic of what has been exposed; a share of his attention must at the same time be given to the disposal of spoil by an unskilled labour force. The initial precedent for this kind of procedure was, of course, set by the Germans at Babylon and Ashur in the years preceding my own birth. But, 80 years later, it is interesting to detect in

Koldewey's and Andrae's letters, symptoms of violent dissension when the
epigraphical conclusions of their sponsors in Berlin were firmly refuted by the
material evidence of discoveries made by their architects *in situ*.

A situation, which may be regarded as the reverse of the above, arose during
my earliest years in Iraq. In the spring of 1933, after the conclusion of
Frankfort's second season at Tell Asmar, a short collaboration was arranged
between myself and Thorkild Jacobsen (later doyen of American Assyriolo-
gists), to investigate some unidentified ruins at Jerwan, about 24 km north of
Khorsabad. Their existence had been noted by early travellers, including
Layard, King and Bachmann, none of whom could satisfactorily explain their
origin. But Jacobsen, on a visit during the previous year, had succeeded not only
in reading the name of Sennacherib on a fallen stone but in learning from another
fragmentary inscription something more about the structure to which they
belonged. The vital passage (later completed), read as follows:

I caused a canal to be dug to the meadows of Nineveh.
Over deep ravines I spanned a bridge of white stone blocks.
Those waters I caused to pass over upon it.

Our permit to excavate was limited to one month only. By the end of that time
we had been able to expose and record the astonishing remains of Sennacherib's
aqueduct, still standing to a height of almost seven metres. To quote from our
publication (Jacobsen and Lloyd 1935):

As the width of the aqueduct without its buttresses is 22 m and its length more than 280
m, it will be realized that a great mass of masonry is involved. If we assume the blocks of
stone to average rather less than 50 cm cubed, the number of stones would be well in
excess of two million.

The surface over which the water flowed was paved with stone over a layer of
concrete, not only graded to an exact incline, but smoothly chamfered,
presumably to allow the passage of wheeled vehicles when dry. A stream in the
bed of the *wâdi* flowed beneath four corbelled arches. The façades of neat ashlar
masonry were ornamented with repetitive inscriptions. From these Jacobsen
was able to learn that the canal had its source on the Gomel river, at a spot near
Bavian, well known for its rock-carvings. From there, by a route which the
inscription enabled him to trace, it brought fresh water to Nineveh almost 50
miles away.

The Assyrian rock-carvings in the gorge through which the Gomel river
passes at Hinnes above Bavian, were at that time already known and published.
In comparing their accompanying inscriptions with those found on the
aqueduct, it became clear to Jacobsen that here indeed was the head of
Sennacherib's canal. According to one text, the whole operation was completed
and an inaugural ceremony performed in the year 690 BC. Intriguing also was
the mention in Sennacherib's official account of a mishap which took place on

1   Gordon Childe (second from left) at the Congress of Prehistoric and Protohistoric Sciences, 1950. Flanking him, from left to right: Kathleen Kenyon, R.J.C. Atkinson, Stuart Piggott, Grahame Clark and Christopher Hawkes; by the door, R.J. Braidwood.

2 Stuart Piggott and
H.St.G. Gray at the
Thickthorn Down
long barrow
excavation, 1933.

3 Gordon Childe
visiting Stuart
Piggott's excavations
at Dorchester-on-
Thames in 1946.

4   Glyn Daniel (centre), Stuart Piggott (left of GD) and Terence Powell (same row, far right) with some other members of the Central Photographic Interpretation Section staff in India during the Second World War.

5,6 Charles Phillips (*above*) in a trench at Sutton Hoo, July 1939, where he uncovered the remains of a great Anglo-Saxon ship burial (*below*).

7   Christopher Hawkes in 1954.

8 Tell Agrab, Iraq, in the 1930s: left to right, Gordon Loud, Pinhas Delougaz, Henri Frankfort, Thorkild Jacobsen and Seton Lloyd.

9 The Shah of Iran visits the Iraq Museum in the 1940s; Seton Lloyd at the back, far right.

10   Seton Lloyd (second from right) with Sir Archibald Creswell and Naji al-Asil in the ruins of the Mustaneiriyah at Baghdad.

11   Tell ʿUqair, 1941: Seton Lloyd (standing, second from right) with Fuad Safar to the left and other members of the excavation team.

12   The original field staff of the Istanbul–Chicago Universities Joint Prehistoric Project at Çayönü, southeastern Turkey: left to right, Linda S. Braidwood, Bruce Howe, Robert J. Braidwood and Halet Çambel.

13   Air view of the excavations at Çayönü in 1982.

14   Gordon Willey in a test pit at Barton Ramie during the innovative Belize Valley project of 1953–6.

15   Sigfried J. de Laet (foreground) and one of his pupils, Louis Vanden Berghe, excavating a Romano-Celtic *fanum* at Hofstade, Belgium, in 1949.

16   C.J. Becker, excavation director at Grøntoft, an early iron age village, 1972.

17   J. Desmond Clark at Berkeley, 1979.

18   Clark with Glynn Isaac on the 1967 Pan–African Congress excursion to the Mauretanian Sahara.

19   Shelter 2, Fromm's Landing, Murray River, South Australia: D.J. Mulvaney and 5,000 years of occupation deposit excavated during the first season in 1956.

20   Rhys Jones and D.J.
Mulvaney at the entrance to
Kutikina (Fraser) cave, 1982.

21   Second season of
excavations at Fromm's
Landing, 1958.

22 Tailpiece: John Mulvaney's photograph of a Cambridge student field class, Stonehenge, 1953, with Grahame Clark and Stuart Piggott at apparent loggerheads.

this particular occasion. 'Before the engineers in charge were ready to open the sluices, the pressure became too great and a breach occurred, presumably behind them.' Fortunately, the King was persuaded that this did not portend any displeasure on the part of the gods whose help he had invoked. On the contrary, over-anxious to see the canal in use, they had 'caused the water to dig'. The breach was accordingly repaired, the architects rewarded and the images of the gods carved on the rocks above the canal's 'mouth'.

Anxious to study the scene of these events, we returned there in the following spring and were able to spend three weeks in surveying the Hinnes gorge and recopying its inscriptions. The results, which appear in the plan and diagrams of our report (Jacobsen and Lloyd 1935), make every detail of the Assyrian record comprehensible. Near the weir by which the river was diverted, there is a spacious quarry: evidently the source of the stone used for the Jerwan aqueduct. From this point (where a stone monument still lies half-submerged in the river), we traced a paved upper reach of the canal down to the narrow outlet of the gorge: the site of the dam which could, when required, create a reservoir. It was here that a few hours' excavation revealed a tunnel, cut through a spur of the rock, in which the sluices had been constructed. When the results of this short survey were added to our report on the aqueduct and published in the following year, a pattern was set in my mind for future 'combined operations' of the same sort.

In the later years of the Chicago Expedition, Jacobsen and I were separated: he to excavate the Diyala site called Ischali (Neribtum), assisted by the late Harold Hill, a fine draughtsman from Harvard. My own assignment was the great Shara Temple at Tell Agrab where I worked alone, returning each evening to headquarters at Tell Asmar (32 km cross-desert). I must by then, I think, have attained qualifications as an excavator, conforming to current standards of method and professional ethics; for I was able later to comment as follows on the success of this project:

The combined work of supervising, surveying and controlling labour on a dig where over 100 local workmen were employed, would normally be considered over much responsibility for one person. But I had completed a topographical survey of the mound before excavating and, for the rest, was supported by a team of specialists at the Asmar base: draughtsmen, photographers, conservators, etc., who were available to assist me on demand. In fact, the whole excavating system had been so perfected during the past six years of work together, that no procedural detail was neglected.

Whether this claim was justified, readers of the final publication (Delougaz and Lloyd 1942) will long ago have judged for themselves. These 'satellite' excavations (Agrab, Ischali and Khafaje), served in some degree to justify the lavish scale on which Frankfort's headquarters at Tell Asmar were designed and equipped. In its remote desert setting, tiled bathrooms with running hot water, library, laboratory and so forth did not escape the notice of our less fortunate foreign colleagues. The Germans for instance, in their modest accommodation at Uruk/Warka, paraphrasing the title of our first publication (Frankfort *et al.* 1940), referred to it as the 'Palace of the Excavators at Tell Asmar'. Their irony would, in fact, have been more perceptively directed to the Oriental Institute's contemporary establishments in neighbouring countries: to Chicago House at Luxor; to the Syrian Expedition's dig-house at Rihaniyah (where the ceilings proved too low for the American beds with their mosquito-proof superstructures): or to Megiddo in Palestine, where P. L. O. Guy spent a quarter of his generous budget on the installation of a kite-balloon, to photograph the wrongly identified remains of 'Solomon's Stables'. For a similar purpose at Asmar, I effectively substituted two 'Naval' kites and a box camera with a delayed release, at a cost of £18.

During the two final years of the inter-war period, I was given the opportunity to work in a new environment and the experience of adapting myself to a different type of excavation. At Mersin in Cilicia, I assisted John Garstang in his stratigraphic investigation of a mound occupied from the Early Neolithic to the Iron Age; the buildings being in this case predominantly constructed of stone. Among our discoveries in 30-or-so occupation levels, perhaps the most memorable of all was the miniature fortress crowning the mound at Level XVI, dated around 4000 BC (Garstang 1953). The outer profile of its defences, with a powerful wall protected by a steep *glacis*, was exposed during our first season by a sounding in the flank of the hill. Built against the inside face of the wall, later excavation revealed a range of uniformly planned dwellings for the garrison, each with a pair of 'slit-windows' facing the countryside. In one, the crushed remains of reed-and-clay fittings for food storage and cooking, proved identical with those which I had noted and drawn some months earlier, while staying in one of the 'domed villages' of North Syria (Lloyd 1935; Garstang 1953).

In Iraq meanwhile, the Oriental Institute's excavations had come to an end and Frankfort was dividing his time between concurrent professorial responsibilities in the universities of Chicago and Amsterdam. During my own interlude in Turkey, I suffered – perhaps more than I realized at the time – as a result of my separation from him. He had till now been my mentor, steering my activities with a characteristically gentle hand, and sustaining in me an awareness of the true purpose and significance of the occupation which I had now permanently adopted. I admired him no less as a man than as a scholar; for in both capacities, as has been said of him posthumously, he was deeply concerned with cultural and human values: 'Quick to rise in defence when these values were neglected through ignorance, indifference or insincerity he would speak out clearly, impatiently and succinctly: a brisk, clear wind cutting through fog' (Delougaz and Jacobsen 1955). The same writers have perceptively added, 'It was impossible to work under him; one always found one was working with him.' Of certain more senior colleagues however, whose theories he considered antiquated, he would speak with humorous disparagement, and to a query regarding the whereabouts of one or another, would reply, 'Still, I think, whitening his perch at Munich' or elsewhere. No less characteristically, my wife and I remember him in his garden at Kimmeridge, thoughtfully contemplating a tiny seedling: 'Man, how does this *know* to be a tobacco-plant?'

The outbreak of war in 1939 occurred some months after my appointment to replace Julius Jordan (Sidney Smith's German successor as adviser to the Iraq Department of Antiquities). War experiences are of course extraneous to my present subject; though it is hard to forget the abortive visit of the Luftwaffe to the country in 1941, which interrupted my partnership with Fuad Safar in the excavation of our fourth-millennium 'Painted Temple' at Tell 'Uair; or later, when a German attack from the north appeared imminent, my discovery that the Royal Engineers were about to install a mammoth fuel-tank in the convenient depths of the Kuyunjik mound at Nineveh: a potential target for enemy bombing. Meanwhile, the mention of 'Uqair brings to mind a more professional reflexion. The discovery of that site serves to emphasize the important rôle played by local authority in controlling the overall strategy of archaeological research in any particular country. 'Uqair for instance, and later Hassuna, were both objectives judiciously chosen from an immense catalogue of sites (listed and identified chronologically by the Department's mobile team of inspectors), on account of their relevance to a specific channel of enquiry. By contrast, to major sites in a different category: Eridu and 'Aqar Qûf, being already well known, were wisely given primary attention for reasons not unrelated to national *amour propre*. During the full ten years of my appointment in Iraq there were of course minor excavations in other localities, chosen to provide experience for younger Iraqis whose competence to operate independently became increasingly evident. At Tell Harmal (Shaduppum, an administrative outpost of Eshnunna), an unique archive of tablets was handled and published by our epigraphist, Taha Baqir, and a widespread programme of conservation and restoration occupied other staff members. In earlier days, publication of our archaeological findings presented formidable difficulties owing to the inadequacies of the local press, and English translation required careful scrutiny. In 1941, when I returned from temporary war duties in Palestine, I found that a report in English on the Department's excavations at Samarra was already in proof. In its historical preamble, a line of Arabic poetry referring to the city's ultimate disintegration, was rendered: 'He die as elephant die whose meat is pulled off his rest.' One of the halftone illustrations appeared twice – the second time upside-down.

When the war in Europe drew to a close, the first symptom became apparent of foreign interest in our own work and in the eventual possibility of renewed collaboration. By then however, I knew that my own future lay elsewhere. Mallowan's return to Baghdad in 1949, to reactivate the long suspended functions of the British School of Archaeology in Iraq, coincided with my removal to Ankara, where I had agreed to take charge of an Institute newly founded for the same purpose. I was more than sad to leave Iraq, which had become a second home to me, but glad that the memory of Gertrude Bell could now be revived by the institution founded in 1932 which still bore her name.

Returning to Turkey after ten years' absence, I was faced with the untidy aftermath of a particularly severe winter. For the present my duties consisted first in finding and equipping modest premises in Ankara for our embryo research establishment. Secondly, there was much to learn about a country of which my knowledge was restricted to the outer fringes. A long programme of travel loomed ahead; but for the moment this presented formidable difficulties. Properly metalled roads were still lacking; hotels primitive or non-existent and the eastern provinces still closed to foreigners. Even a visit to the Hittite capital at Boghazköy involved the use of a farm waggon. In Ankara meanwhile, we had begun to accumulate a library of our own, from which I could at least supplement my exiguous knowledge of Anatolian history and archaeology. Among Turkish colleagues, I had become aware of a current focus of interest in 'prehistory' (meaning in this case the Early and Middle Bronze Ages), a sensation having recently been caused by Hamit Kosay's discovery of 'royal tombs' at Alaça Hüyük, and new finds in the Assyrian *karum* at Kültepe. I puzzled for some weeks over reports from these sources, with their frequent references to something called a 'Copper Age', and also over Von der Osten's empirical conclusions from his pre-war excavations at Alishar. But patience with other people's reasoning was eventually exhausted, and I was delighted when a more practical approach became feasible. I was permitted to share with a Turkish friend the cost of a stratigraphic sounding in a mound at Polatli, west of Ankara, and taught myself more by a diagrammatic analysis of its pottery sequence than I could have in several further months of library work.

Apart from this experiment in excavation, I did contrive to spend much time during the summer of 1949 in travelling. Thanks to the hospitality of John Cook, I was able to use as a base the attractively situated camp at Bayrakli (Old Smyrna), where he was excavating one of the earliest Greek settlements for the Athens School. I journeyed among the ruined cities of the Aegean coast: 'places', as Herodotus said, 'more favoured by skies and seasons than any country known to us'. But by the following spring, my mind had returned to the austere and less frequented uplands bordering the north Syrian frontier, west of the Euphrates, with their fortress-cities: Urfa, Diyarbakir, Mardin and others. They had not been seen by foreigners, almost since the time of Gertrude Bell. I had visited them briefly *en route* from Mersin to Sinjar in 1938, omitting only the ruins of Harran, which proved inaccessible for military reasons. Now in 1950, with no funds available for excavation, it was the remains of this great 'crossroads city' (briefly described by Lawrence in *Oriental assembly*), which suggested itself for a survey, of the kind which I had managed successfully at Bavian and again (with Gerald Reitlinger), in the Sinjar province of north Iraq (Lloyd 1938). Once more I found a collaborator in the person of William Brice, geographer and archivist, who ably contributed an historical study of the place and its surroundings. Three weeks' work, in the intense heat of July, produced an architectural recording by myself of the huge medieval castle, and Brice's unique plan of the ruins as they appear today (inexplicably destroyed after publication by Gordon Childe who was then editor of *Anatolian Studies* (Lloyd and Brice 1951)).

Minor discoveries at Harran still create vignettes in one's memory: a defaced wall-inscription near the entrance to the Great Mosque, in which Brice recognized the name of Saladin (*Salah-ad-Dunya-wa-ad-Din*); a chamber in the Castle ruins, adapted by a 'Norman' archway for use as a Christian chapel during the Crusader Countship of Edessa (AD 1098–1146); and finally, Jacob's Well (*Bi'r Ya'qub*) – a mile outside the walls, but today the only source of drinking-water. It is still approached by the vaulted ramp, *down* which Rebekah went to draw water for Abraham's servant (*Gen.* 24.25), though a padlocked door in the superstructure now replaces the 'stone' which Jacob rolled away for Rachel (*Gen.* 29.10).

By the spring of 1951, the Institute's budget had increased to a degree where some excavation was again practicable, and a new objective had to be considered. While at Harran I had been continually conscious of the high central mound, beneath which it could be assumed that the ruins of the famous Sin Temple of Assyrian times might well be buried. Being, however, well aware of the prodigious task which its excavation would entail, we cast about for something more manageable among the neighbouring sites from which Assyrian remains were reported. Continued in the following spring, our quest brought us to the promising mound called Sultantepe, standing almost 50 m above the plain between Harran and Urfa. Its excavation was to occupy us for two summer seasons. In my report on the Sultantepe dig, something needed to be said about archaeological method. The unconventional expedients to which we resorted in examining and recording the peripheral chambers of an Assyrian acropolis, beneath 20 m of Hellenistic and Roman overlay, could well have invited some adverse criticism on the grounds of professional ethics (*cf.* Lloyd 1963: 94–5). In the event, our own justification would seem to have been deemed logical, and our discovery of a formidable Assyrian library to be regarded as a mere bonus. Today, it is of some interest to remember the distinguished names of my field staff on that occasion, which, apart from Turkish co-workers, included Oliver Gurney, John Evans, Basil Hennessy and G.R.H. Wright. Michael and Mary Gough simultaneously excavated a fine Roman mosaic, conveniently located near the base of the mound.

After Sultentepe, there was to be one more co-operative survey, pending the accumulation of funds for the prolonged and full-scale excavation of a major Anatolian site. My collaborator this time was the late David Storm Rice, a well-known Islamic art-historian, who was currently operating independently for the SOAS at Harran, making clearances in the Great Mosque and Castle. The joint project which we planned for the summer of 1953 was an historical and architectural study of Alanya: the remarkable fortress and naval base, built by Ala'ud-Dîn Kaykubad on a high rock projecting into the sea near Antalya. Unlike the excavations at Harran, which still remain unpublished owing to Storm Rice's untimely death, our joint work at Alanya became the subject of an attractive book (Lloyd and Rice 1958), of which a Turkish edition has since been produced.

While Storm and I were scrambling precariously over our Seljuk fortifications, world events such as the Coronation, the Conquest of Everest and the Turkish Quincentenary (1953) passed almost unnoticed over our heads. More important for myself in the autumn of that year was the birth of a major project for the Institute. During the summer months, James Mellaart, one of its first scholars, had almost completed his unique mound-survey of south-western Anatolia, and the site now selected for excavation was one which he himself had recommended for consideration. During the decades which have elapsed since that time, repeated attempts to reconstruct the bronze age geography of Anatolia have usually been frustrated by the conflicting evidence of the Hittite texts. From the resulting welter of speculation, one relatively unanimous conclusion has persisted. This concerns the location of Arzawa: a major state well known both to the Hittites and to the Egyptians. The mound called Beycesultan, planted firmly in its presumed centre on the upper Meander river, suggested by its size and shape a major Arzawan city; the surface pottery testifying to its occupation from the Chalcolithic to the Late Bronze Age. Six seasons of excavation (Lloyd and Mellaart, 3 vols. 1962–72) proved, in the absence of any written records, that both these assumptions were correct.

While preparing for the Beycesultan excavations, I felt for the first time obliged to consider changes at home in the current attitude to archaeological teaching and practice: the new judgements which were at that time being freely formulated. Any conscious system of teaching had till that time played little part in my experience of project organization. Under Frankfort or Garstang, and as director of national enterprises in Iraq, the staff of expeditions in which I was concerned had been recruited or co-opted economically for special functions, such as architect/surveyor, draughtsman, conservator, etc. The actual excavations were 'conducted' by the director; any form of teaching being restricted to the inclusion of an assistant supervisor, whose function was that of an apprentice, qualifying for fuller independence.

It was accordingly with some misgivings that I now accepted applications from students – often graduates of the new Regent's Park Institute – to be given field experience on a Near Eastern excavation. They would, I thought, be conditioned to the 'procedural liturgy', advocated by the successors of Pitt-Rivers in Roman Britain, and bewildered by the labour-intensive activity to which we ourselves were accustomed. In the event however, they seemed easily to adapt themselves to the empirical requirements of a different milieu: glad in some cases to escape from the tyranny of geometrical 'balks' and the territorial confinement of 'trench' supervision. Their 'sections' however, were always immaculately recorded (save for one masterpiece – a yard long – which proved afterwards to be constructed on an arbitrary baseline, unrelated in any way to the system of levels recorded elsewhere by my surveyors).

Beycesultan in retrospect: apart from the establishment of a definitive pottery sequence for south-west Anatolia in the fifth to second millennia, it is the elucidation of the building remains which should always be remembered as having provided a task of unparalleled complexity. Where the middle bronze age palace was concerned, one must imagine a building of a hundred-or-so rooms in two storeys, for whose construction a comparison could be found in the 'half-timber' mansions of Tudor England, totally destroyed by fire and its ruins briefly occupied by squatters. Our drawn reconstruction (Lloyd and Mellaart 1965: 30), owes very little to conjecture. In this and other tasks presented to us at that site, the ability and enthusiasm of my staff provided a welcome bonus. Each is still associated in my memory with the solution of one problem or another, and their names – even when stripped of their subsequent titles – make a formidable list. Stronach, Mellaart, Burney, Goff, Wright, Beasley, Carswell, Macqueen, Wilson, Harrison, Burton-Brown, H. Smith and Ballance all contributed. One should add that the paucity in successive years of 'removable antiquities' has since found compensation in the reaction of specialists to our harvest of environmental evidence. One privilege bestowed on me in this connexion was a stimulating correspondence with Hans Helbaek, the gifted Danish paleobotanist, of whose sad death we learnt in February 1981. In our 'Burnt Palace' at Beyce, the collapsed upper floors of some minor chambers had been bedded at regular intervals with straw and rushes, now conveniently compressed and lightly carbonized. Helbaek was characteristically enthusiastic about the bulky samples which I was able to send him, and provided an uniquely comprehensive report, listing both the details of contemporary crops and of the weeds which proliferated among them. The fire, he said, had occurred in the spring.

As the final seasons at Beycesultan drew to an end, interest shifted to the prehistoric site called Hacilar, which James Mellaart was concurrently exploring with such striking success, and subsequently to his sensational discoveries at Çatal Hüyük. The last of these corresponded in time to my own relinquishment of the Ankara directorship, which thereafter remained in the competent hands of the late Michael Gough. I myself spent the first of these years concentrating on the final publication of the Beyce results, enjoying for the first time since the war, the opportunity for a prolonged stay in my own Berkshire home. At one moment, this seemed likely to be terminated by an invitation from the Egypt Exploration Society to take charge of a rescue operation at Qasr Ibrîm: a site due to be flooded by the new 'High Dam'. In the event however, my serious doubt about the wisdom of returning once more to fieldwork in Egypt was resolved by a startling telephone call from Max Mallowan, reminding me of his own imminent retirement from the chair of Western Asiatic Archaeology at the London Institute. His suggestion, that I should offer myself as his successor at first revived residual misgivings regarding my capacity as a teacher. My eventual decision to apply for the post owed much to the advice and encouragement of my closest colleagues, and my unexpected appointment brought renewed confidence.

Certainly, among memories of my seven years' work at the London Institute of Archaeology, stronger recollections remain of what I learnt than of what I taught. When I retired in 1969 – 40 years after my first meeting with Frankfort at Tell-el-Amarna – I found myself at last convinced of my ability to speak and write with authority on my own subject.

References

DELOUGAZ, P. & T. JACOBSEN. 1955 Henri Frankfort memorial issue, *Journal of Near Eastern Studies* 14: 1–3.

DELOUGAZ, P. & S. LLOYD. 1942. *Pre-Sargonid temples in the Diyala region.* Oriental Institute Publications 58. Chicago: University of Chicago Press.

FRANKFORT, H. *et al.* 1940. *The Gimilsin temple and palace of the rulers at Tell Asmar.* Oriental Institute Publications 43. Chicago: University of Chicago Press.

GARSTANG, J. 1953. *Prehistoric Mersin.* Oxford: Clarendon Press.

HUMPHREYS, J. 1918. The Elizabethan estate book of Grafton Manor, *Transactions of the Birmingham Archaeological Society* 44: 1–124.

JACOBSEN, T. & S. LLOYD. 1935. *Sennacherib's aqueduct at Jerwan.* Oriental Institute Publications 24. Chicago: Chicago University Press.

LEWIS, R. & A. MAUDE. 1949. *The English middle classes.* London: Phoenix House.

LLOYD, S. 1933. Model of a Tell-el-Amarna house, *Journal of Egyptian Archaeology*, 19: 1–7.

1935. An Arab house in Terib, north Syria, *The Architect and Building News* (London, 28 June).

1938. Some ancient sites in the Jebel Sinjar district, *Iraq* 5: 123–142.

1963. *Mounds of the Near East.* Edinburgh: Edinburgh University Press.

LLOYD, S. & W. BRICE. 1951. Harran, *Anatolian Studies* 1: 77–111.

LLOYD, S. & O.S. RICE. 1958. *Alanya/Ala'yya.* London: British Institute of Archaeology at Ankara.

LLOYD, S. & J. MELLAART. 1962–72. *Beycesultan.* 3 vols. London: British Institute of Archaeology at Ankara.

PENDLEBURY, J.D.S. & H. FRANKFORT. 1933. *The city of Akhanaten* II. Oxford: Clarendon Press.

SAYERS, R.S. 1957. *Lloyds Bank in the history of English banking.* Oxford: Clarendon Press.

6

Robert J. Braidwood

It is initially flattering to receive an invitation to be retrospective in ANTIQUITY. The moment of truth comes soon, however, as thought about writing begins. Was the growth of one's career and ideas about archaeology so smoothly flowing and well reasoned as casual and doubtless fatuous fancy first recalls? How fairly have earlier attempts at retrospection (and I've attempted several: 1972a; 1972b; 1974) corresponded to reality, and what, if anything, remains to be said? What follows, therefore, is offered most diffidently. My old teacher, Henri Frankfort, claimed the most important element in the formation of a career was good luck: I have certainly had my share of it.

I was born in Detroit, Michigan in 1907. My mother was an Ontario Scot (in fact, all four grandparents came from Scotland). My father, a pharmacist, had a country doctor brother who made a sizable collection of Indian artifacts in central Michigan. This uncle's interest and a secondary school course called 'general science' were the first exposures toward anything resembling archaeology which I recall. Certainly in the earlier 1920s, the press was full of Tutankhamun and the Ur Royal Tombs but I don't think I was much affected.

I entered the College of Architecture at the University of Michigan, but the combination of wretched scholarship and the onset of the Great Depression augured ill for a career in architecture. In January 1930, I shifted to a combined curriculum in ancient history and anthropology, thus inducing a humanities-social sciences personality split which has persisted. At the end of that summer my even very modest abilities as a draughtsman and surveyor brought an invitation to become a junior on Michigan's field staff at Selucia-on-Tigris, south of Baghdad. That did it. I've earned my living at archaeology ever since.

I remained at Michigan until finishing an MA in 1933. It was during this time that Peake & Fleure's *Corridor of time* series and especially Childe's *The most ancient East* had their effect on me. Just why the early Near East had such a pull on my imagination I've never known. At Michigan, however, further study after the MA would then have had to be either in classics and cuneiform studies or in New World archaeology, and neither course attracted me. I've often wondered whether my innate incompetence at language study helped focus my early interests on preliterate societies: if they didn't write anything, I'd not have to learn to read it!

In the autumn of 1933, after a summer on an Indian site in Illinois, I was taken on as field assistant by the University of Chicago Oriental Institute's so-called

Syrian-Hittite expedition in the Amouq, the Plain of Antioch. This was one of a dozen Orinst (= Oriental Institute) operations in Egypt and southwestern Asia which flourished because its founder, James Henry Breasted, had a remarkable ability to fire the imaginations of wealthy donors. I was, incidentally, by no means the only Depression-enforced drop-out from architecture on Orinst's roster in those years. My Amouq job primarily concerned pottery and burials as well as general dig duties: Richard C. Haines (1971) was the staff architect and an excellent one. By 1935 I was allowed to undertake a base cut and a top-to-bottom stratigraphic test, by means of a step trench. The step-trench's yield also served as a yard-stick for a site survey of the valley (Braidwood 1937).

The Amouq expedition was very well housed and supplied in those earlier days. Typical of prevailing practice, a staff of five or six worked 300 and often many more local workmen. We had a nine months' season, mid September to mid June, doing indoor processing of materials when the winter weather was bad. All Orinst staffs were on yearly salaries but maintained themselves when they were not in their field camps. Thus Frankfort's Iraq Expedition, working in far hotter country south of Baghdad, had – perforce – only a four- or five-month field season. By offering free maintenance (and 'a bottle a week') we normally doubled our Amouq staff with Iraq Expedition people before and after their own field season. Frankfort himself would stay perhaps a week en route in and out; such younger colleagues as Thorkild Jacobsen and Seton Lloyd gave us most of their available time.

Frankfort had, in our earlier Amouq years, not yet been made a professor in Chicago and there was no possibility anywhere in the States for me to develop a higher degree in Near Eastern prehistory. Frankfort encouraged me to write to Childe. This resulted in Childe's invitation to visit him, which I did in the summer of 1935 while he was working near Ballycastle in northern Ireland. My first impression of Childe was of a face abloom and peeling with sunburn, but also of a most enthusiastic and engaging personality (either unconscious of his frightening appearance or enjoying pretending to be!). He was clearly fascinated with what we were doing in the Amouq. We made tentative plans that I would come to Edinburgh for a doctorate in several years, when I had acquired more field experience and sufficient capital. Thus began a warm relationship which lasted until Childe's death. Bruce Trigger's new biography reminds me vividly of how much Gordon Childe affected my thinking and of how indebted I am to him.

We last saw Childe in London in the early summer of 1955. He seemed in fine spirits. Being driven around the city by him filled us with mind-boggling fright – his mind was everywhere but on the traffic. Linda was happy to be deposited somewhere and I was taken on to dinner at the Athenaeum. It was, as Trigger relates, in the washroom before dinner that Childe called my attention to his wretched trousers, '. . . bought them 25 years ago in Belgrade and aren't they still fine?' There was something delightfully impish about him.

Incidentally, Halet Çambel tells me that when he was at last en route back to Australia, Childe stopped in Istanbul and phoned her. She picked him up, says that he was his usual engaging self and that he particularly wanted to see the Kum Tepe material. It is still difficult for her (as it is for Linda and me) to credit Childe's death to long-premeditated suicide.

That the Edinburgh plans never happened depended on a variety of events of the later 1930s. Breasted's death and the Depression curtailed Orinst field activities. The Iraq expedition closed in 1936 although the Amouq lasted until 1938. In early 1937, Linda and I were married and she joined the Amouq field staff. I was also assured of eventual publication responsibilities in Chicago. Frankfort now had a resident professorship there and the possibility of my doing a doctorate and Linda an MA became real. Indeed, Childe, when he came to the States for a symposium in Philadelphia in 1937, encouraged the new arrangement.

It is, of course, fascinating in recollection to have spanned archaeology's transition, in southwestern Asia, from field practice as it was in 1930 to that of today. With very few exceptions (Mallowan's Arpachiyah being one), sites were still selected because they were believed to be settlements with historically known names. Work on either pleistocene or later prehistoric sites was very rare. I would doubt that field procedures and the proportion of staff size to local crews had yet changed much since the early days of Nineveh or Troy. Non-artifactual categories received little or no attention; architecture, tombs, metals, pottery, fine ground stone and, of course, where they appeared, cuneiform tablets were the standard fare. Given the usual large size of work forces and the considerable areas exposed, the sheer bulk of artifacts tended to overwhelm the abilities of the small staff to process adequately and eventually publish the yield. From the point of view of ease in arranging for permits to work and for help in disputes with local landlords and so on, it was normally very easy for foreign excavators during the days of the mandates. I insist, however, that in my experience, both the British–Iraqi and the French–Syrian antiquities services were strictly fair to all sides, including the end-of-season divisions of antiquities.

Inevitably my pre-war recollections go well beyond archaeology itself. I am very glad I can remember how it was to cross the desert from Damascus to Baghdad following the dust of a Nairn Transport bus, shepherded on from Rutbah Wells by an RAF armoured car. Those were days of sweetly relaxed travel on ocean liners not yet converted to a Caribbean cruise trade which takes the Las Vegas strip as a model. Indeed, finding an Atlantic crossing at all, by boat, is now a real problem. The Orient Express was still in its glory: travel then had human dimensions which airplanes simply cheat one of.

At one of the Amouq sites, we were quite near the Woolleys when they began to work at Atchana. It was a wonderful experience to have Woolley visit your own site. His eyes would sparkle and he would do all the explaining, telling you exactly what had gone on in every room and corner. When the Atchana expedition house was being built, Lady Woolley had the odd notion that she wanted a large picture window with a fireplace directly below it, and the even odder notion that only I knew how to design the fireplace and flue. I did so with great trepidation, I can't remember how, but the fireplace worked and didn't smoke.

Fieldwork terminated in the Amouq in September 1938, and Linda and I came home over a Europe tense with the Czech crisis. (We crossed the Atlantic on the North German Lloyd's *Europa*, finding her stripped and ready to run to Argentina if necessary!). We formally entered the University of Chicago as graduate students. Frankfort's lectures on Near Eastern art and archaeology, and then his remarkable seminar, began in October. The seminar involved the analysis of all available published reports on sites in the Near East and the Aegean with materials prior to *c.* 2000 BC. Almost all of the participants had actually worked in the areas they chose for analysis. Frankfort's seminar lasted until 1945. The original participants were D. E. McCown (Persia), A.L. Perkins, P. Delougaz and T. Jacobsen (Mesopotamia), L. McKaller (Anatolia), R.J. Braidwood (Syria), G.E. Wright (Palestine), H. Kantor, R.A. Parker and J.A. Wilson (Egypt), S. Weinberg (Aegean) and L.S. Braidwood (chipped stone materials generally).

We also attended A.T. Olmstead's lectures in ancient history and I arranged a third of my curriculum in the Department of Anthropology: Old World prehistory, some ethnology and physical anthropology. I was even browbeaten into doing a half year of an ancient Oriental language; I was advised to select Hebrew – both the instructor and I suffered intensely. Linda and I also settled in on final processing for publication, first of the materials we (1940) excavated on the Syrian coast and subsequently on the earlier Amouq materials (1960).

During the summer of 1940, I was asked to act as field superintendent on the Field Museum's excavation of an early village site in highland New Mexico. It was a completely enjoyable experience but I mention it primarily in order to observe that I simply could not, in my imagination, visualize the people who were the site's original inhabitants. The 'pull' which the early peoples of the Near East seem to have for me did not extend to the inhabitants of the American southwest. I do not know why.

When the United States entered the war, I became involved in a meteorology training programme at Chicago. I can't remember much about it: I did hear afterwards that our weather prognostications for the Sicily invasion were sadly wrong. It was possible to moonlight after the hours of the meteorology job. I began teaching Old World prehistory in the Department of Anthropology and completed my Ph.D degree in 1943.

As the war ended, the Department began to re-tool its curriculum for the anticipated return of GIs. Sol Tax (1945), with W.M. Krogman and myself assisting, worked hard on the construction of a year-long course called *Human origins*, complete with an elaborate syllabus and two reading volumes, one of older already published papers and one of original papers. As part of this effort, I sought Gordon Childe's aid and advice and he responded most handsomely. His 'The Orient and Europe' paper was included in the first of the reading volumes and he gave sound criticism on papers Linda and I prepared for the second. The course was given, seminar fashion, around a large round table, and there were always two or sometimes three of us in action.

It was during the preparation of the *Human origins* materials that our ideas for future field work came into final focus. In 1944, we had done a paper on some Samarran pottery from a site on the middle Euphrates (Braidwood *et al.* 1944). The paper included a chart emphasizing a gap in available knowledge between the then-known latest Pleistocene and the earliest village site materials. This 'gap chart', revised and expanded, was used again in one of the *Human origins* papers (*cf.* Braidwood 1972a) and clearly delineated what we saw as a focal point for new field research.

By late 1946, Thorkild Jacobsen, then Orinst's director, began encouraging plans for new field programmes. We proposed returning to Syria, beginning with expanded exposures adjacent to the old French sondages on the same middle Euphrates Samarran site, thence doing survey farther up the river valley. This would put us east but not too far east of the Amouq, with which materials we were usefully familiar. Jacobsen's own prime desire was for a renewed Orinst effort in the literate range of classic southern Mesopotamia. He proposed sending P. Delougaz there and agreed to our plan for Syria. The prevailing political circumstances prevented both plans from working: Delougaz had Zionist connexions about which the Iraqis knew, and Syria, newly independent, was not yet ready to receive foreign excavators. (We are, of course, always wryly amused to think that had Syria agreed, we would probably have turned up a Bouqras or a Mureybet on the middle Euphrates.) Jacobsen then asked us to consider Iraq, to which we agreed if we could do prehistoric excavations hopefully as far to the north and west as possible, again to take advantage of our Amouq experience. We had also been asked by our old friend Seton Lloyd to aid in getting his and Fuad Safar's Hassuna report published. This also whetted our interest in northern Iraq.

Correspondence with Lloyd, then advisor to the Iraqi Directorate of Antiquities, assured us of welcome but indicated that foreigners were not then encouraged to work in the far northwest. Instead, we were particularly invited to consider Matarrah, a Hassuna-type mound on the piedmont just south of Kirkuk, also Jarmo, which he and Safar took to be a 'Mesolithic' site in the Zagros hills east of Kirkuk. I allow myself a dreadful pun only to emphasize that we ourselves did not find Jarmo: we asked for permission for both sites, site unseen, trusting Lloyd's and Safar's judgement.

Our first description of work at Jarmo appeared in ANTIQUITY (1950). The general spirit of the paper had heavy 'gap chart' overtones. The Sialk I, Hassuna, Amouq A-B, Jericho IX and Fayum A types of assemblages were assumed to be those of the earliest then available villages and were contrasted with the far simpler Natufian assemblage. We firmly asserted that the Jarmo assemblage fell within the gap between. The phrase 'the hilly flanks of Breasted's "Fertile Crescent"' was first used, it being claimed that each of the western Asiatic assemblages came from above the present 250 mm or even the 500 mm isohyet. We said that our recovered plant and animal remains had been put in the hands of such interested natural science colleagues as we could find and one radiocarbon age assay was reported; C-113 at 6707±320 b.p., one of Willard Libby's first runs on unknowns.

Being handy in Chicago in those years, we had served as minor midwives' assistants in Libby's developing radiocarbon programme. We were, of course, innocently convinced that big SCIENCE would now solve all chronological problems. Although the *Human origins* 'gap chart' had provided pre-radiocarbon guess dates for the beginning of the gap (end Natufian) at '*c.* 7000 b.c. ± 1,000 years' and its end (Hassuna, Amouq A-B, etc.) at '*c.* 5500 b.c. ± 500 years' – not bad for guessing, I still think – our ANTIQUITY paper tried to justify C-113, the *c.* 4750 b.c. radiocarbon assay for Jarmo. We reasoned, on the analogy of a much accelerated pace of technological development following the industrial revolution, that rapid technological (and cultural) acceleration would have followed the appearance of food-production, which we accepted without question as a revolution. Thus, we reasoned, food-production could have started much later than we had first thought but, when it once started – wow! Childe liked the whole idea, warning us only that there would be great difficulty in identifying the very start, the first sub-era of food-production which we presently came to think of as a range of incipience. And, although the C-113 sample was of shell, two samples of Jarmo charcoal flecks were subsequently run by Libby, all by the old dry carbon method, and Frederik Zeuner's counter also ran two samples. The results all averaged out close to 4750 b.c. and the case for very rapid acceleration, given food-production, seemed crystal clear.

Our 1950–51 field season at Jarmo saw the most extensive exposures of our three seasons there. Bruce Howe began his clearances at the still earlier (incipient sub-era) site of Karim Shahir. Herbert E. Wright, Jr, had his first geological field season with the Prehistoric Project (which we were now beginning to call it). Frederic Barth, because of earlier studies in palaeontology, served with us as field zoologist, then stayed on to begin his Kurdish studies. Further, we had not been long in camp before I received a letter from Hans Helbaek, referring to the 1950 ANTIQUITY article and asking whether he could possibly be sent samples of Jarmo plant remains.

Helbaek did not reach Iraq itself until our 1954–5 season, which was also Charles A. Reed's first season as staff zoologist. We spent the autumn of 1954 doing survey and a few tests (at Banahilk, M'lefaat, etc.) in the Erbil region, returning to Jarmo in the spring of 1955. The much-increased size of that season's staff was due to our first grant from the National Science Foundation (NSF). Having learned of our interest in the field participation of natural scientists to gain understanding of an ancient environmental situation, NSF actually invited us to apply for a field grant. We have had aid from NSF ever since, supplemented by Wenner Gren and American Schools of Oriental Research grants as well as our University's fundings.

It was following the third Iraqi field season that the so-called Jarmo–Jericho controversy boiled over. Kathleen Kenyon reported the first radiocarbon assays for her PPNB (Pre-Pottery Neolithic B) assemblage (technologically quite analogous to that of Jarmo although different in detail) at about 6000 b.c. Our two papers in ANTIQUITY (1957: 73ff) record Braidwood's outrage, basically, at not being allowed to keep his late but fast-paced acceleration and Kenyon's stout defence of an early birth of 'urbanism' at Jericho. In retrospect, I'm sure both our positions grossly exaggerated the then-available evidence. I also think, however, that such academic storms in teacups help draw interest towards a research focus. Certainly, from that time onwards the search for early village sites in southwestern Asia became a very fashionable activity which has had fruitful results.

As to Jarmo's radiocarbon age determinations, assays made in six different laboratories on 18 different samples now span a range between 5266 ± 450 b.p. and 11240 ± 300 b.p. (in Libby half life, uncalibrated, terms). I'm myself convinced that as a single-phase site, Jarmo's occupation cannot have been over 500 years. My own inclination is to think, in uncalibrated Libby terms, of about 6750 ± 250 b.c., based in part on one particular cluster of assays and in part on my sense of the Jarmo assemblage's analogies with other early village materials which have age determinations. Our friend H.T. Waterbolk (1971) favours about 6000 b.c. and suggests that the broad range of the assays may well be due to bitumen contamination.

It was our firm intention to return to the Iraqi Zagros, but in 1958 the monarchy fell and troubles resumed in the northern hill country; a new permit to work was not forthcoming. After being declined permission to work in southeastern Turkey, we gladly accepted the suggestion of an old student, Ezat Negahban, that we try the Iranian Zagros. Negahban worked jointly with us near Kermanshah, where we spent the 1959–60 field year doing survey and test excavations. The agronomist, Jack R. Harlan, was added to the staff and, on a grant of her own, Patty Jo Watson (1979) tried her hand at ethnoarchaeology. Bruce Howe tested two caves and Asiab, an incipient village site; our main exposures (of no great size) were on Sarab, a village mound yielding an assemblage of basically Jarmo-like aspect but somewhat more developed and later.

That we did not continue field work in Iran resulted from two circumstances. First, we our selves discovered, late in 1962, that a joint effort with Halet Çambel of Istanbul University, in archaeologically unknown (and politically restricted) southeastern Turkey, would be possible. Second, what was almost an archaeological population explosion was taking place in the Iranian Zagros. To name but a few, Cuyler Young's Toronto expedition, already at work east of Kermanshah, was soon joined by P.E.L. Smith at Ganj Dareh and subsequently by Louis Levine in the Mahidasht valley. Orinst helped our former student assistants, Frank Hole and Kent Flannery, begin at Ali Kosh and the Danes started work at Tepe Guran.

In all probability the most significant achievement of our own 1959–60 Iranian season was the beginning of Wright's palynological investigations, especially at Lake Zeribar. Willem van Zeist joined Wright in the early analysis of the Zeribar results, and in 1963 they both returned to the lake for more coring. For the first time, solid evidence for a climatic and vegetational history of inland southwestern Asia, for the last 40,000 years, began to build up (Wright 1968; van Zeist and Bottema 1977). In the trans-Euphrates stretches at least, the evidence clearly indicated a cold dry *Artemisia* steppe condition in the hill country until about 11,000 years ago. Our earlier position, reflected in various papers, including Wright's own, in the preliminary Iraqi field reports (Braidwood, Howe *et al.* 1960) had been that the environmental conditions within which food-production began must have been essentially similar to those of today. This was, of course, contrary to Childe's older idea of a riverine-oasis origin for agriculture. Indeed, in my earlier 1950s enthusiasm for already modern types of environmental zones in southwestern Asia in the late Pleistocene, I suggested a rather limited and specific 'natural habitat zone' for the potential domesticates on the 'hilly flanks of the crescent'. By 1960, however, I was already hedging my bets somewhat (Braidwood and Willey 1962: 337).

The beginnings of the Istanbul–Chicago Universities' Joint Prehistoric Project are described more fully elsewhere (Braidwood 1972a; Çambel & Braidwood 1980). Robert B. Stewart and Barbara Lawrence were added to the Project as botanist and zoologist respectively, and a Ford Foundation training grant for archaeology students helped us greatly. Following a regional survey in the Siirt, Diyarbakir and Urfa provinces in the autumn of 1963, we selected a site called Çayönü, near the town of Ergani, for excavation. Çayönü's main (and prehistoric) phase has an inventory roughly analogous, in general aspect, to both the Zagros (e.g., Jarmo, etc. type) and the Levant (e.g. PPNB, etc. type) early village materials. It has also yielded a well behaved series of radiocarbon assays which cluster in the general range of 7000±250 b.c. (Libby, uncalibrated). Six field seasons of work have resulted in substantial areas of exposure, a respectable sample of artifactual and non-artifactual inventory, and evidence that the Çayönü people gave very considerable attention to their architecture. One type of non-domestic structure, which approaches the monumental in both plan conception and detail, appears to have persisted, while different but also remarkable domestic plan types succeeded each other.

Curiously, our autumn 1963 survey did not yield evidence of the sub-era of incipience of pre-village-farming communities such as Karim Shahir, Asiab and the Solecki's Zawi Chemi in the Zagros and the Natufian in the Levant. Our permission to survey did not (for political reasons) include the regions south of a line through the towns of Urfa-Diyarbakir-Siirt, although our hunch already was that traces of the earlier sub-era of incipience would lie further south and at lower elevations. Then, in 1964, Maurits van Loon tested

Mureybet – since exposed in greater detail by Jacques and Marie-Claire Cauvin (Cauvin 1977). Thus the hunch about a more southerly and lower altitude location for incipience was evidenced: *sic transit gloria* for the 'hilly flanks of the crescent'? I'm not sure – I still think some important things went on there.

Perhaps the later 1960s and the 1970s are still a bit too close to allow clear retrospective focus. Certain things do concern me. One is tardy publication: we ourselves are a particularly bad example of this. Our early Amouq volume is dated 1960, thus making 22 years between the end of digging and its appearance. Although a fairly substantial group of preliminary reports on our Iraqi season did appear fairly promptly (Braidwood, Howe *et al.* 1960), our final Iraqi site reports are only now seeing printer's ink, 25 years after we left Iraq. The very bulk of Jarmo, etc., materials to be processed (although we seldom worked more than 30 men) was certainly greater than that from the earlier Amouq phases. Linda and I had come to need more time for both familial and other academic duties and it was far simpler for me to orchestrate the efforts of staff in the field than for several of us to get some 24 different reports, by 18 different authors, produced and edited to any schedule. For Iran, the Sarab materials have been turned over to the Royal Ontario Museum, and Mary McDonald (one of Cuyler Young's assistants) has assumed their publication and herself did a short re-testing of the site in 1978. Sandor Bökönyi (1977) has already reported on the animal bones. Also, the first Çambel–Braidwood volume of the Istanbul University series is at this moment in corrected page proof. All this is not, however, a publication record of which to be greatly proud.

My feelings about the 'new' archaeology have changed little over the last dozen years. In an earlier paper (1972b), I remarked that the 'new' seemed to have '. . . much of the eager, very earnest, quite humorless fervour of a new religious movement.' I think that in the US at least, the growth of the 'new' archaeology, with all its scientism, will eventually be understood in part as a response to the growth of the NSF as a source for substantial financial support for archaeology in the anthropological tradition. It was important to behave and to talk like a scientist. Aid for field work in the humanistic tradition has only come much more recently, with the development of the National Endowment for the Humanities (NEH).

I feel certain, too, that in the US, the obstreperous spirit of many of the 'new' archaeology's leaders reflected the unrest of the Viet Nam years. These people belonged to the 'don't trust anybody over 30' generation (they are, of course, themselves well beyond that now!). It was declared publicly at association meetings, for example, that 'nothing written before 1960 is worth reading' and, given the development of the movement's own new jargon, it was difficult for many of the 'new' archaeologists and their students to *understand* anything written before 1960.

Those of us who were well over 30 in the critical years survived the movement's swaddling years with a combination of wry amusement and no great anticipation of monumental breakthroughs in contributions to knowledge. I do have a rueful feeling that at least some of the writings of the 'new' archaeologists may have brought confusion to students and younger colleagues beyond North America and western Europe.

A final thought about the later prehistory of southwestern Asia. Although investigation of the origins and early consequences of a food-producing way of life has indeed become a very fashionable focus of field investigation, our information is still very incomplete and fragmented. Our theories tend to be plagued by priorities given to sites and materials which – quite accidentally – happen to have been excavated first. Indeed, had Syria permitted us to work along the Euphrates in 1947–8, the importance first given Jarmo – because of its priority of discovery – would not have skewed the record to whatever extent it may have. It seems to me, too, that in theorizing (especially by those who do not know the area or what is in process but as yet unpublished), there is a tendency to give equal weight to site names *per se*, especially when they are already published, with no great thought for the size of areas exposed and the bulk of materials responsibly reclaimed and processed. Not long ago, I wrote something like this to a younger colleague:

The wise archaeologist digs only one small unit for only one season. Then everything is and remains clear for him.

But, unhappily, it is not and should not be that simple.

Just following our second field season in Iraq, I was invited to do a pair of lectures (subsequently published, 1952) at the University of Oregon. Jarmo and Bruce Howe's Karim Shahir were then the only exposures available of sites of their time and cultural level – at least anywhere beyond the Levant. What a picture I was able to paint; no contradictory evidence stood in the way! Very soon, however, as other early village site excavations began, my pretty picture showed its inadequacies.

I close with thoughts that have grown ever stronger, beginning even before our joint effort began in Turkey: joint efforts can be very successful and highly gratifying. I am sure that Halet Çambel would agree with me: neither one of us, with our respective assistants and students, could have made a great thing of the Çayönü operation. Together, our efforts have added up to much more – for now and for the future on archaeology in Turkey – than the simple sum of two parts.

Note as of May 1987

The final report on Jarmo (L.S. Braidwood *et al.* 1983) has now appeared. The two most recent descriptions of the work at Çayönü appear in the Bittel Festschrift volume (Çambel & Braidwood 1983; Schirmer 1983). Our present general speculations concerning the incipient sub-era appear in the Mellink Festschrift (L.S. & R.J. Braidwood 1986).

References

BÖKÖNYI, S. 1977. *Animal remains from the Kermanshah valley, Iran.* Oxford: British Archaeological Reports. International Series 34.

BRAIDWOOD, L.S. and R.J. 1986. Prelude to the appearance of village farming communities in southwestern Asia, in J.V. Vorys *et al.* (eds.), *Ancient Anatolia: aspects of change and cultural development*: 3–11. Madison: University of Wisconsin Press.

BRAIDWOOD, R.J. 1937. *Mounds in the Plain of Antioch: an archaeological survey.* Oriental Institute Publication 48. Chicago: Chicago University Press.

1952. *The Near East and the foundations for civilization* Eugene.

1957. Jericho and its setting in Near Eastern prehistory, *Antiquity* 31: 73–81.

1972a. Prehistoric investigations in southwestern Asia, *Proceedings of the American Philosophical Society* 116: 310–20.

1972b. Archaeology: view from southwestern Asia, *American Anthropological Association Annual Report*, 1972: 43–52.

1974. The Iraq Jarmo project, in G.R. Willey (ed.), *Archaeological researches in retrospect:* 61–83. Cambridge (MA): Winthrop.

BRAIDWOOD, R.J. & L.S. BRAIDWOOD. 1940. Report on two sondages on the coast of Syria, south of Tartous, *Syria* 21: 183–226.

1950. Jarmo: a village of early farmers in Iraq, *Antiquity* 24: 189–95.

1960. *Excavations in the Plain of Antioch I: The earlier assemblages, A-J.* Oriental Institute Publications 61. Chicago: Chicago University Press.

BRAIDWOOD, R.J., L.S. BRAIDWOOD, E. TULANE & A.L. PERKINS. 1944. New Chalcolithic material of Samarran type and its implications, *Journal of Near Eastern Studies* 3: 47–72.

BRAIDWOOD, R.J., B. HOWE *et al.* 1960. *Prehistoric investigations in Iraqi Kurdistan.* Chicago: Chicago University Press. Studies in Ancient Oriental Civilisation 31.

BRAIDWOOD, R.J. & G. R. WILLEY (eds.). 1962. *Courses toward urban life.* Chicago: Chicago University Press. Viking Fund Publications in Anthropology 32.

ÇAMBEL, H. & R.J. BRAIDWOOD. 1980. *Prehistoric research in Southeastern Anatolia I.* Istanbul: University of Istanbul, Faculty of Letters Press. Publication 2589.

ÇAMBEL, H. & R. J. BRAIDWOOD. 1983. Çayönü Tepesi: Schritte zu neunen Lebensweisen, in R.H. Boehmer & H. Hauptmann (eds.), *Beitrage zur altertumskunde Kleinasiens*: 156-166. Mainz am Rhein: von Zabern.

CAUVIN, J. 1977. Les fouilles de Mureybet (1971–1974) et leur signification pour les origines de la sédentarisation au Proche-Orient, *Annual of the American School of Oriental Research* 44: 19–48.

HAINES, R.C. 1971. *Excavations in the Plain of Antioch II: The structural remains of the later phases.* Chicago: University of Chicago Press. Oriental Institute Publications 95.

KENYON, K. 1957. Reply to Professor Braidwood, *Antiquity* 31: 82–4.

SCHIRMER, W. 1983. Drei bauten des Çayönü Tepesi, in R.H. Boehmer & H. Hauptmann (ed.), *Beitrage zur altertumskunde Kleinasiens*. Mainz am Rhein: von Zabern.

TAX, S. (ed.). 1945. *Human origins: an introductory general course in anthropology.* Chicago: University of Chicago Press.

VAN ZEIST, W. & S. BOTTEMA. 1977. Palynological investigations in western Iran, *Paleohistoria* 19: 19–85.

WATERBOLK, H.T. 1971. Working with radiocarbon dates, *Proceedings of the Prehistoric Society* 37: 15–33.

WATSON, P.J. 1979. *Archaeological ethnology in western Iran*, Viking Fund Publications in Anthropology.57. Tucson: University of Arizona Press.

WRIGHT, H.E., Jr. 1968. Natural environment of early food production north of Mesopotamia, *Science* 161: 334–9.

7

Gordon R. Willey

Although I am not altogether sure just how one's genealogy relates to one's career, let me begin that way. The history of my particular branch of the Willey family, at least on this side of the Atlantic, begins with three brothers, soldiers in the army of Lord Cornwallis who surrendered to the Americans at Yorktown. After a brief internment as prisoners of war, they chose to become citizens of the new republic in exchange for lands on its western frontiers. There was a generation-to-generation westerly movement, first Pennsylvania, then Ohio, and then Iowa. My grandfather, William Willey, settled in Iowa in 1855, with a large farm holding in the Mississippi bottomlands. My father was born there in 1876, the twelfth of thirteen children. Apparently, the farm property was not large enough to share among so many, so after two years at the agricultural school at Iowa State University, he decided to go into pharmacy. To continue with this genealogical sketch, his mother was of Scots descent; and on my mother's side my grandfather came direct from Scotland while my grandmother was from Amsterdam. To come to me, I was born on 7 March 1913, in Chariton, a small county-seat town in southern Iowa, where my father was the moderately prosperous owner of a drug store. All this places me, I would assume, as a middle class 'wasp' from the middle of the middle class and the middle of the Middle West.

In 1925 my parents and I (an only child) moved to Long Beach, California, completing the westerly migratory track of the Willey family, although this time the journey was made in a Packard sedan rather than a covered-wagon. Our middle class, middle western ambience was not greatly changed, however, by this move to California for in those days Long Beach was considered a kind of 'Iowa-by-the-Sea'. My father bought another drug store there, and I went to the public schools. In due time, I was to reverse the traditional westward movement of my forbears and start back east.

I have a very clear recollection of just when it was that I decided to be an archaeologist. This was in the spring of 1929 when, in a high school English class, we were asked to write the usual essay on 'my intended career'. Previously, I had always disposed of such assignments by declaring my intention to be a writer, but this time I announced that I was going to be an archaeologist. As I think back, I knew almost nothing about the subject, but I believe my father had pointed me toward the idea, deriving whatever familiarity he had with archaeology from the popular press. Earlier, as I recall, he and I had both been fascinated by the Tut-ankh-amen discoveries.

I stuck with my choice of archaeology, and when it came time to go to college my mother supported me, although I think that by this time my father must have had his doubts. He would have preferred it if I had selected something more conventional, such as the law. The high school counsellor for guidance on college and university curricula, on learning of my desires, took down the catalogue for the University of California, at Berkeley, where I wanted to go and where many of my friends were going, but advised me, sadly, that there was no 'Department of Archaeology' at the institution. It was to be some years before I found that archaeology often was subsumed, variously, under the academic headings of anthropology, classics, or fine arts. When I did find this out, I was nonplussed to learn that Berkeley had a top-quality Department of Anthropology, with archaeological offerings, headed by a gentleman named A.L. Kroeber. At that moment, however, the counsellor brought down from her shelf the catalogue of the University of Arizona, another near-by seat of learning, and they did have a Department of Archaeology so I went off to Tucson, Arizona, in 1931.

In reflecting back upon all of this, I sometimes wonder if my choice of a university at that time was really such a crucial decision. To be sure, I can say, rightly enough, that I decided upon archaeology as a career at a very early age; but I knew very little about the field, and, I am afraid, I did very little to really find out much about it, or to address myself very seriously to it until I was virtually finished with my undergraduate years. As a boy, I had had no interest in such pursuits as arrowhead collecting. Nor did it ever dawn on me that there might have been such a thing as California archaeology. It seems I was fired only by a rather shallow romanticism, by dreams of ancient Egypt or other far-off places.

As an undergraduate at Arizona, I was a reasonably good student and did well enough in the archaeology and anthropology courses offered by Professor Byron Cummings, the head of the department, and by Clara Lee Fraps and John Provinse; but I never became truly interested in the local Southwestern archaeology, and my teachers must often have despaired of my seriousness. I lived in a fraternity house and entered fully into the life there. I devoted a lot of time and effort in trying to become a track star. Every spring semester I missed a fair number of classes by being away on intercollegiate trips; and on late afternoons, when I should have been working in the museum laboratories, I was out running around the track. I remember it well because the windows of the pottery laboratory, which was housed under the athletic stadium, were on a level with the track, and I could see my more diligent student colleagues down there, working away, as I sped past. It always gave me a twinge of guilt. Besides this, I failed to participate in the summer field school excavations which were held each year in the White Mountains of Arizona. Instead, up until my last year, I went home to California each summer to spend my time on the beach. In retrospect, I can only thank Professor Cummings for his patience with me in those years.

Fortunately, at least for my career in archaeology, I changed. I cannot pinpoint any single reason for, or event making, the change, but I suppose it had something to do with growing up. After graduation in 1935, I did go to the summer field school. This was at the Kinishba ruin, a Pueblo IV, Salado-affiliated site in the White Mountains, where Professor Cummings had a student group and also a crew of Apache Indian diggers. It was the first time I had ever done any sustained fieldwork in archaeology, and I enjoyed myself immensely and learned a lot. Toward the end of the summer, I talked with Professor Cummings about what I might do in the fall. Although I was beginning to know something about Southwestern archaeology, I was still enamoured of Egypt and the Near East so he advised me to write to the Oriental Institute at Chicago for admission there. I did this but was turned down so I returned to the University of Arizona for their MA graduate programme.

In 1935 there were about a half-dozen of us in the graduate archaeological programme. My most memorable activities for the year were participating in Cummings's seminar on Middle American archaeology, a field that captured my imagination as much as that of the Old World's ancient civilizations, working with Professor A.E. Douglass in dendrochronology, and writing a Master's dissertation on archaeological excavation methods. Considering my limited experience in the field, my decision to write a thesis on 'excavation methods' was a demonstration of the temerity of youth. I think the thing that prompted me to take up the subject was my restiveness in feeling that all archaeological courses were directed only toward the substantive aspects of prehistory. What were the 'principles' of the discipline? Rather naïvely, I thought that these might lie in 'how to dig'. I was not aware of problems in typology and classification, let alone those of culture change and process. Still, a review of digging techniques was not altogether a waste of time for a tyro. I tried to range world–wide in my survey although most of my data came from Southwestern archaeology. I learned how very little had been written on excavation procedures, *per se*, at that time. One of the profitable by-products of my research was visiting the Gila Pueblo research foundation at Globe, Arizona and talking with Emil W. Haury, fresh from the Snaketown excavations and emerging as the leading Southwestern archaeologist.

During the year, I had been thinking about the future, and I sought scholarships at other universities with advanced programmes in anthropology/ archaeology. I tried again at the Oriental Institute; I looked for museum assistantships – all to no avail. Sometime in the spring, Professor Cummings called me into his office and gave me a notice of the Laboratory of Anthropology (Santa Fe) Summer Field Fellowships in Archaeology, suggesting that I apply, which I did. Late in the spring, not long before my MA graduation, I received a letter from Santa Fe telling me that I had been selected as one of six students for their summer programme. This was, indeed, a crucial turning point in my attempts to become a professional archaeologist. Small as the fellowship was,

and it covered only the summer months of 1936, there was no other possibility open to me. If I had not received it I would have had to give up
archaeology.

In June I left Tucson for Santa Fe, where I was to pick up the Laboratory of
Anthropology station wagon and drive it back to Macon, Georgia, the scene of
the summer excavations that year. I found the prospect particularly exciting. I
knew nothing of Eastern United States archaeology; it was to be a completely
new experience. Macon was the location of a Federal Relief (WPA) archaeological project which had been going since 1933. The work there was centred at a
large Indian mound group on the outskirts of that middle-sized southern city.
The director of the project was Dr Arthur R. Kelly, a Harvard Ph.D and a
former professor of physical anthropology and archaeology at the University of
Illinois. He had kindly consented to take on the Laboratory of Anthropology
group for the summer and to integrate us into his on-going operations. These
operations were considerable. The relief rolls in Macon and surrounding
territory were swollen in 1936, the depths of the depression, and Kelly had
several hundred men, armed with picks, shovels, and trowels, at his command.
Many of these were concentrated on the Macon site proper; others were
scattered around at various smaller archaeological sites in the county. At the
beginning of the excavations, in 1933, Kelly had had James A. Ford as an
assistant, but when the Laboratory of Anthropology group arrived in 1936 Ford
was no longer there and Kelly had to rely on non-archaeological help for his
supervisors. Some of these were very good at their jobs, however, particularly
two college-trained young engineers, of about our age, who gave us valuable
instruction in the use of the transit, alidade, and plane table.

Our student group, except for myself, were all from eastern universities,
Harvard, Yale, Columbia, and Pennsylvania. We were evenly distributed in
anthropology's sub-disciplines: J.B. Birdsell and Lawrence Angel, in physical
anthropology; Charles Wagley and H.Y. Feng, in ethnology; and Walter Taylor
and myself, in archaeology. It turned out to be a most congenial crowd, and it
was a real learning experience for us all. None of us had ever been in the deep
south before, let alone to do archaeology there. There was some archaeological
literature then on the Southeastern United States – the writings of C.C. Jones,
W.K. Moorehead, and C.B. Moore – but none of us was familiar with it so the
mysteries of burial tumuli, platform mounds, and complicated stamped pottery
rushed in upon all of us in a bewildering way. Unable to comprehend much of
the culture history of the area, we, nevertheless, had many good arguments and
discussions over the proper ways to excavate complex mound structures and
properly expose burials. I was saddened to see the summer end. All of my
colleagues were returning to graduate schools; only I had no place to go.
Fortunately, and at the last minute, Dr Kelly agreed to take me on as his
assistant. This was to be for both excavation work and also to explore the
possibilities of developing a dendrochronological, or tree-ring, sequence for
central Georgia. On the first of September, after a railroad station farewell to my

summer friends, I entered upon my first job, employment in archaeology, complete with a salary, small as it was.

I stayed in Macon for two years. My dendrochronological work was confined to living trees. I was able to develop a ring sequence back to about AD 1800, with a few 'checking rings or ring patterns', but the Georgia pines seemed too 'complacent' in their ring growths to make further investigations worthwhile. This research did allow me, however, to publish my first article (Willey 1937). In the spring of 1937, the National Park Service, with Civilizan Conservation Corp assistance, took over the Macon archaeological site which had been renamed Ocmulgee National Monument; and Kelly, I, and the two engineers were taken into the new administrative structure. I was given more duties as an excavation supervisor, and I began to learn about Southeastern pottery in a detailed way. In 1938, Dr Kelly was transferred by the National Park Service from Macon to Washington, DC. He was my first boss, and an extraordinarily kind and warm-hearted man. I was sorry to see him go. Fortunately, he was replaced by J.D. Jennings, a good archaeologist who became a good friend and who was kind enough to serve as best man at my wedding.

During 1937 and 1938, James Ford visited Macon frequently, and, for a time, was employed by the National Park Service in restoring the Macon Ceremonial Earth Lodge. Ford had worked extensively in Mississippi and Louisiana archaeology and was very knowledgeable about Southeastern pottery. He, Preston Holder, who was doing WPA digging on St Simon's Island on the Georgia coast, A.J. Waring, Jr of Savannah, and I, had numerous long discussions about Southeastern ceramic typology.

In the fall of 1938, I married Katharine Whaley, of Macon, and shortly thereafter we moved to New Orleans where I joined Ford in his WPA project in Louisiana archaeology. Katharine was neither archaeologist nor anthropologist, and it was in a social, rather than professional, context that we met. But she was no mean artist, and although she did not pursue her talent professionally she has, at various times, done some pen-and-ink work for me for archaeological illustrations. She also accompanied me on one expedition to Peru, two to Guatemala and two to Honduras. She helped with lab work, especially pottery restoration at which she has real skill, and also with drawings. All of this was in addition to raising two daughters.

Ford and I had fieldwork going on at two locations, at the Crooks Mound, and the better known site of Marksville. W.T. Mulloy and Arden King ran the Crooks Mound operation, and R.S. Neitzel, the dig at Marksville. I was in charge of the New Orleans Laboratory, and Ford was the overall director. This experience continued to expand my knowledge of Southeastern archaeo-logy, and particularly, Southeastern ceramics. Ford and I completed the manuscript on the Crooks Mound (Ford & Willey 1940) by mid 1939, and were beginning on other writing projects, but after three years in the field in the Southeast, I felt that I should go back to graduate school.

Actually, I had tried each year to enter into graduate work somewhere, but I had been unable to secure the necessary scholarship aid. Perhaps it was just as well for I needed the field experience of those three years. But in 1939 my applications were at last successful, and I was offered tuition scholarships at both Columbia and the University of Chicago. The latter was in response to application to their Department of Anthropology, for by this time I had given up on Near Eastern archaeology. Having done real research in another part of the world, I was sufficiently engrossed with my new area to forget the lures of faraway places. I finally chose Columbia. The scholarship stipend was a little better, and Katharine knew New York. I began there in the fall of 1939, with Duncan Strong as my major professor. He had come there only recently after a period at Nebraska where he had distinguished himself in Plains archaeology. His seminar that first year was in Southeastern United States archaeology, and I revelled in it. Albert Spaulding was a fellow student, and he, too, had come from Southeastern Federal Relief archaeology. As a follow up to that academic year, Strong arranged for Dick Woodbury and myself to spend the summer on a Florida coastal archaeological survey. That summer's work formed the nexus of my monograph, *Archaeology of the Florida Coast* (Willey 1949), which came out a good many years later. In this Florida study, my previous experience in, and knowledge of, Georgia and Louisiana archaeology stood me in good stead.

One of the advantages of graduate school at Columbia was the proximity of the American Museum of Natural History and the anthropologists there. Both Harry Shapiro (physical anthropology) and George Vaillant (Middle American archaeology) taught in the department at Columbia, and I had courses with both. In 1941, Vaillant was instrumental, through his friendship with Nelson Rockefeller, to arrange for a substantial sum to be contributed by Rockefeller's Office of the Coordinator for Interamerican Affairs to the Institute of Andean Research to do archaeology in Latin America. Ten projects were planned, reaching from Mexico down to Chile; and Strong, who had long been interested in Peru, was named to head one of the field parties for that country. He picked me for his assistant. After completing my doctoral examinations that May, Katharine and I, along with Junius and Peggy Bird, who were bound for a similar mission in Chile, sailed from New York on the Grace Line's SS *Santa Elena* in early June. At last I was to have the opportunity to see a 'high culture' at first hand, not Mesopotamia nor Mesoamerica, but something that sounded almost as good, Peru.

Duncan, Junius, and I surveyed the Peruvian coast for two weeks until Junius and Peggy resumed their journey to Chile; then we were invited by J.C. Tello, Peru's leading prehistorian, to dig at Pachacamac. Pachacamac, not far south of Lima, is one of Peru's great ruins. It was a pilgrimage shrine of the Inca when the Spanish first entered the country, but it had a much longer history, or prehistory, as Max Uhle (1903) had demonstrated almost 40 years before our arrival there. Our goal, as Strong had explained to Tello, was refuse-heap stratigraphy. Uhle and Kroeber had made a good beginning in developing an archaeological chronology for Peru from stylistic seriations of grave lot pottery, but we felt this could be improved upon, or at least greatly augmented, by potsherd stratigraphy which would refine the chronology and also expand our knowledge of Peruvian pottery beyond the fancier funerary ceramics. Tello advised us that if we were looking for refuse heaps, he knew just the place. He took us out to Pachacamac, where his own excavation crews were working at another part of that vast site, and showed us a great, shaggy-looking, grey-black pile situated on a slope below the pyramid known as the Inca 'Temple of the Sun'. With a small crew of workmen, we began a test trench in this 'haystack' on the following day. I use the word 'haystack' advisedly for beneath a few centimetres of surface dust we began cutting through a firmly packed mass of maize stalks, other vegetal fibres, peanut shells, scraps of textiles, and miscellaneous, semi-decayed debris. The Peruvian rainless coast is known for such remarkable preservation, and to some extent the degree of preservation, or the lack of it, is a rough clue to the relative age of a deposit. Our 'haystack' was purely Imperial Inca, probably no more than 500 years old. To one who had known only North American archaeology, this kind of preservation of prehistoric materials was almost too much to contend with. I will never forget the day when one workman, having injured his bare foot slightly, pulled a textile fragment out of the profile to use as a bandage. The Inca debris turned out to be several metres thick. It was underlain by a light coloured, dusty soil through which we continued to dig. The sherds from these depths were radically different from those of the Inca dump and pertained to what Uhle had called the 'Interlocking Fish or Serpent' painted style, representative of an archaeological culture that he had identified as being pre-Tiahuanaco. So far, so good, we had pottery stratigraphy. It was hardly a chronological breakthrough, but, nevertheless, in the lowermost pottery-bearing levels of the Interlocking style refuse we noted certain differences in the pottery, and in the frequency counts among the various types, that offered suggestions of where we might do some further digging on the Peruvian coast.

Strong returned to the States in September of that year, leaving me to carry on the work in Peru. In this, I was joined by John Corbett, another young archaeologist, and one who had been working in Ecuador, and by Marshall Newman, a physical anthropologist who was a part of the Institute of Andean Research programme in Peru. But to return to ceramic chronology on the Peruvian coast, I had been reading accounts of Uhle's work in the Chancay Valley (in Kroeber 1926), a short distance to the north of Lima, and it struck me that stratigraphic procedures might help clear up the relationship between the Interlocking style, as found in that valley, and another style known as the 'White-on-red'. Uhle had argued that the Interlocking style was the earlier of the two, but his line of reasoning for this had not been a strong one. In the Pachacamac excavations, we had noted that there were a few White-on-red sherds mixed in with the lower Interlocking style levels. With this hint in mind, I shifted our operations to the Chancay and to Uhle's old site of Cerro

Trinidad. This was a complex of adobe structures and refuse whose considerable depths were indicated by the road cut of the Panamerican Highway. For our stratigraphic purposes it proved a good choice. We were able to demonstrate that the White-on-red style was definitely the earlier of the two. Not long after this, Kroeber visited Peru, and I could proudly show him my results, with which, after reviewing the material, he concurred. Later, I used these Chancay data as the core of my doctoral dissertation (Willey 1943).

Corbett, Newman, and I went up to Puerto de Supe after Chancay, still following in Uhle's footsteps, this time to pursue the problem of Chavínoid-appearing pottery which he had found there many years before (in Kroeber 1925). We made some significant Coastal Chavín finds there, including one amazing textile, and the Chavínoid theme also was central to our efforts in subsequent digging in the shell heaps at Ancon (Willey & Corbett 1954). One of the highlights of the Ancon excavations was a visit to the site by Uhle himself. The veteran Peruvianist had been attending an International Congress of Americanists meeting in 1939 and had been trapped in the country by the outbreak of World War II. Well into his eighties, Uhle spent half a day with us at Ancon, photographing the scene of his old activities and discussing pottery styles.

But it was at Supe that we failed to make an important discovery. We excavated for some days at the Aspero site there. Aspero turned out to be a large preceramic midden – something that we were totally unprepared for and found difficult to adjust to. At that time there was no Peruvian 'preceramic period'. Although we found other artifacts in the black, ashy refuse, and even excavated some dwelling structures, we missed, as had Uhle before us, the presence of artificial platform mounds at the site. I looked right at them, concluded they were natural landscape features, and failed to test them (Willey & Corbett 1954). It was not until years later, in 1971 – well after the 'preceramic horizon' had become an established fact of Peruvian archaeology – when on a survey trip with a former student, M.E. Moseley, that I realized what I had missed at Aspero. This was after Moseley had shown me small artificial mounds at Rio Seco, a well-known preceramic site some kilometres south of Supe. I told him then that we had better continue our drive on up the coast and have another look at Aspero. Moseley confirmed my suspicions, especially when he followed up our trip with the later excavation of some of the Aspero mounds (Moseley & Willey 1973). It is an excellent case of not being able to find something if you are not looking for it. By 1971, it had become common Peruvian archaeological knowledge that artificial mound structures were a part of the Peruvian Coastal Preceramic. Thirty years earlier, the idea was unthinkable, and I rejected it. I relate this without any sense whatever of crying *mea culpa*. After all, archaeology is dodgy stuff. Anyone who insists on a record of infallibility is probably trying to fool others and definitely fooling himself.

We returned to the States in May of 1942. The following fall I completed my doctorate and taught for a year (1942–3) at Columbia. In the fall of 1943 I went to the Bureau of American Ethnology in the Smithsonian Institution, in Washington, DC, to be Julian Steward's assistant on the editing of the *Handbook of South American Indians*. Steward, at that time in his early forties, was clearly one of America's leading anthropological theorists. He had already shown this in previous papers in North American ethnology, and he was to bloom forth in some of his long essays in the *Handbook* (Steward 1948; 1949a). The education in archaeology and anthropology, which I had begun with Cummings, Kelly, Ford, and Strong, was to be continued in this association with him. Together with Wendell Bennett we planned the Viru Valley programme in late 1945 and, with additional colleagues, put it into operation in early 1946.

As other young American archaeologists of my generation raised up in the academic house of anthropology, I had always been somewhat awed by my ethnological and social anthropological professors and colleagues. These were the people who controlled the core of theory, and, unwittingly or not, they let us feel that archaeology was something second rate. I can understand that contemporary European prehistorians, Classical scholars, Egyptologists, and Near Eastern archaeologists did not have this same kind of experience, but it was a part of the life of an Americanist archaeologist trained in a department of anthropology. To be sure, Kroeber had time for archaeologists, and did archaeology himself, and even the American 'father' of anthropology, Franz Boas, gave archaeology his occasional blessing; but, by and large, archaeologists did not have a high intellectual rating on the American scene. Clyde Kluckhohn, a leading anthropological theoretician of the 1940s and 1950s, scolded them (Kluckhohn 1940); but Julian Steward began a dialogue with them, and I was one of the first archaeologists to come under his influence.

Steward had done some archaeology, in the North American Great Basin where he also worked as an ethnologist, but he was certainly not primarily an archaeologist. He had a strong culture evolutionary orientation, and in his attempts to achieve an overview grasp of the multitudinous South American *Handbook* data, both ethnographic and archaeological, he leaned in this direction ever more strongly. At the same time, he was uncomfortable with evolutionary thinking in the abstract. He wanted to explore and compare the diverse lines of culture history (Steward 1949b). It was in my many long discussions with Steward that he turned me toward settlement archaeology and, specifically, to the settlement pattern study in the Viru Valley. It should be made clear, however, that the study, as it eventually appeared (Willey 1953), was entirely my own designing. This is not said to detract from Steward's influence, but after the gathering of the field data in 1946, under his very general guidelines that archaeologists should stop being so single-site oriented, and should try to see man's adaptations to natural and social environments over wider landscapes, I was left on my own. Steward departed from the Smithsonian in that same year for a professorial career, first at Columbia and then at the University of Illinois, and I had no further opportunities to discuss the 'settlement pattern approach' with him, especially during the years (1950–51) in which I wrote most of the Viru report. Perhaps I would have done a better job if I had had his counsel, but, instead, I went ahead on my own with no very clear intellectual inspiration beyond what he had given me at the outset. I have already offered one 'retrospect' on this (Willey 1974) and will say no more about it here.

Most of my writing time in the last years before I left the Bureau of American Ethnology was taken up with completing the long, compendium-like report on Florida archaeology, to which I have already referred (Willey 1949). In 1949, I was offered the Bowditch Professorship at Harvard, although my colleagues there allowed me to stay on an extra year in the Smithsonian to complete some obligations with that institution.

When I went to Harvard, in the fall of 1950, my only Central American experience had been a season in Panama with my boss at the Bureau of American Ethnology, Matt Stirling. With this background experience, I wanted to return to Panama and did so in 1952, taking along two Harvard graduate students, C.R. McGimsey and James East. We excavated mainly at the Monagrillo shell mound site, where I had made a beginning in 1948, and the Monagrillo report was published by the Peabody Museum at Harvard (Willey & McGimsey 1954). It had been my intention to return to Panama for still a third season in 1953. I must have had some vague idea in mind of advancing upon the ancient civilizations of Mesoamerica by a gradually creeping process from the south. But A. M. Tozzer, my distinguished predecessor at Harvard, disagreed with this scheme in no uncertain terms. He had been patient while I did my first Harvard fieldwork in Panama, but he told me that it was my duty to gather up my courage and go direct to the Maya area. To be sure, the Bowditch Will, establishing the Bowditch Professorship, had said that 'Mexico and Central America' were to be the purview of the holder of the chair; but, according to Tozzer, Charles P. Bowditch, who had been his patron, and whose spirit was still supervising our activities, meant the Maya, and there were no two ways about it. I bowed to higher wisdom – in retrospect a very good decision on my part – and made preparations for a frontal attack on Maya archaeology.

I think it would be fair to say that Maya archaeology was then the most august field in Americanist studies. It had a long and rich tradition. The great, jungle-shrouded ruins themselves had a certain mystique. A host of distinguished scholars – hieroglyphic experts, students of art and iconography, and, in more recent years, architectural and ceramic specialists – had devoted lifetime careers to the Precolumbian Maya. Not only was Tozzer watching me from the office just across the hall, but there were A.V. Kidder, J. Eric Thompson, and others of the Carnegie Institution archaeological staff – Maya archaeologists all – keeping an eye on me from the Carnegie quarters next door to the Peabody Museum. I thought it would be the better part of valour to lead from what strength I had. I launched a settlement pattern project in the Belize

Valley at a place called Barton Ramie. The location was decided upon because of extensive agricultural clearings which had revealed hundreds of small ruin mounds, putatively 'house mounds', along the river flats. I had seen these mounds in a preliminary scouting trip in 1953. In 1954, I was fortunate enough to receive the first grant for archaeological work ever given by the newly founded National Science Foundation; and, accompanied by graduate students William Bullard and John Glass, we began our mapping and excavations in February of that year.

There had been some incidental concern with settlement patterns in the Maya Lowlands, going back to Ricketson's Uaxactun surveys (Ricketson & Ricketson 1937); and the Carnegie archaeologists had conscientiously mapped all the residential mounds within the walled city of Mayapan (Pollock *et al.* 1962; see also Ashmore & Willey 1981); but our Barton Ramie effort was the first to consider both localized distributions of residential and other mound structures ('micro-patterns') and larger geographic scale distributions and arrangements of site hierarchies (Willey *et al.* 1965). We were lucky at Barton Ramie; the modern agricultural clearings had done some of our job for us. For the most part, dense jungle covers the Lowland and its archaeological sites, especially the small ones. At that date, air photography had been of little help although it was to be in the future. When I initiated my next Maya programme, at Altar de Sacrificios, in the Guatemalan Peten, wide-scale survey was carried out only with difficulty. The site's ceremonial centre was located on what was, in effect, an island in a jungle swamp. Relatively few residential mounds were found in its immediate vicinity. Presumably, Altar's sustaining populations had been located all along the Pasion and Salinas Rivers, extending for several kilometres in several directions from the ceremonial centre. Even now we have no real knowledge of the Pasion–Salinas settlement distributions; it remains as a task for future archaeologists to assemble this information (Willey 1973). At Seibal, farther upstream on the Pasion, where we surveyed and excavated after the work at Altar de Sacrificios, we were on higher ground, and a 5 by 5 km block was laid out around the main site centre and carefully examined for structures of all types (Willey *et al.* 1975). Many of these were excavated, and the forthcoming monograph on this, by Gair Tourtellot III, will take its place, along with similar studies from Tikal, Dzibilchaltun, Cobá, and elsewhere, as a major Maya settlement contribution.

Our labours at Altar de Sacrificios and Seibal lasted for ten field seasons, from 1959 until 1968. For the whole time, A. Ledyard Smith, an old Maya hand from the Carnegie Institution's archaeological staff, and a brilliant architectural excavator, served as my field director. He not only directed much of the work but was in complete charge of setting up and maintaining our field camps. He has also written important monographs on the work at Altar and Seibal (Smith 1972; 1982). Several graduate students – John A. Graham, R.E.W. Adams, Frank Saul, J.A. Sabloff, and Gair Tourtellot derived doctoral dissertations from their work at these two sites; and many other Mayanists, now distinguished in the field, such as E. W. Andrews V, Ian Graham, Norman Hammond, and Arthur Miller, served on our staff.

My most recent fieldwork, and probably my last, was in Honduras. For a long time I had wanted to go into the north-eastern part of that country, one of the last regional archaeological blank spots of Central America; but, after some preliminary excursions, the attempt was aborted when the Honduran government refused to issue me an excavation permit. Some results eventually came out of the venture, however, in that Paul Healy, who had been my student assistant, was able to go back in subsequent seasons when he obtained permission to dig. He has since brought out some of the results (Healy 1974; 1975). Then, in 1975, the Hondurans invited me to begin a settlement pattern survey in the environs of Copan, in the southwestern part of that country. This was carried out in 1975 through 1977, with Richard Leventhal and William Fash as my assistants (Willey, Leventhal & Fash 1978). Since then, this survey has been continued under Honduran governmental auspices by Claude Baudez and William Sanders.

This fieldwork chronicle, while certainly summarizing an important part of my career, has not been all of my life as an archaeologist. I have said little of my base, the Peabody Museum and the Department of Anthropology at Harvard University, where I have been for a third of a century. The associations I have had there, with archaeologists of many different interests, as well as with members of other branches of the anthropological family, have been important stimuli for all aspects of my work. It was with Philip Phillips, whom I had first known in the context of Southeastern United States archaeology, that I wrote *Method and theory in American archaeology* (1958). My students at Harvard have been equally significant in my development as an archaeologist. I am too old-fashioned to hold with the modern saying that the professor always learns as much from the student as the latter from the former; but, in my own case, this has been true on occasion. I have already mentioned some of these students, in connexion with the field programmes, and there have been a host of others of high quality. Both graduate and undergraduate teaching led me to produce a two-volume work, *An introduction to American archaeology* (1966–71), which, incidentally, was actually written on two leaves which I spent in Cambridge, England. I enjoyed my stay there in many ways, especially my associations with Geoffrey Bushnell, Grahame Clark, and Glyn Daniel. It was Daniel who asked me to write *A history of American archaeology* (1974), which I completed with Jeremy Sabloff.

In looking back over what I have written here, I am afraid I have not been very explicit about what I think about archaeology. What is my theoretical stance? I am not sure that I can answer this in any very succinct way. Fifty years in archaeology – as a student, a practitioner, and a professor – have left me with the feeling that it is a very difficult discipline: fascinating, to be sure, but difficult. This does not mean that I am no longer optimistic about it.

Indeed, without optimism archaeology would be impossible: we address the remote past with the confidence that eventually, by some means or other, we will come to understand it. It is when one tries to set down unchallengeable guidelines for doing this that the difficulties arise.

I do not know if we will ever come up with any processual or behavioural 'universals' in archaeology or not. If so, I have no very clear idea as to just what form these might take. I will remain hopeful; but, meanwhile, the best advice I could offer would be that the archaeologist must be immersed in the culture-historical contexts pertinent to the problems at hand. This may seem a commonplace; and some would say: 'We take this for granted; we are now ready to go beyond simple data control.' I only reply that we are never really able to go beyond such control for problems, questions, and hypotheses are inextricably enmeshed in the data of history.

A second suggestion may seem the opposite of what I have just said. This is that the archaeologist, whatever the specific historical context in which he or she is working, will be better prepared to deal with the specific in the light of knowledge about other culture-historical contexts. Clearly, no one can be a 'world archaeologist', at least not on the level of front-line research. Still, knowledge of other areas, of other cultures than the one under primary study, gives one insights into one's own archaeological bailiwick. In other words, the advice is to be comfortable with a comparative point of view, with the anthropologist's cross-cultural perspective. And this applies not only to other archaeological cultures but to the resources of written history and ethnography.

Finally, and most controversially, while I am offering advice, I would recommend approaching causality with caution. Do not be faint of heart, but at the same time, remember that the search for cause seems to have a way of channelling one's outlook, of convincing the searcher that one approach, one basic philosophy has all the answers. There is an unavoidable tension in archaeological research, a tension between the material remains we study and our attempts to grasp the ideas which once created, shaped, and arranged these remains. This is a tension the archaeologist must learn to live with as he goes about trying to resolve it.

References

Ashmore, W. & G.R. Willey. 1981. A historical introduction to the study of Lowland Maya Settlement Patterns, in W. Ashmore (ed.), *Lowland Maya settlement patterns*: 3–19. Albuquerque: University of New Mexico Press.

Ford, J.A. & G.R. Willey. 1940. *Crooks Site: a Marksville Period burial mound in LaSalle Parish, Louisiana*. New Orleans: Department of Conservation, Louisiana Geological Survey. Anthropological Study 3.

Healy, F.F. 1974. The Cuyamel Caves: Preclassic sites in northeast Honduras, *American Antiquity*, 39: 435–47.
1975. H-CN-4 (Williams Ranch Site): preliminary report on a Selin Period site in the Department of Colon, northeast Honduras, *Vinculos* 1(2): 61–102.

KLUCKHOHN, C. 1940. *The conceptual structure in Middle American studies: the Maya and their neighbors.* New York.

KROEBER, A.L. 1925. *The Uhle pottery collections from Supe.* University of California Publication in American Archaeology and Ethnology 21: 235–64.

1926. *The Uhle pottery collections from Chancay.* University of California Publications in American Archaeology and Ethnology 21: 265–304.

MOSELEY, M.E. & G.R. WILLEY. 1973. Aspero, Peru: A reexamination of the site and its implications, *American Antiquity* 38: 452–68.

POLLOCK, H.E.D., R.L. ROYS, T. PROSKOURIAROFF & A.L. SMITH. 1962. *Mayapan, Yucatan, Mexico.* Washington, DC: Carnegie Institution. Carnegie Institution Publication 619.

RICKETSON, O.G., Jr & E.B. RICKETSON. 1937. *Uaxactun, Guatemala Group E-1926-1931.* Washington (DC): Carnegie Institution. Carnegie Institution Publication 477.

SMITH, A.L. 1972. *Excavations at Altar de Sacrificios: architecture, settlement, burials, and caches.* Cambridge (MA): Peabody Museum. Peabody Museum Papers 62 (2).

1982. *Excavations at Seibal: major architecture and caches.* Cambridge (MA): Peabody Museum. Memoirs 15(1).

STEWARD, J. H. 1948. The circum-Caribbean tribes: an introduction, in J.H. Steward (ed.), *Handbook of South American Indians* 5: 1–42. Washington (DC). Bureau of American Ethnology, Smithsonian Institution, Bulletin 143, vol. 5.

1949a. South American cultures: an interpretative summary, in J.H. Steward (ed.), *Handbook of South American Indians* 5: 669–772. Washington (DC). Bureau of American Ethnology, Smithsonian Institution, Bulletin 143, vol. 5.

1949b. Cultural causality and law: a trial formulation of the development of early civilizations, *American Anthropologist* 51: 1–27.

UHLE, M 1903. *Pachatanlac.* Philadelphia: Department of Archaeology, University of Pennsylvania.

WILLEY, G.R. 1937. Notes on Central Georgia dendrochronology, *Tree Ring Bulletin* 4(2).

1943. Excavations in the Chancay Valley, in W. L . Strong, G. R. Willey & J.M. Corbett, *Archaeological studies in Peru.* New York: Columbia University Press. Columbia University Studies in Archaeology and Ethnology, vol. 1, no. 3.

1949. *Archaeology of the Florida Gulf Coast.* Washington (DC): Smithsonian Institution. Smithsonian Miscellaneous Collections, vol. 113.

1953. *Prehistoric settlement patterns in the Viru Valley, Peru.* Washington (DC): Smithsonian Institution. Bureau of American Ethnology, Bulletin 155

1973. *The Altar de Sacrificios excavations: general summary and conclusions.* Cambridge (MA): Peabody Museum. Peabody Museum Papers 64(3).

1974. The Viru Valley settlement pattern study, in G.R. Willey (ed.), *Archaeological researches in retrospect,* 149–79. Cambridge (MA): Winthrop.

WILLEY, G.R., V.R. BULLARD, Jr, J.S. GLASS, & J.C. GIFFORD 1965. *Prehistoric Maya settlements in the Belize Valley.* Cambridge (MA): Peabody Museum. Peabody Museum Papers 54.

WILLEY, G.R. & J.M. CORBETT. 1954. *Early Ancon and Early Supe Culture: Chavín Horizon sites of the Central Peruvian Coast.* New York: Columbia University Press. Columbia Studies in Archaeology and Ethnology 3.

WILLEY, G.R., R.U. LEVENTHAL & W.L. FASH, Jr. 1978. Maya settlement in the Copan Valley, *Archaeology* 31(4): 32–44.

WILLEY, G.R. & C.R. MCGIMSEY. 1954. *The Monagrillo Culture of Panama.* Cambridge (MA): Peabody Museum. Peabody Museum Papers 49(2).

8

C.J. Becker

The first phase in the history of prehistoric archaeology in Denmark covering the time of C. J. Thomsen and J.J.A. Worsaae, that is up until 1885, is well known (Daniel 1975). Developments during the next fifty years have also been made known to international circles (Klindt-Jensen 1975), but progress in the last roughly fifty years has been only scantily treated, mainly in Danish and often somewhat subjective articles. Therefore I am grateful to the Editor for offering me this opportunity to review the time in which I have been personally involved – though it, too, must needs be seen from a subjective angle.

Some details of my personal background may be appropriate. I was born in 1915 in Copenhagen where my father was a lawyer, who could afford to educate his three children without economic hardship. He would have preferred me to study law and this was in fact the idea up until a few months before I sat my university entrance examination in 1933. However I chose to follow my interest in Danish antiquity which had absorbed me for some time, and in September of that year I entered Copenhagen University as a student of archaeology.

My interest in antiquity had been aroused quite by chance. When I was about 12 years old I went exploring in the attic of my home among furniture from my grandparents' house and I came upon a chest containing some two hundred antiquities. These objects had been collected by my paternal grandfather (1824–1902) during the latter half of the 19th century when he had been administrator of a small estate on the island of Zealand. Some people today suppose that personal interests (and characteristics) are inheritable but that they often skip a generation. This never seems to have been proved but, if correct, my interest in history could just as well originate from my maternal grandfather, I.C. Døcker (1860–1938), who had owned a large farm in Jutland but moved to Copenhagen because of his work as a member of the Danish 'Rigsdag' for many years. He was a widower when I knew him and therefore a frequent visitor to our home where he showed a warm interest in us children. He it was who gave me my first books on antiquity and took me to the museums, first and foremost the National Museum. At that time its vast collections were exhibited in their entirety – leaving little room for the public to view them. Every visit was an experience for me but best were those in summer: in winter prehistoric darkness filled the densely crowded display halls. Boys of twelve to fifteen years of age frequently take up many interests only to drop them again. I did this too, but antiquity remained a lasting interest for me and I was gradually reading more systematically on the subject. Sometimes I sat and read for a couple of hours after school in the Royal Library, sometimes I borrowed books from there. I recall that some works attracted me greatly: for example those of Sophus Müller on the Stone Age and E. Vedel's books on the prehistory of Bornholm (and I still set just as great store by them now).

My grandfather's collection had long been arranged in a bookcase in my room and now I enlarged it, for example by a few excavations. My first 'larger' excavation was of an overploughed barrow at Tjørnemark in north-west Zealand in 1932 and here I had beginner's luck. This insignificant barrow contained a number of Stone and Bronze Age graves (eventually published by Aner & Kersten 1975, II, No. 988). I made a report on these discoveries and showed it, together with the finds, to Johannes Brøndsted at the National Museum. My report constituted for me a kind of introduction to professional archaeology.

At that time the National Museum still had its old authoritarian position and was – just as fifty years earlier – Denmark's only archaeological research institute and thus the place of training for Nordic archaeologists. As late as 1930 none of the many local museums had professionally trained leaders, and only few of them were able to conduct minor excavations. At Copenhagen University it was not possible to study any branch of archaeology except classical archaeology.

Perhaps the monopoly of the Museum was acceptable in a small country during the 19th century, and thus matters remained so long as Sophus Müller (1846–1934) was its forceful leader. In his later years, however, and particularly after his retirement in 1921, this monopoly resulted in a period of torpor for Danish archaeology, both locally and internationally. The situation seems specially mediocre when considering progress at this time in the other Nordic countries: here archaeology had long been represented at the universities where scholars with a European outlook were able to train new archaeologists. Throughout the 1920s Nordic archaeology was making its mark – but without much contribution from Denmark.

At this time there were four permanently employed archaeologists (plus varying assistants) in the Department of Prehistory at the National Museum in Copenhagen. None of the staff had any academic qualifications in archaeology: Carl Neergaard, keeper from 1921–33, had read history in his youth (but without obtaining a degree), Hans Kjær had a degree in Greek and in history, while H.C. Broholm and J. Brøndsted had degrees in classical languages (when Kjær died and Neergaard retired their places were taken by Therkel Mathiassen (natural history) and M.B. Mackeprang (classical archaeology)). Only after taking up a position in the Museum did it become necessary to learn archaeology somehow or other. Fifty years earlier Sophus Müller had shown that this could be done; he, too, was a classical scholar.

Brøndsted became keeper of the Department at the beginning of 1933 and his efforts were to prove epoch-making for the history of our discipline. During the short span of four or five years he was able to revive our national archaeology. He made closer contact with the university (and thus with the educational sector), renewed research activities, began to develop the local museums (for example by decentralizing excavations) and – just to round off matters – laid the foundations for legislation to protect field monuments. At the same time Therkel Mathiassen, an archaeologist renowned for his work in Greenland, was attached to the Museum and immediately initiated major projects relating to the Danish Stone Age.

It was decisive for my own situation that it became possible to study Nordic archaeology at this time. Brøndsted had already been appointed lecturer in the subject at the University in 1930, and in 1932 he obtained official sanction for a degree course that was to take six years of exclusively archaeological studies. In 1933 there were only two older students reading Nordic archaeology in this way and a few others who combined it with history or another subject. Many of the latter recall Brøndsted as an inspiring teacher; in 1932 he had just completed an extensive series of lectures on Danish prehistory. His teaching of students on the full degree course, on the other hand, consisted mainly of personal tutoring. He set his students massive written assignments that often took several months to complete, whereafter the work was presented for general debate and criticism – Brøndsted did not always find time to read it himself! For the rest his students had to look after themselves. Nevertheless the fine Museum library and archives were at our disposal both night and day for Brøndsted was head of this department too. Believe it or not, during all my years of study I had the opportunity to attend only one regular series of lectures given by Brøndsted – on Tacitus' *Germania*.

In contrast there was excellent teaching of Greek and Italian prehistory, also required material for the examination. Professor Knud Friis Johansen delivered carefully prepared and updated lectures (though perhaps not in a greatly inspiring way), supplementing these by demonstrations using the abundant collections of the Museum's Department of Antiquities. Friis Johansen had earlier been keeper of this department but had had to participate in fieldwork and research in Danish prehistory too. Thus he was author of some of the few good specialized articles that appeared between 1912 and 1923 on subjects ranging from the Maglemose culture to the Viking era. He had continued to keep in contact with Nordic archaeology and dutifully supported this field and its students as well as his own. I enjoyed his support on several occasions, also fifteen years later when we became faculty colleagues.

The teaching of prehistoric archaeology at that time must appear somewhat strange compared with what it is today. A further factor was the lack of help obtainable from other fields – sciences or humanities. In this connexion neither ethnography nor European ethnology was yet represented at the University. It was an advantage for me that I had read so much archaeology on my own as a schoolboy and thus had some practice at working by myself. Nonetheless, I am grateful that to start with I received much help from the older students, both those reading archaeology and those reading history. First and foremost to help me were P. V. Glob (1911–85) who became professor of Nordic archaeology at the University of Århus in 1949 and later head of the entire National Museum, and Hans Norling-Christensen (1909–70), later keeper of the Department of Prehistory at the Museum. This helpful attitude can be confirmed by students from the following 'classes'; among these was Ole Klindt-Jensen (1918–80), who at his death was professor at Århus and director of the museum at Moesgård. It is interesting to note the later achievements of some of my fellow students (such as those mentioned above) as Brøndsted always warned his students against making a vocational study of Nordic archaeology because, he explained, there was no future in the field. It seems that even he could be mistaken.

What then were the possibilities for us to study European archaeology in the 1930s? The examination requirements included a solid grounding in the prehistory of the whole of Europe, and that was quite a job. A few years earlier a group of Nordic archaeologists under the leadership of Friis Johansen (1927) had published an 800-page handbook containing several excellent surveys, for example on the Neolithic (C. A. Nordman), the Iron Age (H. Shetelig), East Europe (T. J. Arne), Greece (Chr. Blinkenberg) and Italy (Friis Johansen). This volume appeared in the Scandinavian languages only, remaining virtually unknown in international circles. In a small country with a language of limited distribution, one has to be able to read at least three main languages. In this way possibilities were legion and the difficulty was to choose and evaluate the material. We had no idea of scientific theory and we wasted no time on analysing methods and theories. We took what we thought was useful and at first that which corresponded to the attitudes of our teachers. Both the archaeological and the ethnological fields were dominated at that time by (moderate) diffusionist models and 'culture circle' ideas. The evolutionist theories of the previous century had survived only in the politically endorsed archaeology of the Soviet Union, but we had little or no contact with this.

In a paper presented to one of the many present-day symposia on methods, Colin Renfrew (1982) termed the period *c.* 1875–*c.* 1955 'the long sleep'. When considering archaeology in continental Europe and the dominance of literature in German, a rather different picture emerges of the 1920s and 1930s. For geographical reasons Germany was important to us. Research at German universities and museums was by then well advanced but split up into different schools of thought, most strongly in the north. In opposition to the Germanic-nationalistic theories of Gustaf Kossinna (1858–1931) were those of Carl Schuchhardt (1859–1943), whose basic idea was that the Orient and South Europe had always been leaders of development. Today it is easy to overlook the fact that Kossinna's '*siedlungs-archäologische*' methods were epoch-making for the whole profession. Some of his first pupils (for instance, E. Blume, M. Jahn, J. Kostrzewski) wrote excellent books that are still in use and these do not express the extreme views of Kossinna: it was first during the 1930s that they became so politically and racially orientated. Although a (too) biased dismissal of Kossinna's work was customary in Denmark, Brøndsted did recommend us to take a look at it too. This liberal attitude in research is one that we have sought to foster in the next generation.

The proximity of Kiel was particularly important for here was Gustav Schwantes (1881–1960), a likeable university teacher (of self-educated type) and museum head. He was personally interested in close collaboration with the Nordic area and his pupils followed his example. During the 1930s we established yet other contacts that were perhaps more significant in the long run. These were with our contemporaries of the 'Marburg school', that is the pupils of Gero v. Merhardt. As is well known this group of scholars were to put their stamp on German archaeology in excellent and more homogeneous fashion in the following generation. With respect to research there ran from Marburg a line directly back to the third 'great' name of German archaeology in the 1920s – Paul Reinecke (1872–1958). Last but not least Max Ebert deserves mention for his splendid *Reallexicon der Vorgeschichte* that appeared in the years 1924–32. This more than made up for our lack of lectures in European prehistory.

There were also more advanced schools of thought in European archaeology at that time, for example the 'Vienna school' and Oswald Menghin's *Weltgeschichte der Steinzeit* (1931). Some of us read this book (or at least parts of it). It is a complex work containing a partly self-invented terminology and theories in which philosophy, linguistics, ethnology and archaeology are ingeniously woven together. The author interprets material from the whole world – however erratically assembled – on the basis of one common model: this was the 'New archaeology' of that time; but it found little support.

Obviously we also kept ourselves informed of progress in British archaeology – once it was discovered that prehistory also existed on the far side of the North Sea. Two scholars were specially important for us in the 1930s. One was V. Gordon Childe with his book *The Danube in prehistory*, as well as his handbooks on the prehistory of Europe and the Near East. The other was Grahame Clark, whose book *The Mesolithic settlement of northern Europe* (1936) was given an enthusiastic reception – also by our older colleagues – because large-scale primary research in this period had just been initiated in Denmark.

What was the state of Nordic archaeology during the same span of time? In fact there was much for us to gather here. Research flourished in Norway: A. W. Brøgger's broadly based books on cultural history were just as exciting to us as the masterly studies of H. Shetelig (particularly those on the history of style in the Viking era). It was as if these different personalities and their pupils – one group in Oslo, the other in Bergen – were driving each other on in friendly competition.

Perhaps the same might be said about the situation in Sweden although the tone was some what more aggressive there. Considerable research was going on in this country at that time and subjects of special interest were chronology and the history of style in a European background using the rich Iron Age material of Sweden as a basis. In Stockholm Nils Åberg studied every period of European prehistory; he followed almost fanatically in the footsteps of Montelius and his typological method, while in Uppsala newer ideas were represented by Sune Lindqvist with whose pupils we had direct contact – these were the scholars who left their mark on further progress in Sweden. A third Swedish scholar, only a few years older than the group of students in Copenhagen, deserves mention: J.-E. Forssander, who was attached throughout his all too brief career to Lund university where he died, a professor, only 40 years old. He did not belong to any central Swedish school of thought and was a scholar of great intellect and charm whose inspiring books dealt with subjects ranging from the Neolithic to the Viking era. It was probably significant that Lund and Copenhagen were – and still are – very close archaeological neighbours.

Since 1916 Nordic archaeologists have held regular gatherings and in 1937 it was the turn of Denmark to host the congress, which had attracted many participants. Here met Brøgger and Shetelig, Åberg, Lindqvist and Forssander, and from Finland came C.A. Nordman and Ella Kivikoski, among all the others both young and old. It was an experience for us students when the names attached to books and articles took shape as living people.

Although we did read current Danish archaeology (Brøndsted's work on the prehistory of Denmark appeared first in 1938–40), it was the older works published prior to about 1920 that attracted our attention most. For example, I have always felt myself much indebted to the scholarship of Sophus Müller (1846–1934). Far later, as a teacher, I discovered that the following generation can be taught just as well – or better – through what one writes as what one lectures. The wide-ranging research and penetrating analyses of Müller, and not least his profound respect for source material, seem to me to have perpetuated a certain tradition in Denmark.

Quite by chance I received a personal and very vivid impression of the old master. In spite of his advanced age he continued to study at the Museum where, during the winter of 1933–4, I was working on some Iron Age finds. When passing my place he might stop, look at the material I had on hand and let fall a few comments. Now and again this involved a 10–15 minute long monologue that rapidly led to the problem on which he was currently working (because of his deafness no dialogue was possible). In particular I recall his warning against studying 'artless' Iron Age objects and pottery of the type that then lay on my table because, he said, they would not be of any value to prehistoric research during the next fifty years at the earliest – fortunately it did not take quite so long.

My rather mixed picture of what was going on in European prehistory is no attempt at a history of this discipline but just a brief comment on some of the possibilities that I sought to exploit in the 1930s and which constituted the background for my later research. Of course outside impulses have remained of vital importance to me and I have gained inspiration from many sides:

perhaps this can be detected more obviously in the work that I have produced since 1947. I have chosen to describe the pre-war situation in such detail for two reasons. First, it should be emphasized that European archaeology in the 1920s and 1930s was developing so vigorously and excitingly, and secondly I have come to realize that my youngest colleagues know little of the background on which they are to build, or have already built.

In 1939 I obtained my degree (that of 'magister' in prehistoric archaeology). Throughout my years of study I had spent a few hours daily working as an assistant at the Museum and this employment I continued until, in 1941, I obtained the post of assistant-keeper when Brøndsted was appointed to the newly-established chair of Nordic archaeology and left the Museum. Eleven years later he was to return as head of the whole institution on the sudden death of Poul Nørlund in 1951. I then applied for and was appointed to Brøndsted's chair at the university, and here I have worked ever since.

Under normal circumstances, after obtaining my degree, I would have supplemented my theoretical knowledge with foreign travel but obviously this was impossible during the war and in the years immediately after. In 1936 and 1939 I had published a couple of longish articles dealing with Stone Age finds in the *Aarbøger for nordisk Oldkyndighed*, but then there was a gap before I woke again to renewed research activity in 1945. I found a good subject among the finds that had come to light in bogs when peat was being dug during the war. My choice was the many exciting finds of Neolithic pottery: this study led to renewed evaluation of the first stages of the Neolithic in Denmark (i.e., the Funnel-beaker culture = TRB) and an attempt to rearrange the closely related Central European groups. The latter work had to be based on the literature though. Gradually I expanded my material into a thesis for the doctorate that I defended in 1948 (Becker 1948). Even though the thesis appeared in Danish (with a short summary in English), it received a certain amount of attention abroad. For example, Gordon Childe wrote me a long letter with many comments, material which he also used for an article on the subject (ANTI-QUITY 1949). My work gave rise to continued debate as can be seen (Böhm *et al.* 1961) in the report on the Neolithic Symposium held in Prague/Liblice in 1959, and elsewhere. For this reason there is no need for more detailed mention of it.

The rich Danish find material, both that found earlier and more recently, had been so little exploited that there lay research openings everywhere. For my part, over the next twenty years, I wrote a number of papers on subjects ranging from the Palaeolithic to the Viking era. On the other hand, I had little desire to write surveys or reference books and at that time there was no need for such because Brøndsted revised his work in 1957–60. However I have frequently had to hear later on that I should have produced a new survey of Danish prehistory: but this will not be forthcoming from me. There are still unexploited research areas offering chances of new primary studies: most recently I ventured into Danish numismatics of the 11th century (Becker 1981) and this put me in contact with a whole new circle of colleagues both at home and abroad – coins should really be a primary area of study for the archaeologist. Such a scattering of research objectives demands time if the work is to be done fairly satisfactorily, and I have always had to carry out my research in addition to other duties, first at the Museum and then at the University and elsewhere. Everything has a price and in my case it was probably my family who paid. I married in 1949 and my wife and our three daughters have patiently endured that too little time has been left over for them.

Perhaps it sounds as if I just continued to sit at home and write on the basis of the literature. As soon as it was possible I travelled to meet colleagues and to view the material. In 1947 and 1948 I visited the other Nordic countries, while in 1949 I had the chance, under the auspices of the British Council, to participate in a six-week exchange programme for four British and four Danish archaeologists. We learnt an incredible amount and were given the opportunity to meet many older and younger British colleagues. One special course – Stuart Piggott referred to it in his article in the present series (ANTIQUITY 1983: 36; above, page 32) – was just one of many experiences. A few years later I was awarded a bursary by the New Carlsberg Foundation and this was used for a three-month study tour in West Europe. On this occasion my special interest was the Palaeolithic which I studied in Paris, in the vicinity of Les Eyzies, and in Austria. Later I got to know the countries of Eastern Europe.

In any profession the education of the following generation must be of paramount importance. As touched upon earlier, in the 1920s and 1930s Denmark lagged behind many European countries in this respect, even though university education in prehistoric archaeology did become possible in 1930. The establishment of the chair for this subject (1941) made no great alteration: there was no increase in the volume of teaching and students had still to find room to work in the Museum library and other premises. It was only in 1949 (on the initiative of the students themselves) that a 'reading room' with three or four hundred books was set up in the name of the University but still in Museum premises.

When I took up my appointment at the university in 1952 one of my first tasks was to establish an institute with a usable library. This was no easy undertaking as the University's funds for the humanities were microscopic at that time. I was a 'single-handed' professor for thirteen years; there were no other teachers and not even a secretary. Things gradually improved and from 1965 four permanent posts for lecturers and one for a secretary were established in rapid succession. Better premises became available to us but still in the Museum building. In 1969 the University purchased a building quite close to the Museum for the use of all archaeological disciplines. The number of students has much increased over the years and since 1952 some 80 'magisters' have completed their studies at our institute: most are now employed in their special field by the universities, by regional and local museums, and by libraries.

Of course this brief survey of the last thirty years of prehistoric archaeology in Copenhagen is but part of the total picture in Denmark. In 1949 a chair of prehistoric archaeology was established at Århus university and here it took only a short span of time for P. V. Glob and then Ole Klindt-Jensen to create an extraordinarily live environment through combining a university institute with a central museum for Jutland – both now installed in the old manor house of Moesgård south of the city of Århus.

Archaeological excavation in Denmark has developed just as rapidly during the last fifty years. As mentioned, up to about 1936 the National Museum was the only institution able to carry out proper scientific investigations – that is 'proper' according to the standards of that time. The staff of four archaeologists in the Department of Prehistory was supplemented by a few colleagues from other departments and by the young assistants. Already in 1934 I was employed by the Museum as a student, and by chance I became senior assistant the year after. I was involved in almost everything going on in the Department including, for example, standing in for the only secretary and using her (and the Department's) only typewriter. It was more important, and far more exciting, to collect new finds and to carry out minor excavations (the first being a Bronze Age barrow (Aner & Kersten 1975, II, No. 1067). As a rule this work was on Zealand so one could return to Copenhagen by bus or train in the evening. In 1936 I purchased a large motorcycle with sidecar – the first attempt to motorize the Department. Quite soon I was entrusted with rather larger excavations round about the country. During holidays too I was able to investigate two Stone Age settlements (published in *Aarbøger for nordisk Oldkyndighed* 1939 and 1952) near my parents' summer cottage. But what was my practical training? It was good enough according to the standards of those years. In 1934, with the two other students, I had participated in an excavation of a Bronze Age barrow under Brøndsted's direction. This took three days and then I spent some ten days with Broholm excavating an Iron Age cemetery in North Schleswig. However, already the previous year, I had had a stroke of luck when allowed to participate in one of Gudmund Hatt's investigations of Iron Age houses at Ginderup in north-west Jutland. Brøndsted arranged this for me (as a result of my earlier-mentioned 'private' excavation). Hatt had earlier held a position at the National Museum but he had been appointed to the chair of human geography at the University in 1929. He continued, however, his outstanding studies of Iron Age settlements and fields in Denmark. Influenced by van Giffen in the Netherlands, he had developed a new technique for excavating the sites of structures. His broad-based geographical outlook imparted valuable impulses to Danish archaeology, while his almost fanatical enthusiasm for each task was bound to affect all his co-workers, even though his fiery temperament could make us keep a low profile on occasion. In 1933 I had no idea that, a generation later, I was to continue Hatt's research into Iron Age society.

Hatt's excavations of the 1930s should be set against the background of the

National Museum's excavation technique in which I had been trained. This had been established by Sophus Müller in the 1890s: at that time it had been modern and efficient, forty years later it was out of date, to put it mildly. A barrow was studied by means of a quadrangular sector in the centre (4–6 m long on each side according to the size of the barrow) and paying no attention to profiles. Settlements of all ages were excavated in sectors of one square metre, inside these in strata 20 cm thick, but without regard to stratigraphy. In addition to these inadequacies the Museum had only scant financial resources, so only few, and generally far too hastily completed, excavations could be carried out. For these reasons one of the most important staff jobs was a heavy-handed assignment of priorities so that as many tasks as possible could be dealt with. Nevertheless, let me hasten to add, the really large and important finds were treated with all possible care – for example, the pre-Roman vessel at Hjortspring and the Viking ship at Ladby. Both these were excavated by the chief conservator, G. Rosenberg, who was the Museum's finest field archaeologist. The Viking stronghold at Trelleborg should also be mentioned here: this was excavated by Poul Nørlund of the Mediaeval Department because it was thought at first to date from the 16th century.

One of these large projects was of special significance for me. This was Jelling, where the two impressive barrows are associated with the first Danish royal dynasty of the 10th century. In the first years of the war state finance was made available for various large projects in order to provide employment, and Nørlund took this chance to plan a new investigation of our monuments. Einar Dyggve was appointed head of this work: he was an experienced and conscientious field archaeologist whose investigations of Early Christian structures in Yugoslavia and Italy had been disrupted by the war. As a permanent member of the Museum staff, and as its representative, I was ordered to assist Dyggve in 1941 and 1942. In all I spent six months working at Jelling – a time I recall with great pleasure. Dyggve was one of the finest people that I have been privileged to meet and it was on this project that I (and different assistants) learnt modern techniques. For Danish archaeology this excavation was therefore of greater importance than most realize, but strictly speaking the methods employed were only those that had been used internationally for several years. Personally I was soon to find good use for my new experience as in 1944 I was to excavate several Bronze Age barrows on one of the airfields that the German Wehrmacht was busy establishing in Jutland. However odd it sounds, the National Museum was permitted on its own to excavate field monuments on German military bases. Here a few Museum staff found themselves with major but often problematic assignments. I worked inside the Hansted fortress in Thy as well as on the airfield at Skrydstrup in North Schleswig (the results are best published in Aner & Kersten, vol. VII, Nos. 3519, 21, 22, 30).

Another challenge taken up by Danish archaeologists in the war years was related to the widespread digging for peat in Danish bogs because of the lack of other fuel. Here too some museum staff – particularly the younger ones – were kept very busy. The innumerable finds that came to light had to be rescued: far too rarely was there any opportunity of proper investigation. In the incredibly rich Store Åmose bog in West Zealand the newly set up Scientific Department of the Museum did manage, however, to excavate and save a vast amount of Mesolithic and Neolithic material. In other places rather rougher methods were used to save as much as possible: the excavations that I carried out in 1943–5 of the Maglemose settlements on Zealand (Svaerdborg, Lundby, and Holmegård) fall into the latter category (Henriksen 1976; 1980). After the liberation in 1945 larger research projects could again be started up: many more Museum staff now carried out important excavations of sites ranging in time from the late Palaeolithic (Bromme) via the Neolithic (Barkaer) to the Viking era (Fyrkat and Aggersborg) and the Middle Ages (Store Valby). Space does not permit detailed discussion of this work, nor of my own excavations of Iron Age sites in West Jutland and on Bornholm where, for example, we carried out the first total excavation of a cemetery containing more than 500 cremation graves (Nørre Sandegård, see *Germania* 1962).

I continued excavating after moving to the University in 1952, but for practical reasons this work was still carried out in close collaboration with and in the name of the Museum. There was, though, the difference that to a greater extent I could choose my own projects as part of my research, and that this work was partly financed by the Carlsberg Foundation and other institutions. Examples of my work at that time are the first large Neolithic flint-mines in North Jutland; a further project was the so-called stone-packing graves of the late TRB culture, an almost unknown form of grave at that time. I came upon the track of them by accident and since 1962 in parts of Jutland we have been able to excavate large burial grounds that contain up to a good hundred structures laid out in long rows in the landscape. This work led to a re-evaluation of the late TRB culture in Jutland, the graves being a point in the debate on this group (Becker 1970; Jørgensen 1977).

Once again, quite fortuitously, I came into contact with an area in which I had never dreamed of doing any primary research: Iron Age settlements, later those of the Bronze Age too. In 1960 one of our experienced local museum leaders, J. Dalgaard-Knudsen from Ringkøbing, requested my help after applying unsuccessfully to the National Museum and to Århus. For special reasons an investigation had to be made of a largish Iron Age settlement (Grøntoft). I took on the task and decided to tackle it by using machinery – a tractor and scoop – with which we removed the thin layer of humus containing the already destroyed structures. I did not expect any results but I was mistaken. When the first 3-metre-wide strip was uncovered, the lines of the walls and posts of the houses appeared more clearly against the pale subsoil than I had ever seen on a plan. We rapidly systemized this discovery, making it possible to uncover swiftly and simply not only the plans of houses but of whole villages (Becker, *Acta Archaeologica* 36, 39, 42; Steen Hvass, *Acta Archaeologica* 46, 49). It was of much help that soon after I could set up a committee under the State Research Council, from whom we received excellent financial support for excavations carried out solely for research purposes. Up until the present day the efforts of some of my colleagues and students have totally changed our picture of settlements, farmsteads and villages throughout the later Bronze Age and the whole of the Iron Age, that is up to and including the Viking era; even large, rich men's farms have been uncovered in this manner (Becker *et al.*, *Acta Archaeologica* 50). In brief, throughout the 1960s and 1970s conventional archaeology made the most surprising and, let it be noted, well-documented contribution to our knowledge of the social history and economy of Denmark in antiquity. I have let colleagues deal with theoretical ideas and imported socio-anthropological models.

In other words there was an increase in my excavation activities from about 1957. It is not because there was a lack of offers, nor of too narrow a personal horizon, that I have only discussed work in Denmark and not major projects carried out abroad. In the same period of time one large expedition after another left Denmark for the Near Orient, Nubia, Thailand and not least the countries surrounding the Persian Gulf. The numerous participants in these projects were recruited in the main from among Nordic archaeologists and this paralysed efforts on the home front – although there were plenty of exciting tasks here and just as great a need to save sites threatened by destruction as was the case abroad. It was on these grounds that I concentrated on problems at home.

Since 1974 I have done no excavating myself – a decision that was planned. Teaching and administrative obligations both at the University and for different councils (e.g. the Danish Research Council) as well as editorial commitments (*Acta Archaeologica* 1948–84, and the monograph series of the institute *Arkaeologiske Studier* since 1973) gradually made it difficult to lead excavations in person on a site – and this is something that must be done there and not from a remote office. Moreover over the years I have collected a large amount of important material that must appear in published form. It is no good teaching that an excavation is first complete on its publication unless one practises what one preaches. Far too much information on Danish projects, my own included, is still inaccessible.

As mentioned in my introduction, it was not my intention to describe developments in all spheres of our profession, space limitations preclude this. However one factor of much significance for Danish archaeology is the widespread decentralization of activities that has taken place in the last twenty years. At the present time more than a hundred professional archaeologists are working at museums and institutions all over the country, and it is important that all of them have had the same good university training as their colleagues who are to continue the work of the National Museum and not least that of the

Universities. Fifty years ago we had far too few professional archaeologists in Denmark. Do we have too many today?

References

ANER, E. & K. KERSTEN. 1973–84. *Die Funde der älteren Bronzezeit des nordischen kreises in Dänemark, Schleswig-Holstein und Niedersachsen* 1-7. Copenhagen: Neumünster.

BECKER, C.J. 1948. *Mosefundne Lerkar fra yngre Stenalder.* Copenhagen (also *Aarboger nord. Oldkyndighed* 1947).

1970. Die Steinpackungsgräber der dänischen Trichterbecherkultur. *Actes du 7ième Congrès International des Sciences Pré- et Protohistoriques, Prague 1966*, 1: 512–15.

1981. The coinages of Harthacnut and Magnus the Good at Lund *c.* 1040–*c.* 1046. Copenhagen. Studies in Northern Coinages of the eleventh century. Kong. Danske Vid. Selsk. Hist.-Fil. Schrifter 9: 4.

BOHM, J. & S. DE LAET (eds.). 1961. *L'Europe à la fin de l'âge de la pierre: Symposium Prague–Liblice–Brno 1959.* Prague.

BRØNDSTED, J. 1957–60. *Danmarks Oldtid* I–III. 2nd edition. Copenhagen.

DANIEL, G. 1975. *150 years of archaeology.* London: Duckworth.

FRIIS JOHANSEN, K. (ed.) 1927. *De forhistoriske tider i Europa* I–II. Copenhagen.

HENRICKSEN, B. 1976. Svaerdborg I, excavations 1943–44. *Arkaeologiske Studier* 3.

1980. Lundby-Holmen. Copenhagen. *Nordiske Fortidsminder*, ser. B 6.

JØRGENSEN, E. 1977. Hagebrogård-Vroue-Koldkur, Neolithische Gräberfelder aus NW Jütland. *Arkaeologiske Studier* 4.

KLINDT-JENSEN, O. 1975. *A history of Scandinavian archaeology.* London: Thames & Hudson.

RENFREW, C. 1982. Explanation revisited, in C. Renfew, M.J. Rowlands & B. Abbott Segraves (eds.), *Theory and explanation in archaeology: the Southampton conference*: 5–23. New York: Academic Press.

9

Sigfried J. De Laet

Pure luck played an important part in determining my scientific career. As far as I can remember, when a schoolboy I never seriously considered devoting myself to historical studies, let alone to archaeology and prehistory. In fact, I then had no clear predilection for any particular, well-defined field. I was a rather good pupil in most subjects; only physics inspired a profound dislike in me and this barred the road to the exact sciences. My father made his living as a teacher and probably without realizing it, I wanted to follow in his footsteps. The influence of a few excellent teachers eventually made me decide to read classics at the University of Ghent, my birthplace. Soon however, I grew strongly disappointed by my chosen subject and my professors could not kindle in me any fervent love for the endless rehashing of antique texts or for critical text-editions. Luckily I was attracted almost immediately by a remarkable man, Hubert Van de Weerd, whose extensive courses included not only the whole range of ancient history but also the archaeology and art history of that same period. His personal interest, however, was in Gallo-Roman archaeology, and precisely at the time when I first met him he had just finished the first large-scale operation undertaken in Belgium, to wit the excavation of the townwall of Tongeren, the antique *Atuatuca Tungrorum*. In the course of his academic career, Van de Weerd spent the best part of his time and efforts on the training of his students; he thus created a solid school of historians and archaeologists, the best of whom were to occupy important positions in Flemish intellectual life. Under his direction, I specialized in Roman history, but already as a student I devoted much time to provincial Roman archaeology. In 1936 I obtained the licence-degree and only one year later I also obtained the doctor's degree with the presentation of a thesis on the composition of the Roman Senate. This thesis was published as a book in 1941. As far as my archaeological training was concerned, my lack of excavation experience was important: these were the dark years of the great economic crisis and no funds were available for fieldwork.

In 1939, I had obtained a travel grant which was to be used to go and work for a year in Budapest under the direction of A. Alföldi. But the German invasion of May 1940 put a stop to these plans. During the early occupation days, I was told that this grant could be used only for a study-tour at a German university, an offer which I, of course, refused. Since 1937, I had been a teacher at the Aalst Athenaeum. At first, the favourable geographical location of this small town, which lies halfway between Ghent and Brussels, made it easy for me to spend my free time in the libraries of both towns and to do scientific research. But the German occupation soon also put a stop to this: the train-connexions were slow and few, while the libraries would no longer loan books. What I then considered to be a major disaster eventually proved to be crucial in my further career. On the advice of Van de Weerd, I went browsing in the small museum of Aalst, where I discovered a collection of unpublished material dug up long ago – about 1875 – by an amateur archaeologist on the site of a Gallo-Roman *vicus* in Asse. Henceforth, I spent all my free time on the study of these remains. Owing to the absence of excavation diaries, drawings and plans, it was not an easy task, but it sharpened my critical sense of what could not be learned from this type of find. My first archaeological contributions were published in 1942.

In October 1942, I returned to Ghent University as a research fellow of the National Fund for Scientific Research, and the year after, I became Van de Weerd's assistant. Naturally, I resumed my research in the field of Roman history, but I retained a lively interest in archaeology. The German occupation authorities had forced a number of 'guest-professors' on the University, among them the German prehistorian K. Tackenberg. At the time, quite a number of papers on prehistory were published in periodicals and weeklies which were at the service of the 'New Order', and many of these contributions were written in the spirit of the notorious *Germanenforschung*. Immediately I became very critical of these papers, and I became more and more interested in prehistory and in the problems of the real possibilities and limitations of archaeology. I tried to discover the flaws in the reasoning of the supporters of the ethnic interpretation of prehistoric cultures and thus further sharpened my sense for thorough criticism, which I have kept till the present day.

Soon after the liberation, I obtained a research grant from the British Council and, one stormy day in October 1945, I embarked for England, where I stayed for a few months in Magdalene College, Cambridge. This study-tour was most fruitful for my work. The very restful atmosphere allowed me to draft the larger part of a study of the Roman customs, *Portorium*. This substantial volume – probably the most solid one I ever wrote – was published in 1949 and an anastatic reprint was published in New York 25 years later. In Cambridge, I had contacts mainly with two leading historians of antiquity, F. E. Adcock and M. P. Charlesworth, but here too my interest in archaeology remained as lively as ever before. I felt my limited knowledge of classical archaeology to be a flaw, and therefore I regularly followed the courses given by A. W. Lawrence and Jocelyn Toynbee. Almost every weekend I went to London to visit the museums. Because of the war, many books published in Great Britain since 1939 were still unknown in Belgium, and I read many of these, particularly those concerning archaeology.

During the Easter holidays of 1946, I was all of a sudden telephoned by the Rector of Ghent University; he asked me to suspend immediately my Cambridge stay and return forthwith to Ghent in order to give – in the short period between the Easter holidays and the first examinations – an important

number of courses and thus to fill in temporarily for two professors who had
been taken ill. In Ghent the preparation of these courses took the larger part of
my time and during the following academic year, this temporary duty was
continued. Still, I found time to finish my *Portorium*.

Of great importance were the regular contacts I had had since 1946 with A.E.
van Giffen, who then towered over the whole range of Dutch archaeology. He
invited me to take part in some of his most important post-war excavations,
such as those of the Roman *castella* in Vechten and in Valkenburg and those of
the bronze age barrows of Toterfout-Halve Mijl. I accepted his invitation and
this allowed me to complete and refine my then still limited experience in field
archaeology and excavation techniques. I consider van Giffen to be among the
most important of my mentors, together with Van de Weerd, and until his
death, I remained a good friend of his. On the occasion of his final lecture, I had
the privilege to congratulate him on behalf of his foreign colleagues.

In 1947, I was appointed as a lecturer at Ghent University and four years later,
I was promoted as an *ordinarius*. I had the chair of West European archaeology
(from the earliest times to the Migration period). At a later date, new courses in
medieval archaeology were added to the list. Thus I was confronted with the
near-impossible task of giving lectures on *Homo erectus* as well as on medieval
town-archaeology. Luckily, I had been able to train a few good students in the
meantime, and the academic authorities granted me a few posts of assistant
which they could fill: as teachers and later as colleagues, they helped me
considerably. Archaeology became a growing success with the students.
Indeed, at the end of my career, I can look back on a list of almost 100 students
who prepared a licence-dissertation under my direction and furthermore, some
ten of these obtained the doctor's degree. In my teaching, I always strove to
develop a sharp sense of criticism in my students. I tried to show them what can
and what cannot be attained through archaeology, seen as a historical discipline.
In 1950 I wrote a small booklet on the subject for the use of the undergraduates.
In 1954, a rephrased, improved and expanded version of this was published in
French. Glyn Daniel published a review of it in ANTIQUITY and, as a result of
this, an English edition was published in 1957 (*Archaeology and its problems*). In
quick succession, a new Dutch edition and Danish, Spanish, Italian, Swedish
and Polish translations followed.

In 1945, the situation of Belgian national archaeology was far from
satisfactory. My chair was the very first one in non-classical archaeology. Only
in Liège University had limited tuition in *préhistoire* – in the French sense of the
word – been provided since 1926: these courses exclusively concerned the Stone
Age, while the Metal Ages were not even mentioned. Since then, the situation
has much improved and, partly after the example set by the Ghent model, most
Belgian universities now provide a fully developed education in national
archaeology, ranging from the palaeolithic period up to and including the
Middle Ages. As far as excavations were concerned, Belgium equally lagged far
behind Great Britain, the Netherlands and Scandinavia. At the time, only a

small excavation service, attached to the Royal Museums in Brussels, existed; it was far easier to obtain important grants to excavate in the Near East, in Egypt or in Italy than to secure a small state grant to excavate in our own country. By sheer force of will and with much daring, I succeeded in creating a small excavation service, attached to my chair at the University. At first I had to confine my activities to a few rescue excavations of limited proportions, but slowly I succeeded in convincing the authorities of the cultural importance of national archaeology and gradually I obtained more financial support, not however from the State but from the provincial and communal authorities, from the University and from the National Fund for Scientific Research. This allowed me to switch to 'thematic' excavations of greater importance and planned with the specific aim of solving well-defined problems. As an example of these were the excavations in Destelbergen near Ghent, where systematic excavation work has steadily been carried out since 1960 with the purpose of gaining radically new information concerning the Gallo-Roman origins of Ghent.

At the start of my professorial career, there was – not only in Ghent, but in the whole of Belgium – a painful lack of facilities to publish the results of scientific archaeological research. Therefore, one of my first concerns was to create the *Dissertationes Archaeologicae Gandenses*, a series of monographs, the first of which was published in 1953. 1986 saw the publication of volume 23. For shorter contributions, I could use the periodical *L'Antiquité Classique*, of which I was editorial secretary, but this periodical was restricted to the publication of papers concerning the Roman period. Other universities faced the same problem. For these reasons, I consulted with my colleagues Danthine (Liège), Glasbergen (Amsterdam) and Waterbolk (Groningen), and on 25 May 1959, the periodical *Helinium* was founded. The first fascicle was published in the spring of 1961. Very soon, *Helinium* became widely accepted as the leading archaeological periodical of the Low Countries.

In 1959, together with a number of colleagues from other universities and institutions, I helped with the creation of the National Centre for Archaeological Research in Belgium, of which I was the first Chairman. The NCARB aims – amongst other things – at the systematic publication of bibliographical repertoires concerning all the finds and discoveries in Belgium and the Grand-Duchy of Luxemburg; it also publishes catalogues of private collections. Finally, some years ago, I also helped with the creation of a national post-graduate teaching programme in archaeology; it works under the auspices of the National Fund for Scientific Research and is carried out jointly with other Belgian universities.

I also considered it to be a moral duty to publish text-books for the use of my students. On the occasion of the Zurich and particularly of the Madrid congresses, I became a close friend of several prehistorians and under their influence my personal interest gradually shifted from the Roman period to earlier times. I was much interested by problems of acculturation and continuity, and it was clear to me that in order to understand the Gallo-Roman civilization in our part of the world, one needed a thorough knowledge not only of the classical Roman civilization, but also of the earlier, autochthonous Celtic culture on which the Roman was grafted. I also understood that it serves no purpose to study a particular culture within the present state-borders, and that these cultures had to be approached in the context of the whole of their territorial setting. A few of my books reflect this. My *Préhistoire de l'Europe* was published in 1967, but at an earlier date I had already written a survey of the prehistory of the Low Countries. This was done at the instance of Glyn Daniel, whom I met in Brussels on the occasion of one of his famous TV broadcasts *Animal, vegetable, mineral?* which he presented that day to the audience from the Brussels museums. We were sitting on one of the Brussels pub-terraces, together with Stuart Piggott, when all of a sudden he suggested that I should write a survey of the prehistory of the Low Countries to be published in his newly created series *Ancient Peoples and Places*. Rather rashly, I accepted, but the volume cost me numerous headaches, mainly because of the fact that the editor authorized only a limited number of words: I had to restrict myself to the broad outlines of the story and retain only the highlights. *The Low Countries* was published in 1958 and was well received, although it remained slightly too limited to be of use to students in archaeology. Only a few days after the publication of this book, my Amsterdam colleague Glasbergen proposed that he and I together publish a more detailed Dutch version. *De Voorgeschiedenis der Lage Landen* saw the light in 1959; it was still of a small format but it was about twice as long, and after only one year it was already sold out. We then conceived the plan to publish a far more detailed analytical work, consisting of two parts: Glasbergen would take care of the area north of the Great Rivers, while I would concern myself with the rest of Benelux. Unfortunately, owing to the beginning of the illness which would eventually carry him away much too soon, Glasbergen could not complete his part. My own voluminous contribution, *Prehistorische Kulturen in het Zuiden der Lage Landen*, was published in 1974 (followed by a new, expanded edition in 1979). A French translation, *La Belgique d'avant les Romains*, which in fact constitutes a third, expanded edition, came out in 1982; it has grown into a mammoth work of about 800 pages. Whether this made my students feel happier is another question. . . .

Since 1931, the most important international organization in the field of prehistory had been the *Congrès international des Sciences préhistoriques et protohistoriques* (CISPP). It had grown from a schism within the *Congrès international d'Anthropologie et d'Archéologie préhistoriques*, where the anthropologists had gradually relegated the prehistorians to the background. But the war had paralysed the activities of CISPP. Furthermore, during the second conference, in Oslo in 1936, grave difficulties had risen within the CISPP. These were caused by the German Nazi government, which had demanded the resignation of a few German colleagues, who did not share the racist theories of the Kossinna school. J. Bøe, secretary of the Oslo congress, took the initiative of convening the *Conseil Permanent* (CP) of the CISPP in Copenhagen in 1948. It was the occasion to fill the gaps in the ranks of the CP, many members of which had died since 1936. Thus, I was co-opted as one of the Belgian representatives. It was decided that the third conference, as had already been planned in 1936, would take place in Budapest, but a few months later political events caused Hungary to renounce the organization of this meeting. Switzerland immediately proposed that the congress take place in Zurich in 1950. It was a great success. There were 244 participants coming from 30 different countries: the conference still had 'human' dimensions, but in the future, our congresses would become more 'mammoth'-sized, which would cause organizational problems. A drawback was the absence of our colleagues from the so-called Eastern Bloc: the Cold War was raging. Until then, the CISPP had been concerned only with the organization of congresses. The Zurich meeting changed that. The CP had to consider a proposal made by P. Bosch-Gimpera to join the *International Council for Philosophy and Humanistic Studies* (CIPSH), an organization founded in 1949 and closely linked with Unesco. The CIPSH grouped a number of international, non-governmental organizations active in the fields of philosophy and humanistic studies (e.g. the *Union Académique Internationale*, the philosophers, the historians, the linguists, etc.; at present, in 1983, 13 organizations of this kind are part of the CIPSH). Bosch-Gimpera's proposal faced strong opposition from a number of older prehistorians, who had not forgotten the interventions of the Nazi government in 1936, and who were wary of all organizations which – like Unesco – were of a governmental nature and which could, theoretically at least, intervene in the free organization of the CISPP. The younger generation, on the other hand, was interested in the perspective of a broader efficacy and wider action of the CISPP, made possible by the grants to be obtained from Unesco via the CIPSH. Among other things, these grants would make possible enterprises which required wide international cooperation. Eventually, the CP decided to create a *Comité exécutif* (CE), which would convene every two years; its task consisted of studying the problems of joining the CIPSH and of broadening the activities of the CISPP. The election of the members of the new CE presented no difficulties, but nobody was found willing to take charge of the secretarial duties; eventually, the resigning chairman, E. Vogt, agreed to fill in temporarily, until the next meeting of the CP. In 1952, the CP met in Namur, and following suggestions of the CE, it was decided to apply officially for formal admission to the CIPSH and to grant CISPP patronage to a number of international ventures, such as the *Inventaria Archaeologica*, a commission on spectral analysis, a commission on the study of prehistoric art, etc. It was also at Namur that chairman L. Pericot asked me to accept the post of secretary of the CE. After long hesitation, I finally accepted, on the condition that it would not mean too much supplementary work and that the job would only be a short-time one. In fact, I did it for 14 years and co-operated closely with the successive presidents: L. Pericot, G. Bersu, M. Pallottino and J. Filip in the preparation for the congresses in Madrid (1954), Hamburg (1958), Rome (1962) and Prague (1966). In Madrid it was decided that henceforth the secretary of the CE would also be the secretary of the CP, in order to ensure better coordination, and that he would have the title of secretary-general. Naturally, it is impossible to relate here all that happened during this long period of 14 years and I have to confine myself to mentioning the most important of the problems which I helped solve. First of all, there was the matter of the geographic expansion of the CISPP: I wanted to change the almost exclusively European nature of our organization and strove for universalism. In 1954, only 45 nations were represented in the CISPP. As a first step I succeeded in convincing the Eastern Bloc countries to participate again in our activities: their representatives were again present at a meeting of the CP in Lund in 1956, and the year after the USSR joined the CISPP and Soviet colleagues attended the 1958 Hamburg congress. In 1968, no less than 85 countries had joined our organization (at present they number more than one hundred). Only in the case of China did I remain unsuccessful and today this remains the only important gap.

Our joining the CIPSH also presented difficulties: during the general meeting of the CIPSH in 1953, our application for membership faced strong opposition from the representative of the anthropologists, who had not yet digested the 1931 divorce between prehistorians and anthropologists. It was suggested that the CISPP – while keeping a certain amount of internal autonomy – should again place itself in the care of the anthropologists. In Madrid, the CP rejected this proposal; G. Bersu was asked to attend the third general meeting of the CIPSH in 1955 as an observer and to defend our interests on this occasion. He performed this duty with complete success, as the general assembly co-opted us with overwhelming majority as a full member of the CIPSH. Our joining the CIPSH also caused us to change the name of our organization: the word *Congrès* was replaced by the term *Union*, in order to make clear that the UISPP (this being the new abbreviation) would henceforward have a much wider range of activities. Our membership of the CIPSH also made us the only international organization in the field of prehistoric sciences to be officially recognized by Unesco; for this reason, the UISPP also contacted other organizations, such as the *Congrès panafricain de préhistoire*, the *Far Eastern Prehistory Association*, *INQUA*, the *Congrès international d'archéologie slave*, etc., which pursued goals similar to ours, but which had a more limited geographical or chronological base. Through the intervention of the UISPP, these organizations could now also obtain grants from Unesco via the CIPSH. All this made clear the necessity to change and adapt radically the statutes of the UISPP. This task was given to G. Bersu and myself. The new statutes were accepted on the occasion of the Hamburg congress; since then they have been changed very little and are still operative.

134		*Sigfried J. De Laet*

Earlier, I mentioned the international enterprises which had been granted our patronage. Over the years, their number has grown, but as secretary-general, I had no control over their activity. Some of them are directed intelligently and are still prospering; others, however, some of which had been created in a hurry and without adequate preparation, died an inglorious death. More important to my mind was the creation and organization of specialized colloquia. The first of these, organized under the auspices of the UISPP, concerned the late Neolithic period in Europe and took place in 1959 in Liblice and in Brno. It was a great success and pointed the way to the future: colloquia of this type, which concern the detailed discussion of well-defined subjects, are to my mind of greater scientific importance than large congresses, where all the available time is generally taken by short communications and none is left for discussion. This is the very important problem of the 'giant' congresses. In Zurich there were only 244 participants and everything went smoothly. But in Madrid, already some 500 participants turned up; in Hamburg, there were more than a thousand of them, and *c.* 1,400 attended the Prague meeting. The problem was discussed by the CP in Madrid and again in Hamburg. In Hamburg it was decided that henceforth – and following the example set by the large conferences of the historians, where this procedure had become a tradition – a number of specific subjects would be selected and that competent archaeologists would be asked to prepare a report, to be printed and circulated before the conference; such reports would then serve as suitable bases for detailed discussion. This was done for the 1962 Rome congress and the initiative met with general approval. But the actual realization of this procedure had been so difficult that the principle was abandoned. This, to my mind, was a mistake. Later, on the occasion of the Nice congress in 1976, where more than 2,000 participants turned up, another solution was thought to have been found: within the general framework of the conference, some 25 colloquia were organized. This too proved to be a lop-sided answer to the problem. Indeed, of those participants who wished to present a contribution not falling into one of these colloquia, each had three(!) minutes in which to present his work. The result was chaos! In 1981, the congress was organized for the first time outside Europe, in Mexico. Because of the high travelling expenses, the number of participants remained limited. But for future congresses, the problem of gigantic attendances remains very real and urgently requires a suitable solution.

In Rome, I had accepted that my mandate as secretary-general would finally be renewed for four years. In 1964, in Zaragoza, the CP elected my friend Ole Klindt-Jensen as my successor, and in 1966, at the start of the Prague congress, he took over. He too would have discharged this duty for 14 years or more, but for his sudden death in 1980. The members of the CE then urgently asked me to step in, as an interregnum could have been disastrous in view of the nearing Mexico congress. I convened the CE in Mainz and there the measures required to guarantee the continuity of the UISPP were taken.

In 1959, the CE had decided that henceforth the secretary-general would represent the UISPP in the general assembly of the CIPSH: this would ensure a certain amount of continuity. As a result of that decision, I attended the meetings in 1961 (Tokyo), 1963 (Mexico) and 1965 (Copenhagen); from 1967 onwards, Klindt-Jensen, of course, became our representative. In 1971, however, I received a personal invitation to attend the general assembly of CIPSH in Salzburg. To my surprise, I was then elected treasurer of the CIPSH. Since then I have been re-elected regularly up to 1984 at the Bangkok meeting, when I retired voluntarily, thinking that a younger man would be more efficient. Within the CIPSH, I could defend the interest not only of the UISPP, but also of other organizations – such as the UAI, the classicists, the orientalists, the anthropologists, etc., also active in the field of archaeology.

It was also through the CIPSH that I was able to build up closer contacts with Unesco. The aims of this organization deserve everybody's support, and significant results have been achieved, but Unesco suffers from two ailments which grow worse every year: a deplorable augmentation of political impact and impending bureaucracy. I co-operated in some of the ventures of Unesco and recently I was appointed director of Volume 1 of the new edition of Unesco's *Scientific and cultural history of mankind*. I contacted more than 40 colleagues from all over the world and the venture would be most stimulating indeed, if one had not to wage a continuous guerilla warfare against this bureaucratic frame of mind.

In 1975 the Belgian National Fund for Scientific Research appointed me as its representative in the *ad hoc* committee for archaeology of the European Science Foundation, a quite young non-governmental organization founded in 1974, and grouping academies and research councils which are responsible for supporting scientific research at a national level. The task of this *ad hoc* committee was to draw up the list of laboratories and institutes in the 18 member-states of the ESF, which provide services to archaeologists, particularly in the field of the natural sciences and archaeometry. It was also to analyse critically the present general situation in this field. This work resulted in a three-volume repertory, drafted by F. Verhaeghe (*Archaeology, natural science and technology: the European situation*) and published in 1979. In 1980, the present sub-committee for archaeology was created within the framework of the standing committee for the humanities and I was appointed chairman. This sub-committee has several well-defined tasks: it has to devise means and ways to promote the co-operation between archaeology and the natural sciences (to achieve this, it organized a few colloquia and workshops and prepared a series of small handbooks); it has to analyse the archaeological legislation in the different member-countries and to formulate general recommendations; it has to study the possibilities of rationalizing archaeological publications (e.g. by the publication of series of abstracts); finally, it has to study how the relatively unsatisfactory relationship between history and archaeology can be improved. The importance of this sub-committee also lies in the fact that it groups representatives from all branches of archaeology (prehistorians, classical archaeologists and representatives of the natural sciences). It is the only organization of this kind in Europe. Therefore – and although the mandate of the sub-committee expired in 1984 – its existence should be continued. But this brings us to future perspectives, and these hardly belong to the present retrospect.

Did I, in the course of my life-time, do something that is valuable enough to be written down here? It is a question I cannot answer. But one single thing remains to be said: I followed a trade which I deeply like and this presents a real advantage: I have, indeed, enjoyed it very much.

10

J. Desmond Clark

Does one, I wonder, inherit with one's genes the shortcomings, the idiosyncra-
sies and the interests of one's forebears? Sometimes, maybe; maybe not. Often it
works the other way round and it seemed to me that the libertines among the
boys at school were the sons of parsons though here, no doubt, it is environment
that is overriding. I did, however, have a grandfather who had strong
antiquarian interests and perhaps it was out of this, nurtured by one or two
superb teachers, that my own interest in prehistory developed.

My father's family had been small landowners, farmers, on the boundaries of
Buckinghamshire and Oxfordshire for some few hundred years. My great
grandfather ran cattle on an uncle's farm near Oving in Buckinghamshire, and
walked them up to London to sell there. He had had a raw deal as, being the
youngest son with seven other brothers and sisters, he was turned out when his
father died intestate and his eldest brother took everything. My grandfather was
a chemist who turned to pharmacy and ran a relatively lucrative business in
north London and patented and manufactured an early cosmetic cream. He
travelled widely on the continent, particularly enjoying, as his photos show, the
classical antiquities. My father trained as an electrical engineer at Faraday House
and, after serving on the Western Front in the First World War, he took over the
cosmetic business. By the time this was sold after his death, he had probably put
more into it than he got out of it. One of his interests was in history as this could
be seen in the numerous vestiges surviving in England and Wales and my
brother, sister and I visited with him many a castle, monastery, Roman villa or
ancient hillfort and, since the Upper and Lower Icknield Ways were less than
three miles from where we lived, we would go for long walks down them.

My mother was a Wynne. The family came originally from Wales but went
over to northern Ireland with Cromwell and settled near Sligo. They seem to
have been mainly soldiers and churchmen, some of distinction. I was born in
1916 in London and the family removed after the war to Northend, a hamlet in
the parish of Turville in the Chiltern Hills some forty miles west of London and
eight miles from Henley-on-Thames. This was superb country, most of it still
covered in beechwoods, where I acquired a deep interest in and, indeed, love of
the English countryside, the animals and plants. These were most happy days –
watching the bodgers make chairlegs that were then carried to High Wycombe
to be made into Windsor chairs; or listening to the local inhabitants discussing

others' peccadilloes or various technical problems, when we brought a horse down to the blacksmith's for shoeing.

By the age of 6½ I was considered to be too intractable for those who looked after me so was sent to a boarding school at Portishead near Bristol. This required a train journey from Paddington and a cab ride to the school. I loathed the parting from my family and was wildly elated when returning home for the holidays. Whatever anyone says about boarding school, I am absolutely certain that it makes one appreciate one's family and family life so much more than being with them all the time does. I learned nothing very much at Portishead except to swim and, on the annual walk to Cadbury Camp, a general interest in Iron Age hillforts. From there I was sent to Swanbourne House, a preparatory school for Bradfield in Buckinghamshire, where at last I really began to learn something that would enable me to clear some of the hurdles of exams. I passed the Common Entrance and went on to Monkton Combe School just outside Bath. Looking back on my time there, I can see now that this is where I started to become what I am today and my archaeological interests began to form. I had a maths master, A.T. Wicks, who was a local antiquarian who did his best also to teach me maths; a history master, Maurice Howells, who taught us to look for cause and effect and not just to memorize the bare facts; and a house master, A.F. Lace, outwardly austere, but who took a very real interest in all of us in his charge. Monkton is a rowing school and did well at Henley Regatta where we went in for the Ladies' Plate; in my last year in the VIII we got to the semi-finals. I rowed at Cambridge, of course, and was lucky enough to find the Zambezi Boat Club at Livingstone where I continued to row regularly up to 1961 when I came to Berkeley. It taught one good team work which is of the essence, whether in rowing or as part of an archaeological team in the field in Africa.

My interests at Monkton were in the humanities, in history and things archaeological but not in classical languages which I was never much good at. I remember going to see Sydney Smith, the Keeper of Egyptian and Assyrian Antiquities at the British Museum, when I was around sixteen, to ask about the job possibilities in Egyptology. I was told that unless I could be certain of a first in Greek and Latin I could forget about it – I did just that. I got my School Certificate all right but did not take Higher Certificate, I think because of something to do with timing; but I took Littlego instead to go to Cambridge where I was accepted at Christ's and went up in 1934. Christ's had been A.C. Haddon's college and it was he who had really got anthropology going at Cambridge. I met him only once, later, with Louis Clarke in the Museum of Archaeology and Ethnology (as it then was!). I read history for two years and received a 2(2) in the Tripos and then went on to read the Archaeology and Anthropology Tripos under Miles Burkitt and Grahame Clark. This is really where my interest began to focus on prehistoric archaeology and, in particular, on the Palaeolithic. Miles was a superb teacher. I don't think his knowledge of the subject was all that profound but he had vast enthusiasm for it and was a born teacher who embellished his tutorials at Merton House with many an anecdote relating to some prominent archaeologist or anthropologist. I was one of, I think, six undergraduates that year; Charles McBurney was another and we became fast friends. I still remember with much pleasure the day excursions to sites in East Anglia that Miles took us on, ranging from gravel pits at Girton (not the most interesting things to see at Girton), to flint-knappers at Brandon and a day's paddling in the sea at Walton-on-the-Naze searching the submerged Neolithic/Early Bronze Age land surface; or a day at the cliffs at Cromer looking for 'Cromerian' artifacts.

If it was Miles who gave us the enthusiasm, it was Grahame who showed us the need for precision in archaeology; how to study an assemblage and, what was most important, to study it within its environmental setting. For me, Grahame's emphasis on palaeo-ecology has been all important since, without an understanding of the habitat of any prehistoric group, it is impossible to begin to understand their behaviour – why particular resources were being used, why they chose to do so in the way they did and how the changes in climate and environment brought about the particular adaptations that resulted. Grahame gave us people, Miles instilled an interest in the artifacts through knowledge of those who dug them up and of the history of the discipline.

My fieldwork initiation was with Sir Mortimer Wheeler at Maiden Castle for the 1936 season and a shorter time in 1937. I have always been grateful for this introduction to the rigorous field methods he adopted. They certainly set a new standard in Britain – and in India also, as I was able to see for myself a few years ago. I was put to work on Iron Age pits at Maiden Castle with John Waechter, who had been working in the Middle East, as my site supervisor; he was a kindly and stimulating instructor and we became lifelong friends.

I was lucky enough to get a First in the Archaeology and Anthropology Tripos and was awarded an Honorary Bachelor Scholarship by Christ's. From there I did voluntary work at the London Museum under Mortimer Wheeler while applying for job openings in museums. At that time I think there were only three permanent non-museum appointments in archaeology in the country – at Cambridge, Edinburgh and the Archaeology Officer at the Ordnance Survey. I suppose one was expected to have some private means if one took a museum job, at any rate the stipend – around £125 a year – was not lavish! I remember applying for one at the British Museum – my knowledge of Byzantine history and art was not good enough – at the Salisbury and Wilts Museum and at Norwich; I was offered none of them. I have never been more grateful since that I was not. Then, at the end of 1937, came the offer of an appointment as Secretary of a newly formed Institute for Social Anthropology – the Rhodes-Livingstone Institute in Northern Rhodesia – and the Curator of the David Livingstone Memorial Museum which had been merged with the Institute. This was for three years with option of a long-term contact. I had no special interest in south-central Africa but, since there was nothing else in the offing, I accepted. I shall always remember my mother's saying, 'It is only for three years, dear, and think of the experience.' I have found that most of the major decisions one takes in one's life are seldom carefully considered and thought out but are the outcome of sudden or unforeseen happenings. Certainly, my going to Africa was one of these.

I sailed from Tilbury on 17 December 1937 and arrived at Cape Town in the first week of January 1938. I just had time to make contact with John Goodwin at Cape Town University before boarding the train for Livingstone. Goodwin had been one of Miles's first students and was the first professional archaeologist to work in South Africa, if not in the whole of the continent south of the Sahara. Arriving in Livingstone three days later, I found that the Museum was housed in the old United Services Club, a pretentious, Palladian-style building that must have made an excellent club, as I was told by various former members who reminisced tenderly over the card rooms (now offices) and the mineral collection (formerly the bar). It made only a somewhat inadequate museum, however, owing to lighting, white ants (termites) and the sparseness of display cases. The Museum had been going for two years before I got there, chiefly through the interest of the then Governor, Sir Hubert Young. It possessed the nucleus of a good collection of early maps of Africa, some David Livingstone memorabilia and letters, the beginnings of an ethnography collection, minerals from Broken Hill and the Copper mines and such things as the bracelets, beads and coins from a crocodile's stomach. One took on all sorts of jobs – like blowing crocodile eggs to send to someone in the United States (not an easy task, I can assure you). Archaeology was represented by several petrol boxes of artifacts from the Mumbwa Caves excavation of Commander Attilio Gatti, a somewhat flamboyant explorer and adventurer, but who had invited Professor Raymond Dart to participate with him in the excavations at Mumbwa. I was able to salvage from these, essentially unlabelled, some Middle Stone Age retouched artifacts in quartz which formed the first exhibit of material from Northern Rhodesia. The Museum remained in the old Club building until after the Second World War when a new Museum was built.

Livingstone, which had been the capital of the country until, in 1935, that was moved to Lusaka, was a small colonial town living in an era, as perhaps most small colonial towns did, some 30 or so years behind what was going on elsewhere, and it was quite often, though not always, conventional and stuffy. It had one very great advantage. It was situated only three miles from the Zambezi and six miles from the Victoria Falls, one of the unforgettable sights of the world. This meant that it was the nearest town to a major tourist attraction and, after the war when flying became relatively easy, we had an endless stream of 'the rich and famous' from all over the world who, having come to visit the Falls, came on, *faute de mieux*, to fill in some time visiting the Museum. In this way, we met Prime Ministers, Archbishops, famous writers and even members of royal families.

My contract gave me a salary of £400 a year, a house with basic furniture and home leave every three years. I had become engaged while at Cambridge and after my arrival in Livingstone, with a special dispensation from the Governor since 'cadets' in their first tour could not marry without it, Betty and I were married in 1938. What I have been able to do in archaeology has been essentially a team effort by the two of us and, if it had not been for her input, it would not have been possible to do half of what we have managed to do between us.

The Zambezi valley gave me my first opportunity to apply what I had learned at Cambridge and over the next two years I was able to work out the geomorphological sequence of terraces and their contained artifact assemblages and, more rarely, faunas. I had to re-learn completely what a gravel deposit looked like, having been used to gravel pits 20–30 ft deep back in England. At the Falls, where the Zambezi was running over a bed-rock base, we were faced with gravel of only 2 or 3 feet, or less. One outcome of this work at the Falls was that I was able to concoct a rough estimate of the rate of recession of the Falls through the gorges back to the present line, based on the kinds of artifacts to be found abraded and left exposed on the old river bed as the Falls receded upstream.

Godfrey Wilson was the first Director of the joint Rhodes-Livingstone Institute and Museum and it was he and his wife Monica who gave me a much deeper appreciation of what archaeologists could gain from ethnography and a deep interest in material culture and the ways in which this, and the activities and people with which it is related, can provide the archaeologist with a basis for understanding how prehistoric peoples behaved. However, I had a problem in getting any money for fieldwork and virtually everything done on the Zambezi was done with my own money and my own, rather rickety, transport. At last, in 1939 I was given £15 a year for fieldwork and with this I spent a month re-excavating at Mumbwa to try to clarify the sequence there since the Gatti work had introduced an iron-smelting furnace sandwiched between two deposits with Stone Age material. Mumbwa had been the first site ever to be excavated in Northern Rhodesia – by F.B. Macrae, a District Commissioner, and also one of Miles Burkitt's students. I was able to define the Iron Age, Later and Middle Stone Age sequences but chiefly I had the opportunity to look at the ecology and possible seasonal occupation of the site since it lay in the ecotone between the plateau savanna and the grasslands of the Kafue Flats. How much more we would have been able to know if the knowledge of game behaviour had been as good then as it is today.

Archaeological research came to an end with the outbreak of the Second World War. For a time I was a member of the Defence Force guarding the Victoria Falls Bridge and then, since I was in general opposed to the taking of life, I joined as a Sergeant the 7th East African Field Ambulance being formed in Northern Rhodesia and attached to the 4th Battalion of the Northern Rhodesia Regiment. As part of the 27th Brigade we were in at the retaking of Berbera in British Somaliland, spent some time on the plateau at Hargeisa and Boroma and then went on to Gondar in northern Ethiopia which was the last battle in the Ethiopian campaign in late 1941. As probably in all wars, our life alternated between long periods when nothing much happened and short but very active, often unpleasant episodes. During the former I had an opportunity to work out the archaeology recorded in the numerous exposures of quaternary sediments in Somaliland and some parts of Ethiopia. Somaliland in particular produced superb collections.

From Ethiopia we went to Diego Suarez in Madagascar where we sat for several months waiting for the Vichy French to declare for de Gaulle. From there I went back to OCTU in Njoro, Kenya where at weekends – the only time off we got in a most strenuous series of courses – I would bicycle to Nellie Grant's to carry out on her farm the only excavation I have ever done in Kenya – a small trial pit in a burial cave, the contents of which were comparable to the large-scale excavations of the Njoro River Cave carried out by Louis and Mary Leakey. While in Kenya I was able to get to know Louis and Mary well and was especially appreciative of the times I was able to spend with them whenever I passed through Nairobi up to the end of the war, visiting their sites and discussing archaeology, often well into the night, in the museum or in their near-by house, surrounded by the Dalmatians that Mary bred so successfully.

I was posted for a time to the Somali Scouts where I did a kind of holding battalion job in British Somalia. There I was able to do some more archaeology and the excavation at Mandera of a Later Stone Age rock shelter. From there I joined the British Military Administration in Somalia (ex Italian Somaliland) and was a Civil Affairs Officer, first at Isha Baidoa, then at Oddur in the southern part of the country and afterwards in the Secretariat in Mogadishu. Here I got to do a lot more archaeology since the job entailed a great deal of 'touring', either by lorry or, more usually, on foot. My nascent interest in ethnography was further stimulated here; I got to appreciate the way the Somalis reacted to circumstances, to admire and envy the independence of pastoralists and to understand a little of the way they responded to and used their surroundings. I was able to immerse myself in trying to understand them better and to see what it means to be a pastoralist or a marginal farmer. I am convinced that an appreciation of the habitat is the basis for understanding behaviour in the past, just as it is for the present and, to this end, in a continent like Africa, one needs to walk through it, discuss it with one's companions as one walks and soak up their lore of plants and animals and their beliefs and customs. One can appreciate the buried past so much more if one has an understanding of comparable environments in the present. On the only local leave I ever had I was able to excavate at Gure Warbei, a rock shelter at Bur Eibe, an isolated 1000 ft granite inselberg, and recovered stratified the main Later, and Later Middle, Stone Age sequence in the region between the Webi Shebeli and the Juba rivers. By 1946 I knew my districts with their archaeological content fairly well and when the time came for my discharge from the army I asked the Chief Administrator, Denis Wickham, a fine, long-time colonial administrator from the Northern Frontier District of Kenya, if I might have a truck and rations for six weeks to visit northern Somalia to look at the archaeology there before leaving. He gave me these and so I was able to locate a number of sites in the centre and north of the country and do some trial excavation there. I had accumulated 22 petrol boxes of artifacts and a batch of field notes from my time in Somalia and Ethiopia and, on finally leaving Nairobi, I had myself made baggage officer so that I could oversee their safe transport all the way to Livingstone. As the lines of communication involved some nine transfers from trains to lake steamers to pontoons and road vehicles some care was needed to ensure that none of them was lost. All arrived safely in Livingstone and eventually made the journey to Cambridge via Cape Town.

My wife had been Acting Curator of the Museum during my absence, Max Gluckman was now the Director of the Institute and shortly after I got back the two became separate institutions. I had accumulated sufficient leave that I was able to get in a full academic year back at Cambridge for my Ph.D residence. The thesis was in two parts: on the prehistoric sequences in the Zambezi valley and the Horn of Africa. I received the degree in 1951 and both parts were subsequently published. I can still remember Mr Black, who had only recently joined the Cambridge University Press, and whose first assignment was *The prehistoric cultures of the Horn of Africa*, saying, 'The Press is part of a tripartite agreement on publishing the Bible and so it is able to publish at least one book a year for which there can be no possible sale.' Incidentally, the book has even been reprinted – but I have never had any royalties!

On my return to Livingstone the Museum Trustees agreed to construct a new building and, with financial help from the British South Africa Company, the Copper Companies, the Beit Trust and the Northern Rhodesia Government, this came about and it was opened in 1951. At the same time we founded a National Monuments Commission to investigate and conserve the historical and national 'Monuments' of the territory and I was appointed its first Secretary. Anything older than 1897, when the administration began, was an historic monument or relic and I well remember one or two of the members of the Commission's being proud of the fact that they too were 'national relics'!

Up to the late 1940s and early 1950s, prehistoric research, especially in the Palaeolithic, had followed more or less conventional lines. That is to say, we concentrated mostly on the taxonomy of the artifacts and on obtaining stratified sequences that could be dated in relative terms only. Assemblages were allocated to one or other of recognized industries, often ill-defined. There was more than an impression that artifacts might, as it were, breed and investigators would produce charts to show the evolution of a particular complex which was believed to be associated with a discrete group of people and so to be an expression of 'culture'. It has taken us quite a while to realize that one cannot understand human cultural behaviour solely on the basis of one small, often unimportant element of the material culture – the imperishable stone tools. Our concern was with relative chronology and with the typology of the artifacts themselves, in particular with what we believed to be 'type fossils'. We had little or no means of relating these artifact assemblages to the hominids who made them and no means at all of estimating how long a period of time a particular industry or complex lasted. Everything was really very imprecise and subjective and almost every assemblage we were looking at was in secondary context, unless it came from a cave or rock shelter, and even these were dug in spits of several centimetres or inches so that we had no basis for beginning to decipher evidence for behaviour. That is not to say, however, that we should view as of little account the way things were done before the Second World War. With hindsight we can see that what we did fell far short of what we should have been doing but, without this basis in stratigraphy and taxonomy, prehistory would not be where it is.

Then, in 1950, Willard Libby gave us the radiocarbon method of dating which meant not only a sure foundation for a timescale within the past 40–50,000 years, but also a method of correlation over wide distances. It was due to this that Iron Age archaeology in Africa received the impetus that intensified research in this time range and has led to the very significant advances that are providing their background history to many of the indigenous populations of the interior of the continent. This all happened after Libby dated a beam from a drain in a wall of the Elliptical Building at Great Zimbabwe to the 7th century AD. Few, until then, believed there was much time-depth to Iron Age archaeology in Africa as the migrations of the first Bantu-speaking agriculturalists were put down as having taken place only in the 14th and 15th centuries AD.

In the 1960s, Jack Evernden and Garniss Curtis gave us Potassium Argon dating and shortly after came Uranium fission-track and the Palaeomagnetic Reversal chronology, all of which gave dates in the Tertiary and early Quaternary. Relative chronology became a thing of the past and we now have a chronological framework in which we can have confidence. In addition to being able to show how long a prehistoric industrial tradition lasted in terms of radiometric years, it was also possible to see the length of time it took for one biological hominid stage to evolve into another. One of the most significant findings to come out of the new chronology was the great time-depth of hominid evolution. In Sir Arthur Keith's time, 500,000 to 1 million years ago was the estimated date for the beginning of the Pleistocene and the appearance of humankind. Now we know that it was probably somewhere between 5 and 6 m. years ago that our early ancestors became bipedal; 2.0–2.5 m. years ago that the first stone tools made their appearance; and 1 m. years ago, give or take a few thousand, that mankind migrated into Eurasia.

Another of our problems was lack of precision in definition and, indeed, in understanding where we were going. There were quite a number of amateur archaeologists in South Africa, relatively few in most other parts of the continent south of the Sahara and even fewer professionals. By the mid 1960s foreign researchers and expeditions were already at work and some valuable site excavations and reports became available. Basil Cooke and Dick Flint had shown the folly of trying to build a chronological framework on inferred climatic changes (Pluvials and Interpluvials) based on evidence from the tectonically most unstable part of the continent – the Great Rift Valley. Radiocarbon and Potassium Argon dating were well under way and the time was ripe to introduce some rigour into African archaeology. Accordingly, a three-week symposium was held at the Wenner-Gren castle in Austria, Burg Wartenstein; Bill Bishop, myself and Clark Howell were the organizers. A core group met one week with geologists, one week with palaeontologists and one week with archaeologists. The input from each of the groups was quite invaluable and the full report of the symposium was published in 1967 by Chicago under the title *Background to evolution in Africa* (ed. Bishop & Clark). This contains a wealth of information, especially in the discussion summaries that are a record of where we were, how much ambiguity we were working with and where and how it seemed important to try to introduce some precision. Our recommendations received general recognition, especially in regard to the need for precise definition of industrial entities and of boundaries whether they be stratigraphic or cultural. The hierarchy of terms proposed is now in general use in the continent.

In the late 1940s Mary and Louis Leakey started excavation at the site of Olorgesailie in the Rift Valley not far south of Nairobi. Mary applied the excavation methods that had been current in Europe for a long while at neolithic and later sites, to the palaeolithic ones at Olorgesailie. Here, fine-grained, old lake and fluvial sediments sealed a series of Acheulian cultural horizons, either on palaeosols or in shallow, low-energy stream channels. These horizons appeared to have suffered minimal disturbance from the time the site was abandoned by the hominids until it became buried by lake sediments. This gave us the added dimension of space and it was possible to study associations between different kinds of artifacts and bone waste which is generally well preserved at the Rift Valley sites. We now had a viable basis for beginning to say something about the activities represented by these artifacts and bones and so to try to look at the behavioural strategies of the early hominids.

In 1953, I discovered the Kalambo Falls site on the Zambezi plateau near the southwest corner of the Lake Tanganyika Rift. Louis Leakey often spoke of 'Leakey's luck' but I think I had my fair share of it as well, certainly in the finding of the long sequence at Kalambo. After a hot scramble through a gorge and nearly falling into a pig-trap, John Hodges, our new Inspector of Monuments, and I came out on to the top of a terrace which clearly terminated in a cliff. In two minds whether to call it a day, but going on the principle that one never passes up an exposure of sediments, we went to look and had literally to fall down the cliff to the base where we found ourselves amongst

Acheulian bifaces in mint condition with carbonized tree trunks sticking out of the same deposit. A trial excavation that year and a full season in 1956 plotting the distribution of everything on the several different horizons showed that the wood and other plant remains were unquestionably contemporary and that we were dealing with a series of occupation horizons with no depth that rested on fine sands and silts and presumably represented seasonal visitations by hominids. Some fluvial resorting was evident but not sufficient to cause significant redistribution of the mint fresh artifacts. The one or two distribution plots published in 1960 were the first, so far as I know, to show what an African Acheulian activity area looked like. Unfortunately the acid nature of the groundwater had caused all bone to disappear relatively rapidly so that none survived in any of the archaeological horizons. What had survived, however, were macro plant remains – wood, seeds, leaves and thorns besides pollens; the reason for their survival being that the deposits containing them had been waterlogged ever since they were laid down. Further full seasons' excavations continued in 1959 and 1963 with some small scale work in 1964. This work was in large part financed by grants from the Wenner-Gren Foundation for Anthropological Research based in New York. There can be few, if any, organizations that have done more to advance the fields of archaeology and anthropology than this Foundation, with its relatively small-sized grants, has done. In particular, the symposia held at Burg Wartenstein, the Foundation's headquarters in Austria, gave us the opportunity, cut off from the world, to immerse ourselves to great advantage in the particular topics, problems and sub-disciplines we were concerned with.

Another major step forward in communication and understanding was the inauguration of the Pan-African Congress on Prehistory and Related Studies, the first of which was organized in 1947 by Louis Leakey in Nairobi. Previous to that time, we had all worked in more or less watertight compartments – mostly because in those days it was not easy to move around all that much. Until the 1950s, I saw John Goodwin only at the Cape, *c*. 1300 miles away, when I was going on or coming from leave; Neville Jones, a former missionary turned professional archaeologist, at the Bulawayo Museum some 300 plus miles away, only a little more often. There was no other professional archaeologist, or amateur for that matter, between myself in Zambia and Louis Leakey in Nairobi some 1500 miles or so to the north. The Nairobi Congress brought together for the first time archaeologists, quaternary geologists and palaeontologists from all parts of the continent and the Pan-African Congress has, until recent times when political overtones have disrupted it and reduced its worth, been of inestimable value as a meeting ground for scholars actively working in African archaeology. Meeting on an average every four years, it has been a forum for exchange of information and discussion, for establishing friendships and team projects and for providing opportunities to visit key sites and localities in the host country. These meetings gave us an appreciation of the vastness of the African continent and of the great variability in its prehistory – a variability that stems from the many adjustments and adaptations in response to the varied nature of the continent's eco-systems, in particular in the savannas where the human race emerged.

Back in Livingstone, the Museum saw considerable development. First, Ray Inskeep and then Brian Fagan joined us as archaeologists. Barrie Reynolds was ethnographer and Clayton Holliday technical officer and natural historian. A new administrative, research and storage wing was added and the collections were considerably expanded owing to field research in archaeology – both Stone and Iron Age – and in ethnography. We spent some time with Hukwe Bushmen in southwestern Zambia; carried out experimental studies in stone flaking, bone bashing and butchery; and we studied the marks resulting from particular usage on some of our experimental pieces. Inskeep and Fagan worked on the Iron Age while I dealt with the Stone Age. From the Nachikufu Cave excavation we recovered the Later Stone Age sequence on the northern plateau that shows the antiquity there of the bored stone (23,000 BP) and the edge-ground axe (*c.* 10,000 BP). Incidentally, it took us quite a while to understand that radiocarbon dates were generally much more accurate than our subjectively conceived age estimates and when the Yale Laboratory first sent us their age for the Nachikufan, I said they must be wrong!

The fifties was a time also that saw the beginning of primate behaviour studies with Sherry Washburn's and Irvine DeVore's work on baboons, Jane Goodall's on the chimpanzees at Gwembe and George Schaller's on the mountain gorilla. Sherry spent several months with us in 1955–6 working at the Falls and in the Wankie Game Reserve. His preparation of baboon specimens in a corrugated aluminium shed in the Museum grounds, well away from the main building, looked and smelled like the chamber of horrors! It was from these beginnings, though, that we have progressed to the understanding of primate, in particular Great Ape, behaviour that has been so vitally important for providing insights into the behaviour of the first protohumans – the Australopithecines and *Homo habilis*.

Most of my fieldwork was carried out in Zambia and covered everything from pre-Acheulian to the Iron Age, including rock art – paintings and engravings – which has long been an interest of mine, and it was somewhat disappointing at first to find that what existed in Northern Rhodesia and Malawi was schematic, rather than naturalistic, such as the superb painting styles in Zimbabwe. What we knew of this art in the 1950s is published in *The rock art of the Federation of Rhodesia and Nyasaland* (ed. Roger Summers). Much of it is contemporary with that in the south but the reason for its schematic and symbolic nature remains unknown. Such schematic art is found widely dispersed in central Africa and some of these symbols are present in the central Tanzanian art groups in the same friezes with the naturalistic paintings. Some are contemporary with Iron Age farming populations but the paintings appear to be connected with groups of indigenous black hunter/gatherers who performed certain rites, such as those of the Butwa secret society, both for themselves and, when consulted, for the farmers. In southwestern Angola, the BaTwa people or, as they are called there, Kuissi, are still painting and performing these rites and it is important, as soon as politics permit, to undertake a thorough study of the motives behind their schematic art.

In 1950 (and again in 1968 and 1972) at the request of the Government, I undertook an archaeological survey in central and northern Malawi (Nyasaland, as it used to be) and did several seasons at the Portuguese diamond mines in northeast Angola where mining operations had cut through deep thicknesses of Kalahari-type sands and many buried horizons of artifacts. The thick vegetation in this high rainfall area reduced erosion to a minimum and, if it had not been for the mining operations, we would have known little about the rich later pleistocene record buried there.

In 1961 I was offered and accepted an appointment at the University of California at Berkeley, joining Sherry Washburn and Ted McCown (who had dug at Tabun and Skhul with Dorothy Garrod). This was a very different appointment from the one in Livingstone and involved full-time teaching which was something I had never done before except for the two-week 'Winter Schools' we had started in Livingstone, and a little at the newly formed University of Rhodesia and Nyasaland in Salisbury. I was teaching African archaeology with the opportunity of training students to work in that continent and of being able to get back there for research most years myself. We were able to develop a good programme which received great new impetus when Glynn Isaac joined us in 1966. From then on, Glynn became a leader in the field of early man studies and was without equal. Trained in the natural sciences as well as anthropology/archaeology, his breadth of understanding introduced new approaches and new methods into African pleistocene archaeology. This is where the main advances in African archaeology have been made over the past twenty years or so, for it is only comparatively recently that Iron Age archaeology has turned from looking at potsherds to uncovering and interpreting settlement patterning and spatial archaeology.

Berkeley enabled me to work more widely in the continent and one result of this was the introductory text *The prehistory of Africa*, published by Thames & Hudson in 1970. Our approaches and understanding have developed so greatly since that time that a new edition, planned for the very near future, will entail virtual rewriting of the complete text. Being able to get back to the field in Africa with students and adequate funding also meant expanded interests and more time devoted to analysis which, with the revolution in quantitative studies, inevitably involved long hours in the laboratory. More work at Kalambo Falls with Maxine Kleindienst and in northern Malawi with Glen Cole, Vance Haynes and John Mawby, gave us understanding of the relative age, faunas and archaeology of the sequence there. One lucky find was the partial remains of an elephant together with the artifacts used to butcher it, on an old land surface >300,000 years old.

In the early 1960s also I had two short seasons in northern Syria. Syrian Antiquities very generously loaned us equipment and we excavated the Acheulian living site of Latamne, north of Hama, that had been found some three years before by Willem van Liere working for FAO. This was a site on a sand bank of the Palaeo-Orontes, here a low-energy stream. The hominid occupation site dated to the Hoxnian Interglacial, on the evidence of the fauna, and it must have been a relatively small group from the spatial distribution of artifacts. What was especially interesting, however, was the configuration of large blocks of limestone that can only have got there by having been carried in, and which might possibly have formed the basis for some kind of shelter and showed, as subsequent finds in other places have confirmed, that structures were, indeed, being made by Lower Palaeolithic man.

My main interests since coming to Berkeley have been in early man research, stimulated to no small degree by the mutual interests Glynn Isaac and I shared in this, and by the input from Sherry Washburn and Clark Howell on the physical side. Another interest was, however, in the origins of agriculture in Africa south of the Sahara which received a considerable boost from a British Expedition, led by Colonel David Hall, to the central Sahara in 1970–71; followed up by a season's excavation of a Late Neolithic and a Mesolithic site on the Upper Nile in the Sudan and a programme in Ethiopia begun in 1974.

With the greater emphasis on ecology and its significance for understanding dynamic systems of human behaviour, an attempt was now being made to look at the distribution of the different prehistoric traditions in relation to existing vegetation, rainfall, soils, etc. and in relation to past changes in these patterns that reflected the onset of glacial and interglacial conditions in the high latitudes. *The atlas of African prehistory*, of which I am the co-ordinator, consisted of a number of geographical and ecological base maps and a series of overlays showing different industrial distributions so far as these were known. This was published by the Chicago University Press with funding from the Wenner-Gren Foundation in 1967. It was a useful step forward as it showed the connexion between environment and culture but it was only partially successful as, in many parts of the continent, the distribution pattern of sites was largely a reflexion of where archaeologists had been working. A more detailed corpus of information, computerized for data retrieval, should prove to have wider potential once it receives the general input it deserves from the national monuments commissions, museums and individual investigators.

The results of all my field studies have appeared in print in some form or another but the book that I think I most enjoyed writing was *The prehistory of southern Africa*, published as a Penguin in 1959 in harness with Sonia Cole's *Prehistory of East Africa* and Charles McBurney's *The Stone Age of North Africa*. Not only did I have to learn a lot of South African archaeology and be lucky enough to visit, with John Goodwin, Peter van Riet Lowe, Berry Malan, the Abbé Breuil and others, some of the key sites there but I had the opportunity to use the wealth of ethnographic literature and to develop the ecological approach to prehistory which I inherited from Grahame Clark and consider all important. The book did, I think, have some effect on the way people began to look at their material and my often-quoted paper on potential wood-working tools is an intimation of the changing ecological emphasis and interests in the behaviour behind the artifacts themselves. Now South African archaeology leads the continent in research into past human behaviour from the later Pleistocene.

The Early Man/Africa Program at Berkeley has produced a number of outstanding prehistorians who are working on special problems relating to recognition of the evidence of the activities of prehistoric peoples and how to distinguish these from the marks of other animal or of geological agencies. From a state almost of naïveté in seeing any association of artifacts and broken bones as being due to hominids, an appreciably more cautious approach is now used so that ascription to hominid activity is only made after other possible agencies can be eliminated and much of the new understanding that is coming about is due to the prehistorians trained in the Berkeley programme.

At Berkeley also we have been able to begin training African nationals to the doctoral level. They will go back to their own countries to assume responsibility as University teachers, Museum Directors and Antiquities and Monuments Commission officers. Glynn and I laid special emphasis on this since it is their own past they will be responsible for investigating and a thorough understanding of the field and research potential is essential. In general, it has worked very well and we can be well satisfied that in six African countries there are now some ten African graduates from Berkeley working.

Over the last twenty years or so, research into the origins of culture has expanded tremendously. In large part this has been due to the team approach to solving the broad problems of understanding of how human culture evolved. These interdisciplinary and international teams of specialists have provided knowledge of the savanna environments in which the human lineage emerged, of the favoured habitats, of dietary preferences, of the evolving biological nature of humankind as this is demonstrated by the fossil record, of the activities and patterns of behaviour that are apparent from the spatial distribution of artifacts, associated remains and features on primary context sites, and of the evolving intellectual and technical skills that resulted in the appearance of Modern Man some 40,000 years ago.

When we are dealing with more archaic forms of hominid we need to be much more cautious in any behavioural assumptions we might make on the basis of what present-day hunter/gatherers, ethnography and ethno-archaeological residues can provide. This is why I have always emphasized the need for sound, empirical data from a series of carefully chosen localities yielding the kind of evidence we need, that must be the basis for any behavioural models we might be able to build. Clark Howell's American and

French team's ten-year field studies in the Omo; Glynn Isaac's work with Richard Leakey in East Turkana; Donald Johanson's and Maurice Taieb's at Hadar; Philip Tobias's and C. K. Brain's long and on-going work in the Transvaal Australopithecine caves and my own work with Martin Williams, Tim White and others in Ethiopia, in particular on the high plains at Gadeb and in the Middle Awash section of the Afar Rift – these and others are providing the essential data which it is for us to try to interpret. Clearly, interpretations must change as new data and new techniques become available; this is, of course, as it should be. Who would have thought, any time in the 1930s, that we would have been able to know one quarter of what we know today? and who, even fifteen years ago, would have thought it would be possible to determine dietary preferences from abrasive patterns on the occlusal surfaces of teeth; from oxygen and nitrogen isotope studies to show how much marine food there was in the diet of a prehistoric population and whether the terrestrial animals they were taking were primarily grazers or browsers? Determination of whether stone and bone have been burned and the temperature to which they have been subjected is now possible and is crucial for understanding when it was that the hominid lineage first made regular use of fire, since very ancient sites in the open no longer preserve charcoals. Polishes on the edge of stone tools as much as $1\frac{1}{2}$ million years old are still identifiable as having been produced by use on different substances – soft plant remains, wood and meat, for example – and I would predict also that it will not be too long before we are able to identify organic traces on the working edges of stone tools.

For me, it has been in part the excitement of learning more about the human past in the continent where it all began – the exhilaration of discovery and excavation of new sites for their confirmation of what we already know or for what they can add to it and the sheer joy of walking and working in a part of the world that has not really changed all that much, so far as vegetation and some animal communities are concerned, since the late Miocene. *Plus ça change, plus c'est la même chose*, for we can see surviving here the kinds of processes, physical and intellectual, and material ways of doing things that can be the clues to more realistic and reliable understanding of the past. The Livingstone Museum (Cecil Rhodes now being out of favour) continues apace with a Berkeley trained archaeologist as its Keeper of Prehistory; and the Early Man/Africa Program will continue – if not at Berkeley, then elsewhere in the States – carried forward to new goals by some of those who enjoy working in Africa as much as I do and in close collaboration with those archaeologists and others, often their fellow graduate students, in the African institutions. It is clearly in the pooling of resources, in the sharing of ideas and information, that African prehistory will continue to advance. If we start to fall back into little watertight compartments, as there has been a tendency to do in the past few years, and if political or other non-scientific discrimination prevents full exchange between academics, then we can expect fragmentation and stagnation. It is, of course, those who practise such discrimination who will suffer most. The overwhelming rejection by the international body of archaeological science of the discriminatory policy put forward by the 'World Archaeological Congress' is an encouraging reminder that it is the science that is all-important and not the colour, religion or politics that dictate whether you may travel here or there, attend this or that meeting or publish this or that book. I look forward to the day when the Pan-African Congress will resume its all-important role of welding more firmly together the archaeological world in Africa and all who work there. What comes from there is always interesting, often new and exciting, and Pliny's *ex Africa semper aliquid novi* is equally true of archaeology there today. Africa gave us the earliest hominid stage and, for a long time, no one believed it; it gives us the beginnings of culture and now it looks more and more as if it had a larger than expected hand in the appearance of Modern Man also. So let us go easy on the theoretical answers until we have some more hard, factual data on which to base them.

11

D.J. Mulvaney

Gordon Childe's *Dawn* illuminated prehistoric European horizons in the year of my birth, although my delayed archaeological education meant that one of my first academic publications was Childe's obituary (Mulvaney 1957). My father, an always penniless rural schoolmaster, emigrated from Ireland in 1908. His transfers around Victorian schools were dictated largely by my educational needs, for I was the eldest of five children. To facilitate my early secondary schooling, we left a village in forested Gippsland for the curiously named Rainbow, a modest centre in marginal wheatlands, then being smothered by drifting sands and a mouse plague. We transferred again so that I might attend year eleven classes, because few schools in depressed rural Victoria of the thirties catered for such levels. Unable to afford the cost of my matriculation year schooling in Melbourne, I spent two unhappy years as a trainee primary teacher.

It was escapism, not patriotism, that motivated me to enlist in the Royal Australian Air Force, during the week in which I turned eighteen. Although I never had crossed the state border, I soon ranged so far that, on my twentieth birthday, I embarked aboard RMS *Aquitania* at Southampton for Sydney, thereby completing a voyage of circumnavigation at the King's expense.

During the momentous interval I graduated as a navigator under the Empire Training Scheme, a term today reserved for realms of science fiction. It was real enough, however, to arrive in England during September 1944. I learned to manipulate radar equipment efficiently, without ever comprehending the mysteries behind the dials. Time and fortune prevented me from dropping any bombs in anger, because Hitler's war ended just as I was posted to a Lancaster bomber base.

My wartime memories are of gentler things, particularly continual visits to historic places, perceived within the wonderment and untutored romantic ambience that a Victorian education then instilled of 'home' (as Britain was termed). British prehistory was unknown to me, but I recall vividly the thrill of my first encounter with the deep past. I was cycling one summer evening from the Moreton-in-Marsh drome, when the brooding, mysterious Rollright Stones suddenly appeared. It is a place to which I returned on all subsequent English visits.

A civilian again, a grateful government offered me university entrance for 1946, under terms of a rehabilitation training programme. The gratitude was all mine, because I was determined never to return to rural school teaching. Having sat requisite aptitude tests, I was advised to study engineering. My results surely were biased by my recent sortie into navigation. Actually I lacked the basic entrance prerequisites, because I abandoned mathematics and science early in my schooling. (One examination is memorable for my eight per cent mark in arithmetic and an unbelievable one hundred per cent for history.) With such restricted options, I entered the University of Melbourne. The only subject which attracted me was history and, to please a helpful sub-dean, I enrolled for the degree at honours level. Next to my marriage in 1954 and my RAAF enlistment, that hesitant move was the most crucial decision of my life. The History department of the forties was one of Australia's intellectual power-houses. It owed much to Professor R.M. Crawford, a broad-minded Renaissance scholar, who championed Australian history and who encouraged Anthropology. His staff espoused tolerance and the critical evaluation of sources, even including 'authorities'. Their enthusiasm for the value of studying the past proved infectious and numerous of my contemporaries today hold senior academic posts at home and abroad. I worked unduly hard to make up for lost schooling, but the effort proved stimulating. I regret that modern undergraduates seldom seem to derive the same sense of excitement and purpose, despite a plethora of publications, computing and technical aids on a scale undreamed of in those penurious times.

My prime mentor was J. L. O'Brien, a classicist who taught Greek and Roman history using translations of the classics. I became fascinated by the detective work of source criticism and reinterpreted some obscure incidents in 5th-century BC Thrace, which O'Brien encouraged me to expound to the class. During my second year, a small group opted to take his seminar on Roman Britain. The class met weekly at 8 p.m. under O'Brien's direction in a college study and it rarely disbanded before midnight. We investigated the data behind R.G. Collingwood's reconstruction, in Collingwood and Myres, *Roman Britain and the English settlements*. In this manner I interested myself in the economy of Iron Age Britain, later comparing Collingwood's practice with his *The idea of history*. I was approaching the fringes of archaeology, although not that of my own continent.

Upon graduation, I accepted a temporary tutorship in Ancient History, combining this with research for a master's degree into the origins of the Australian Labor Party (Mulvaney 1949). I now read Gordon Childe, but only the angry, disillusioned author of *How Labour governs*. My heart was not in political history and, despite my ignorance of classical languages, I turned with relief to Roman Britain for a thesis topic.

My dissertation on 'The Belgae and English economic history' was completed early in 1951 (partly published as Mulvaney 1962). My topic later was judged unsuitable by some English archaeologists. Yet it is not eccentric to research the archaeology of a country from outside. Archaeologists should be assessed by those discoveries which they report, and the manner in which they illustrate and interpret them, rather than through any indigenous mystique or oral transmission within a favoured circle. Besides, imperial ties were so strong that the State Library of Victoria replicates the British Library reading room architecture and, since last century, it subscribed to over 70 British archaeological journals. Immersed in hillfort excavations, ceramic complexes and field systems, I boldy criticized assumptions and methodologies of British archaeology. I sternly dissected Wheeler's *Maiden Castle* saga and queried the Iron Age ABC according to Hawkes.

During my research I discovered Grahame Clark's trail-breaking economic prehistory articles and Glyn Daniel's *A hundred years of archaeology* arrived while I was writing my thesis. In Melbourne there was only John O'Brien with whom to share my excitement over such stimulating 'new' archaeology. Now, convinced that I wanted to experience archaeology in the flesh, I knew that it was to Cambridge that I should venture. I intended to return and apply the lessons in Australia. As far as I am aware, nobody then holding any university or museum post had received academic instruction in archaeological techniques and interpretation relevant to what today would be called hunter–gatherer societies, but which I then knew as stone age.

Academic Australia then consisted of six universities separated from each other by hundreds of miles and by disparate cultural and funding traditions of different states. Despite the abundance of indigenous people in Australia and its Melanesian territories, anthropology was taught only at the University of Sydney. Radcliffe-Brown, the foundation professor in 1926, was not a person to foster the study of past societies, so prehistory was neglected. Sydney also held a monopoly of Classical and Near Eastern archaeology, but that was neither the area nor the methodology of my concern. To a participant, the intellectual gulf apparently separating the two history departments seemed formidable. Melbourne historians were problem oriented; theory, explanation and Carl Hempel were conspicuous decades before the New Archaeology (Crawford 1939; 1947). Sydney historians were reportedly pragmatic, positivist, and scornful of model building. Besides, such was the overwhelming 'cultural cringe' within Australian universities, that an Oxbridge degree was mandatory.

That exciting prospects for fieldwork existed seemed obvious. The most relevant literature on Aboriginal antiquity was associated chiefly with three museum curators, Norman B. Tindale (the South Australian Museum), Frederick D. McCarthy (the Australian Museum, Sydney), and Edmund D. Gill (the National Museum of Victoria). Their enormous range of work was published chiefly in the relative obscurity of their museum serials and it made no impact on the academic community, despite the significance of their material.

Once my master's thesis was completed, I applied for scholarships for overseas study. At this period the newly established Australian National University lacked a physical entity, and its early doctoral candidates voyaged overseas to undertake research. When I received a scholarship, therefore, I requested permission to vary the terms of my award, in order to learn the rudiments of prehistory. I may be the only Ph.D scholar in the history of the

ANU who was permitted to substitute an undergraduate degree.

Accepted as a member of Clare College in October 1951, I read for the Cambridge Tripos in archaeology and anthropology. Because Clare had no archaeology tutor, N.G.L. Hammond, the adaptable and considerate senior tutor, suggested that I nominate my own supervisors. Not surprisingly, Grahame Clark supervised me during my first year and Glyn Daniel during my second. Across both years I was stimulated by Charles McBurney's innovative ideas, both in supervisions and in lectures. His teaching career and my studies commenced during Dorothy Garrod's final year and their contrasting styles and emphases were remarkable.

Cambridge archaeology offered an exciting education, for it combined new ways of looking at the past with innovative fieldwork. There was a sense of immediacy and of relevance. Grahame Clark lectured on his current Star Carr research, while his *Prehistoric Europe: the economic basis* was published in my time; McBurney was re-evaluating the Palaeolithic of Europe and North Africa; Daniel used slides as a teaching aid in a manner superior to anybody within my experience and he stimulated my own interest in the history of archaeology; by way of contrast erudite Toty de Navarro sat behind his desk piled high with books of illustrations – not for him a new-fangled projector – teaching traditional typology as a master of that arcane pursuit; meantime, Tom Lethbridge, evidently John Bull's clone, expounded outrageous but provocative ideas.

I received an immediate introduction to fieldwork as a member of the student society which completed the extensive excavation of the Melbourn Anglo-Saxon cemetery. A fellow enthusiast was David Wilson, with whom I shared Daniel supervisions and wines. The intellectual stimulation provided by visiting speakers is best indicated by naming some, including the Abbé Breuil, Woolley, Wheeler, Piggott, Oakley, Cyril Fox and Ian Richmond. Jack Golson, a graduate student, reported the saga of Axel Steensberg's excavating a Danish medieval cow, while Gordon Childe's venue was a room in the 'Red Cow', stumping off angrily when his slides were misplaced hopelessly, presumably by himself.

As I hankered after the Iron Age but knew that I must return to Stone, I attended classes across an impossibly broad spectrum from the Palaeolithic to medieval society (Postan and Dom David Knowles). I learned wisdom during two years of lectures from Harry Godwin and found companionship with several palynologists, whose heartland was Clare. A brief excavation with fellow students at Hoxne was a warming episode, designed to assist Richard West's research there.

The most pervading influence on my Australian fieldwork was the three months spent on McBurney's 1952 expedition to Haua Fteah, Libya. All five of us travelled in his Austin utility across France and then from Tunis east to Apollonia. The work was tiring, but McBurney drove himself more than his workforce and by the end of that season we were deep into the Mousterian, 9 metres down.

Amongst my debts to McBurney's innovation was the design of his demountable frame and sieves, which I adapted for Australian use, as also his sample collection according to layer and substance. The Haua provided my introduction to radiocarbon dating, of great assistance later. During that dawning radiocarbon age, he strove to ensure the stratigraphic provenance and the uncontaminated purity of samples. These early post-Libby-an samples were collected on teaspoons, smoking was banned, samples were stored in jars washed sterile with petrol and packed in drums filled with soil sieved from the same strata as the samples.

I appreciated the sense of purpose during my Cambridge years, and in fact archaeology embraced Europe and much else, not simply Britain. I also was fortunate in my humane college, the encouragement of my supervisors and in the extent to which one shared field experiences with equally concerned fellow students. Prehistory was still fun. This made annual departmental excursions of staff and students memorable – in my case, the antiquities and pubs of Kent and Wiltshire. Whether students today derive such pleasure from the past, or whether they share information so freely, seems doubtful. My latter-day experiences with humourless theoreticians, or of earnest devotees of specialisms from which they refuse to deviate, troubled me to such an extent that I preferred to leave them to their devices. It was a major factor in my decision to take retirement at age sixty.

In a frantic attempt to gain varied field experience during the 1953 summer, I visited the megalithic problem at Barclodiad y Gawres in Anglesey under the gentle guidance of Glyn Daniel and Terence Powell. Then followed a month in the Irish Iron Age, excavating on the hill of Tara with the wise and enthusiastic Sean P. O'Ríordáin. I was within sight of my father's birthplace. A hurried London visit followed, primarily to lunch with Mortimer Wheeler. Daniel had shown him my Melbourne thesis and, although he could have vanquished me, he spent over an hour strenuously defending Maiden Castle against my verbal attack. I guess that he accepted me as a 'colonial', worth encouraging to work in a distant land. His praise and genuine interest (for he wrote to me months later) are acknowledged with gratitude.

My next diversion was the Danish Neolithic. Firm but friendly J. Troels-Smith instructed me how to uncover hazelnut husks in Aamosen's bog, with the utmost precision, while nourishing me with a gruel which Tollund Man would have recognized. The context of my Australian fieldwork made impractical the application of such important but time-consuming three-dimensional recording. Like McBurney in Libya, I had to temper desirable methodology with realistic goals. Funding, field time and trained assistants were rare during the fifties and sixties. The optimum requirement was to produce a series of dated stratified deposits on a continental canvas, containing artifactual and environmental data. That pattern now is established; funding is available on a moderate scale; and there are many young professional archaeologists. Long-term projects, or those designed to test hypotheses or to solve detailed local problems are required. We need regional archaeology texts rather than broad syntheses. Unfortunately, the means of ensuring such directed research, posts with security of tenure, are a diminishing resource.

Employment opportunities did not exist at all in 1953, as the time approached for my return home. A new lectureship arose in New Zealand, and Grahame Clark tempted me with the offer of expanding the Cambridge archaeological empire to Auckland. But Auckland is as far distant from Melbourne as is Moscow from Cambridge. So, it was Jack Golson who departed on his influential pioneering career in the Antipodes, abandoning English cricket fields and Wharram Percy's buried fields.

Fortunately my former head, Max Crawford, offered me a lectureship in history. In tandem with O'Brien, I taught Greek and Roman history over the next eleven years. Not surprisingly, courses became increasingly diluted with Old World prehistory. About thirty years ago, I introduced an option for honours history students. Named Pacific Prehistory, initially it dealt with Polynesia, but gradually expanded westward. The first class tested the 'evidence' upon which Heyerdahl voyaged *American Indians in the Pacific*. By the time I left Melbourne at the end of 1964, available sources had shifted dramatically away from the lunatic fringe to critical archaeological standards, especially in New Zealand.

Fieldwork became practicable in 1955. Modern students consulting my early reports may deplore their lack of sophistication and the apparent lost opportunities of those unfettered times, free of all legislative control of relics and not a dissident Aboriginal in sight; but neither were funds nor leisure available. Teaching commitments limited fieldwork to vacations; departmental funding was meagre; neither the department nor myself owned a vehicle. As sites needed to be within easy access, this precluded those exotic regions where traditional Aboriginal ways were followed.

The selection of a site resulted from serendipity, in the form of a chance meeting with C.P. Mountford, an Adelaide ethnologist. He later guided me to Fromm's Landing, a group of rock shelters in the limestone cliffs which fringed the Murray River, only 70 miles from Adelaide. My decision to plan a dig there was immediate, as its context was text-book oriented. This was a rich resource zone only 10 miles downstream from Devon Downs, the most important site so far dug in Australia and published 25 years before by the South Australian Museum (Hale and Tindale 1930). Prospects for deep stratigraphy and preservation of organic materials were excellent. The excavation later confirmed this, producing 5 metres of stratigraphy, a 5000-year sequence of carbon dates and varied fauna.

Shortly after my decision to excavate, Tindale (1957) delivered a continent-wide synthesis of Australian culture history at a science congress. As his reconstruction depended essentially upon his interpretation of the Devon Down sequence, it posed a need to test its validity by excavating an adjacent site. Two seasons at Fromm's Landing produced crucial information and led me to question Tindale's model (Mulvaney 1960), for one site was not the yardstick for a continent's prehistory. As background research, I already had surveyed historical records since first European contacts with Australia in 1606, and emphasized changing European perceptions of Aboriginal society (Mulvaney 1958).

A critical evaluation of the present state of knowledge of Aboriginal prehistory was required, using environmental, archaeological, material culture and historical evidence. My paper (Mulvaney 1961) may read negatively today, but it seemed essential to distinguish fact from assertion, and it posed many of the problems for which answers were sought by fieldworkers over the following decade. The title of that Prehistoric Society paper was revealing. 'The Stone Age of Australia' reflected the dead-and-gone-world viewpoint of a European archaeologist, and my paper took little account of existing Aboriginal society or of what was to be termed ethnoarchaeology. Perhaps this was because I had never experienced Aboriginal society and, in fact, I doubt whether I even had met an Aboriginal person.

Except for a handful of museum curators and amateur stone-tool collectors (rugged individualists for the most part), I had few specialist contacts. The two leading authorities of the day, McCarthy and Tindale, were 600 miles and 450 miles distant, respectively. I relied upon advice from abroad, chiefly McBurney, although that brace of Clarks, Desmond and Grahame, also answered queries. Golson's success in New Zealand was an inspiration. Because I lacked early funding, Hallam Movius obtained dates for my first season's radiocarbon samples at Fromm's. The National Physical Laboratory, Teddington, later accepted samples, through the intercession of Harry Godwin and Kenneth Oakley (whom I confronted with a bag crammed with samples).

Visitors to Australia in those days were a rarity. Gordon Childe was the first, on his lonely journey back to his roots. He twice lectured to my classes during 1957 and inspected my Fromm's Landing finds, if not with interest, with encouragement. Jacquetta Hawkes paid a fleeting call, and then Grahame Clark twice visited Australia during the mid sixties. Since the major Congress of Orientalists in 1971, numerous archaeologists have toured Australia, although this seems to have made dispiritingly little impression upon American or European course offerings.

One evening shortly before my first Fromm's Landing expedition, a phone call produced a courteous voice with a slight stammer, requesting permission to visit the site. So commenced ten years' close association with the late Dermot A. Casey, then possibly the only FSA in the country. He brought those photographic, surveying and stratigraphic skills which so facilitated Mortimer Wheeler's British and Pakistan campaigns. I owe much to his cheerful advice and encouragement, and it was in his Landrover and trailer that we twice drove the four-day trek to Kenniff cave. We formed an odd contrast, for he was a man of vast proportions and strength.

The deluge dates from 1961 and I felt isolated no longer. Golson transferred from Auckland to the first archaeological post at the Australian National University. The Anthropology department of the University of Sydney appointed Richard Wright to its first prehistory lectureship, and Vincent Megaw was appointed to teach European prehistory in the Archaeology department. A former Melbourne student, Ian Crawford, completed a London Institute of Archaeology diploma and became a curator at the Western Australian Museum. A year earlier, another Melbourne historian, Isabel McBryde, having completed a Cambridge diploma, combined history teaching at the University of New England, in northern New South Wales, with an impressive regional archaeology campaign.

1961 also witnessed the initial conference, resulting in the foundation of the Australian Institute of Aboriginal Studies (AIAS) by the Commonwealth Government. Henceforth, funds for Australian fieldwork became available on an unprecedented scale, although meagre by American comparison. Although I contributed a state-of-the-art paper on the needs of prehistory at that meeting (1963), I was absent abroad on a Nuffield Foundation Fellowship. That Foundation also granted me field research funds, which first took me and two others to Kenniff cave during 1960 and to the Northern Territory in 1963.

The chief purpose of my Fellowship was to learn conservation techniques at the London Institute of Archaeology. (At that time probably only one museum or art gallery official in Australia had formal conservation training.) I also studied Aboriginal collections in European museums and excavated at La Cotte St Brelade with the talented McBurney field team. It provided the opportunity to cement a firm friendship with young Glynn Isaac. Our families continued to meet periodically in Australia, Kenya, England or California. During the last academic year before his untimely death, I was fortunate to be based in Glynn's Stone Age Lab at Harvard University. His enthusiasm was undiminished and it was reciprocated by his students.

The first specialist meeting of Australian archaeologists was staged early in 1963, with AIAS sponsorship. Almost all professionals and amateurs assembled to discuss better systematics in stone tool typology and cultural nomenclature. More importantly, it provided opportunities for colleagues to meet, many for the first time. Such a meeting might have been held in the proverbial telephone booth a few years earlier, and even then it required only a moderate sized room.

Later that year, Golson and I arranged a joint Canberra-Melbourne expedition to the Katherine region in the Northern Territory. This was my first experience of tropical Australia and my earliest contact with Aboriginal Australians. My small party included Casey and the innovative geomorphologist, Jim Bowler, making his initial contact with archaeology. Bowler went on to contribute enormously to Quaternary studies, and he collaborated with archaeologists. He recognized the environmental significance of the Pleistocene Willandra Lakes system in western New South Wales, and located the first evidence there of human occupation. He also discovered the two Lake Mungo burials, one of them the world's oldest cremation and the other a 30,000-year-old inhumation powdered with ochre. That this region is registered on the World Heritage List is due to Bowler's discernment. During the early seventies we collaborated on excavations on the Mungo lunette, uncovering artifacts and ochre pigment considerably older than 32,000 years, and possibly 40,000. Unfortunately, the full potential of this remarkable region for interdisciplinary effort has not been achieved.

Golson recruited me for the Australian National University in 1965. I had enjoyed introducing the first courses on our region's prehistory in Melbourne and a number of my students have gone on to distinguished academic careers. However, it was frustrating to teach classical history and to undertake Australian research simultaneously. Once in Canberra in a research post, I had the leisure and facilities to complete a number of projects. My first task was to analyse the Kenniff cave finds (Mulvaney & Joyce 1965). By 1962, that site had produced a stratified series of radiocarbon dates, beyond 13,000 years, thereby confirming the Pleistocene occupation of Australia, a breakthrough announced in the pages of ANTIQUITY (Mulvaney 1964). Late Pleistocene sites had been claimed by Gill at Keilor, by Dr Sandor Gallus at Koonalda cave on the Nullabor Plain, and by Tindale at several localities. The importance of Kenniff cave was that unlike those sites, dating, environment and cultural traits were contained within deep stratigraphy, and the stone assemblages were distinguishable by their change through time and remarkable for the presence of most Australian stone tool types within that stratigraphic context. There was a basic separation between a flake tool (scraper) component in lower layers of the deposit, and the appearance during the last 4000 years of various specialized small stone tools, including backed blades, symmetrical points and chisel tips (tula adze).

Analysis of the initial Mungo discoveries by Rhys Jones and Harry Allen (Bowler *et al.* 1970), resulted in the term 'Australian core tool and scraper tradition' to describe assemblages of the lower Kenniff type. Richard Gould (1973) coined the phrase 'Small tool tradition', for the other. These concepts served as a useful model and ready reckoner for stone tool assemblages, but they are so vaguely defined that the term 'tradition' is today questionable. More precise regional typologies and closely dated excavated assemblages are essential, supported by studies of reduction sequences, replications of stone technology, residue and use-wear analysis.

Australia rapidly produced surprises from its newly won Pleistocene past. The 13,000 years minimal age for human presence of 1962, became 20,000 in 1965, it passed 30,000 by 1970 and before that decade ended, 40,000 years was probable. No segment of the history of *Homo sapiens* had been so escalated since Darwin took time off the Mosaic standard. I was present in 1965 at Nawamoyn, one of Carmel (Schrire) White's Arnhem Land rock shelters, when edge-ground stone hatchets were excavated, some encircled by pecked grooves. Years elapsed before many European prehistorians accepted their antiquity of 18,000–23,000 years. A Eurocentric nonsense even rejected the carbon dates because they were 'made in Japan'. Indeed, Australians abroad still find it difficult to impress upon colleagues the significance of this continent and New Guinea for interpretations of world prehistory, or for models of transformations from food collecting to horticultural societies. The excuse offered sometimes is that Australian research is not published in the appropriate journals. Why should some British or American serial be appropriate? It is time that prehistorians included journals such as *Archaeology in Oceania* and *Australian Archaeology* on their list of essential reading.

Bowler led a group of scientists to the Mungo lunette in 1969 to what was an eroding cremation some 26,000 years old. These precious scattered fragments were packed in my suitcase, its contents discarded, pending later excavation of the grave. Almost simultaneously, Alan Thorne uncovered a series of Pleistocene burials at Victoria's Kow Swamp. Their cranial morphology contrasted markedly with the Mungo remains and triggered a major interest in human biology. Also during the sixties, Koonalda cave proved to have been a flint source at the peak of last glacial cold, while its wall markings may be equally ancient. Continued discoveries concerning the age of rock engravings and paintings and their stylistic changes through time, make this art corpus a vital resource for the origins of human creativity.

Late in 1968 Golson and I sought to bring together these discoveries at a symposium. *Aboriginal man and environment in Australia* (Mulvaney & Golson 1971) was a benchmark occasion, it involved state-of-the-art summaries from many disciplines, including scholars who had not previously interacted with prehistorians. It was the first of several major conferences where, increasingly, it has been demonstrated that the interaction between hunter-gatherers and the landscape was subtle, but profound. The traditional dichotomy between Palaeolithic and Neolithic is shown to be meaningless in Australia and New Guinea (Jones 1975; Lourandos 1983).

In 1969 I completed a volume in the *Ancient Peoples and Places* series, *The prehistory of Australia*. Critics found that it concentrated unduly upon stone tools and culture history. Certainly, it was completed before the New Archaeology surged over unredeemed archaeologists. It *did* stress that there was an Australian history before Europeans, a reality then ignored by historians, and it was the first book-sized attempt to depict prehistoric Australia. The pace of discovery and reappraisals, particularly the ideas of Rhys Jones, made my revision of that volume more convincing. An unfortunate distribution policy, never communicated to the author, restricted the Penguin Books *The prehistory of Australia* (1975) to that country. Despite requests from various publishers, I have refused to revise or to write a new version. My two attempts were the earliest in the field and they reflect the activities and concerns of those times. It is appropriate that younger authors, with different preconceptions, formulate their vision of the past. I eagerly await an exposition by some Aboriginal scholar.

My first Canberra year 1965, also facilitated my entry into the intriguing field of protohistory. During the tropical dry season I travelled extensively around Arnhem Land beaches and islands, particularly in Aboriginal boats. With Aboriginal assistance, I identified several sites where Macasson trepangers from Sulawesi (Celebes) during recent centuries processed their catch. I returned bearing pottery, porcelain and glass, proof of massive culture contact. This traffic was described extensively by nineteenth-century observers, although historians ignored its ramifications, an omission for which I condemned them (Mulvaney 1966). The field and literary documentation of this traffic provided one of my first Ph.D scholars, Campbell Macknight (1976), with a major theme, which took him to Indonesia (via Mulvaney & Soejono 1970).

The following year a charter plane deposited another aspiring scholar, F.J. Allen, and myself on deserted Arnhem Land beach, returning to collect us seventeen days later. We surveyed the overgrown and tumbled ruins of the abortive Port Essington settlement of 1838–49, intended as an Australian Singapore. Allen's perceptive research later fixed this forlorn, isolated place on the map of world empires, examined the vagaries of innovation and tradition in a remote colony and traced racial interaction (Allen 1967; 1973).

These northern expeditions convinced our department that island southeast Asia and Australia constituted a single research entity. Ian Glover's doctoral research involved systematic excavations in eastern Timor. During 1969, Glover, Macknight and myself linked with the National Archaeological Institute of Indonesia, when R.P. Soejono and I directed a joint project in Sulawesi, research later extended by Glover. Another vital connection was forged with Indian archaeologists, culminating in an international symposium at Poona in 1978, arranged by V.N. Misra (Misra & Bellwood 1985). My experience of Asian archaeology broadened when I attended the 1966 Pan-Pacific Congress in Tokyo. Subsequently, the Indo-Pacific Prehistory Association has sponsored invaluable regional meetings. My university has trained archaeologists from Asian countries, including Indonesia, Malaysia, Brunei and Thailand.

As a member of the newly created Australian Heritage Commission between 1976 and 1982, I urged upon officialdom, the public and even uncaring historians, that cultural records are precious, even when the material evidence is only a century old. Port Essington was a prime example of a significant archaeological place capable of illuminating both prehistory and the contrast between imperial expectation and colonial reality. Even as Australia moves towards the bicentenary of European settlement in 1988, archaeologists and architects, but not historians, have spearheaded a major public campaign to prevent the New South Wales government selling off land in central Sydney for commercial development, upon which Governor Arthur Phillip built the first substantial European house in Australia. The foundations of that symbolic structure survive and now will be preserved. Significantly, even here past ways and the new interacted. The first Aboriginal whose name is recorded by Europeans, Arabanoo, was buried in Phillip's garden, during a service attended by that governor (Mulvaney 1985a). Australia's recent past may be likened to the interdependence of Roman and Celtic Europe, and its archaeological investigation should not be pigeon-holed into distinct branches – prehistoric, industrial, or historic.

My research also was guided by the belief that prehistorians and historians must take into account the changing intellectual influences and preconceptions which guided the compilation of written sources during different periods or places. The impact of evolutionary biology was particularly profound in conditioning attitudes to the mental and material 'progress' of Aboriginal society. A vogue for cranial morphology and the accumulation of skeletons in museum cupboards was one reflexion of these concerns. In their assumed intellectual superiority and scientific importance, such grave diggers overlooked entirely the wishes of Aborigines, or the ethical issues involved. Pioneer anthropologists, such as A.W. Howitt (Mulvaney 1971) and Baldwin Spencer (Mulvaney & Calaby 1985) emphasized evolutionary aspects of social structure, thereby unintentionally providing a scientific rationale for the racialist dogmas of land-takers and legislators. They assumed that Aboriginal minds were childlike in their simplicity, survivals from primeval times, holding clues for the origins of 'advanced' societies.

They were otherwise kindly humanitarians, but they justified a draconian paternalism in the interests of Eurocentric 'improvement'. The emphasis which Radcliffe-Brown's generation placed upon the comparative analysis of kinship networks, did nothing to alter this abstract notion of a laboratory on a continental scale. The whirlwind is being reaped today, by archaeologists and anthropologists alike, who are condemned by most Aborigines on the basis of inherited and little understood caricature, despite the fact that it is disowned by the present generation of practitioners.

Prehistorians are acutely aware that Australian prehistory is not remote and that, over the past decade or so, it has developed a unique character. Past evidence and present traditions suggest cultural and spiritual continuity. Aboriginal people have their own interpretations and explanations which differ from those of prehistorians, although close consideration may allow reconciliation, for example, between creation myth and field reality. Fieldwork involves the consent of a resurgent Aboriginal culture which attaches no importance to model testing. Neither does it see itself as an experimental population resource, providing earnest but hurried visitors with analogies for a university textbook. In their positive acceptance of this intellectual milieu, some prehistorians feel out of sympathy with overseas concepts. Visitors evidently consider Australians to be unduly pragmatic, often 'sitting down' for long periods with a community and recording apparently mundane matters, without the supposed rigour of a theory or explanation. Critics overlook the fact that, to gain a feel for the ethos of a people, to appreciate its philosophy and its lifeways in depth, is not simply a question of a single-minded, limited stay to test a theory or impose a model.

With the possibility of some 40,000 years of Aboriginal prehistory to interpret, a fine line divides remote, middle range and existing societies, or separates settlement patterns then from land rights now. Theories of artistic origins are complicated by knowledge of the sheer diversity and complexity of traditional ceremonial life – there is no monolithic Aboriginal culture. Where should scientific human biology research end? Given that the decapitated remains of historical figures rest in European museums, their post-mortem treatment illegal under the law, it is difficult for archaeologists not to become involved in present social issues. The greater the empathy with a society, the probability increases that a researcher will become involved in other issues, sometimes beyond disciplinary confines.

Prehistorians are sympathetic to Aboriginal causes, and every Aboriginal activist justifies his tenurial rights by citing the archaeological revelation of 40,000 radiocarbon years of human presence. Many archaeologists act as consultants to communities in documenting their land claims, and a narrow line demarcates such activities from what may be called ethnoarchaeology. Few Aborigines acknowledge this disciplinary contribution however, and even object strenuously to the term 'prehistory'. They equate 'pre-' with 'sub', constituting for them yet another implicit evolutionary down-grading. They demand equal status 'history' with Europeans. In their assertion of cultural identity, they claim an absolute ownership of their past; and they assert that their past extends back to the beginning.

Twenty years ago, this emphatic mingling of past and present did not occur, so I went about my business as a 'stone age' researcher. The dramatic change involved in the reassertion of Aboriginal cultural identity ranks as one of the most significant developments in Australian intellectual history, even though it proves inconvenient and challenging for field workers, and most Australians deride it as self-interested radicalism.

I have attempted to explain the purpose of prehistory to Aborigines for over a decade, because I believe that greater communication is essential. Findings must be interpreted at the grass roots level in addition to overseas congresses. Conciliation rather than confrontation, support for the establishment of Aboriginal committees of advice or management within State Aboriginal sites authorities, assistance to education programmes to train Aboriginal archaeologists and anthropologists, are some of the necessary tasks which partly explain Australian pragmatism.

It also is vital that academic standards be maintained in the face of such pressures. While present societies may provide guides to the interpretation of the past, they are not identical. I am concerned, for example, that the concept of a core and scraper tradition which spans tens of thousands of years is unreal. Similarly, when is an Aboriginal not an Aboriginal? While I consider that it is unethical to exhume for scientific study the remains of known identities, without the consent of relatives, I do not apply the same criterion to the pleistocene Kow Swamp burials, although Aboriginal people do. Where should I draw the line between Pleistocene and present? There is the rub. I also dispute any claims to monopoly, based upon racial grounds, of the ownership of the cultural heritage of prehistoric Australia, both in the near and the remote past. I accept the appropriateness of its custodianship by Aborigines, advised by experts of whatever race or creed. I first raised some of these issues generally at the London Institute of Archaeology in 1977 when, as an Australian, I was honoured to deliver the second Gordon Childe Memorial Lecture (Mulvaney 1978b). For later elaborations (Mulvaney 1979; 1981; 1985b) and an Aboriginal reaction to my stance, see Langford (1983).

The Australian National University established two Prehistory chairs during 1970, Golson became foundation professor in the Research School of Pacific Studies and I was appointed to head a new department (eventually Prehistory and Anthropology) in the Faculty of Arts. We were monopolists for a decade, but four other universities now have professors (two of them ANU research graduates). Prehistory is taught also at another five universities, including the University of Papua New Guinea. Thirty years after my initial Melbourne Pacific Prehistory class of six, hundreds of undergraduates enrol annually in prehistory units. It is appropriate to paraphrase Grahame Clark's celebrated assertion, which stirred emotions during the forties – 'to the peoples of the world generally . . . Palaeolithic Man has more meaning than the Greeks'. Many students in Australasia today take that for granted, but consider that, for the peoples of the Pacific, indigenous prehistory has more meaning than the Europeans.

As a teacher who must take some of the credit for this interest in the region's past, I also am conscious that I am a Fellow of the Australian Academy of the Humanities and a Corresponding Fellow of the British Academy. At a time when prehistory has become increasingly specialized and technical worldwide, I am concerned that its essential humanism and universalism is being overlain by a narrow provincial concentration, or by emphasis upon the shallow, jargon–cluttered 'objectivity', of some favoured specialism. I am proud that at the time of my retirement, and despite expressed student preference for greater local orientation, the department ranged broadly over the Old World and the New in addition to the Indo-Pacific region. Major options also were available in art, material culture, epistemology and history of archaeology, cultural resource management (an awful Americanism, here to stay), and biological anthropology.

During the past 30 years, prehistory has required more than fieldwork and teaching. The initial rarity of practitioners and the vital importance of Australia's rich, but neglected, cultural heritage, necessitated activities with government and in the market place. The first perceived need was for government legislation in every state to protect Aboriginal sites. The AIAS played a major role and I assisted with arrangements for two influential conferences (McCarthy 1970; Edwards 1975). South Australia, in 1965, was the first state to enact laws, and the last was Tasmania, in 1975. Promulgation of laws was an advance, but their implementation through adequate staffing proved another matter, and some states lag. Post-European historical sites have not even received that degree of priority, probably because they have proved less contentious politically. Consequently, in some states important places lack any protection. This problem of public apathy and official neglect has concerned me (Mulvaney 1978a; 1985a).

Between 1964 and 1986, except for two years, I was an elected member of the AIAS Council, including a term as its chairman. When head of its advisory committee on prehistory during the sixties, I edited a handbook on field techniques (Mulvaney 1968), with the intention of raising site recording standards and introducing materials conservation. The book went through three editions under my editorship, but no chapter on excavation techniques was included. I opposed implicitly sanctioning amateur digging before academic institutions taught both techniques and professional ethics. Elitism was mooted, but I preferred that the AIAS was seen not to promote unskilled digging until legislation was in place to ensure that permits to excavate were required.

When the first widespread Aboriginal opposition to fieldwork surfaced during 1971, I was Acting-Principal of the AIAS. Trouble centred around a critical issue, publication of photographs of a secret-sacred ceremonial nature, whose revelation to uninitiated people held life or death potential. The issue was side-stepped by anthropologists hitherto, largely on the dubious assumption that Aborigines never saw publications. I organized a Canberra conference of field workers and administrators on the theme of problems of field access. At the time, researchers had been withdrawn from territory larger than Britain. Assessed from today's more relaxed perspective, the meeting's intention was biased towards assuring academic access, and no Aboriginal representatives were invited – an impossible situation today. It represented a faltering step towards the dialogue which followed during the next few years, particularly as encouraged by the new AIAS Principal, Peter Ucko.

This meeting possibly constituted the first occasion on which a representative group of fieldworkers from various disciplines gathered to ponder ethical issues, or attempted to formalize the obligations of researcher to informants and their communities. It symbolized the approaching end to that heavy handed paternalism, when officials could line up Aboriginal subjects to have blood samples taken, or when eager archaeologists could dig sites without first seeking the permission of traditional owners.

These were the years of the mineral exploration boom, when vehicles tracked across the remotest regions. If sites were to be preserved, whether those of deep spiritual significance to Aboriginal people or places of artistic and archaeological value for all Australians, they must be recorded on site registers. A year after the access conference, the AIAS sponsored a larger meeting, after which it received funding and the responsibility for co-ordinating a national site recording programme (Edwards 1975). It was premature, in that Aborigines did not wish to reveal locations of sacred sites; there existed a shortage of adequately trained fieldworkers; some states already had systems of their own, while others had no intention of collaborating. Yet in the face of the success rate of miners gaining priority over other claims to land use, this urgent project was surely worth prosecuting, and it had my support, in that even a faulty site register was better than nothing. Mineral exploitation prefers a blank site map.

The most intensive project was in the Arnhem Land uranium province, where nature placed uranium in proximity to some of the world's best rock art and scenic beauty. I was a member of the Alligator Rivers Region Scientific and Technical Evaluation Committee in 1972–3, and emphasized the cultural heritage of the region. Around 350 art galleries were recorded, but subsequent field research has increased that number to about 1500. Although uranium mining was sanctioned subject to limitations, the fact that the Kakadu Park has been placed on the World Heritage List owes something to the work of that committee.

The reformist Whitlam Labor government of 1972–5 attempted the first major appraisal of Australia's natural and cultural heritage resources, as an exercise in conservation. The Committee of Inquiry into the National Estate made a far reaching investigation which resulted in the creation of the Australian Heritage Commission. I was appointed one of its first seven commissioners in 1976 and served for two terms. The Commission worked with meagre resources, implacable opposition from some state governments, but with assistance from voluntary conservation bodies, such as the National Trust. The first Register of the National Estate, 6600 places representing the natural environment, buildings and Aboriginal sites, was published in 1981. I wrote an appreciation of the Aboriginal heritage in the massively illustrated book (Heritage 1981).

To complement this concern for the preservation of *in situ* heritage places, a committee was established in 1974 to consider moveable items. I served on this Committee of Inquiry into Museums and National Collections. It revealed a shocking lack of curatorial staff, storage and conservation facilities in Australian museums, great and small. Far reaching improvements have resulted since the report, although there is much room for further improvement. One of the committee's tasks was to report upon the needs, scope and location of a national museum in Canberra. The resulting recommendations for a future Museum of Australia were innovative and challenging. As the complex included a Gallery of Aboriginal Australia, I chaired a planning committee of equal numbers of Aborigines and non-Aborigines, which produced an unorthodox blueprint (Museums 1975). It emphasizes the creativity and the complexity of Aboriginal societies. Recent legislation established the museum, whose planning proceeds.

Unlike Britain, which remains aloof, Australia was an early signatory to the World Heritage Convention. In 1977 I was the chief Australian delegate to a

Paris Unesco meeting which framed the criteria governing inclusion of places on the World Heritage List. My attendance at the 1981 Sydney meeting of States Parties to this Convention therefore proved rewarding. The Kakadu Park and the Willandra Lakes (including Lake Mungo) were entered upon the select list of World Heritage places.

My close association with these matters and my conviction that supreme places of natural or cultural value must be preserved, explain my activities during the campaign to save the Franklin River region of southwestern Tasmania, yet another World Heritage listing (Mulvaney 1983). I opposed publicly the proposal to drown the valley systems, refuge of unique vegetation and site of human habitation 20,000 years ago, at the peak of glacial cold. The scheme for hydro-electricity was outright vandalism, because the power output was trivial and its need non-existent. Most scientists abstained from comment, claiming the fiction that science is above politics. I believed that the importance and rarity of this vegetation, including living trees over 2000 years old, and caves which humans abandoned before Altamira was painted, imposed an obligation upon experts to speak out, despite the consequences.

In the face of the Fraser Federal Government's decision not to prevent dam construction by the Tasmanian state government, I resigned from the Interim Council of the Museum of Australia. I voiced my concern in the media, from the back of a truck outside Parliament House, on the stage of Hobart's Town Hall alongside David Bellamy, and eventually in an affidavit in the High Court of Australia.

With the support of the Australian Conservation Foundation, Rhys Jones and I wrote to a number of overseas scholars, seeking their assistance to save an entire pleistocene archaeological complex. Several wrote to the Prime Minister and other colleagues from Britain, Canada, New Zealand and the United States allowed their names to appear in a full-page newspaper advertisement (*The Australian*, 4 September 1982). The headline asked, 'Do people overseas care more about preserving Australia's treasures than our own government?'

The battle for the Franklin was won after a federal election replaced the government. Because the region was entered on the World Heritage List, the High Court ruled by a narrow margin that Commonwealth obligations to observe foreign treaties over-rode state government concerns. Many people contributed to forcing this dramatic policy reversal, but there is reason to believe that archaeological testimony proved crucial. The response of the overseas correspondents, who eloquently stated the case for preserving the region, offers testimony to the truism that prehistory knows no national boundaries.

170   D.J. Mulvaney

References

ALLEN, F.J. 1967. The technology of colonial expansion: a nineteenth-century military outpost on the north coast of Australia, *Australian Archaeologist* 4: 111–37.
1973. The archaeology of nineteenth-century British imperialism: an Australian case study, *World Archaeology* 5: 44–60.
BOWLER, J.M. *et al.* 1970. Pleistocene human remains from Australia: a living site and human cremation from Lake Mungo, *World Archaeology* 2: 39–60.
CRAWFORD, A.M. 1939. *The study of history.* Melbourne.
1947. History as a science, *Historical Studies (Australia and New Zealand)* 3: 153–75.
EDWARDS, R. 1975. *The preservation of Australia's Aboriginal heritage.* Canberra: Australian Institute for Aboriginal Studies.
GOULD, R.A. 1973. Australian archaeology in ecological and ethnographic perspective. Warner Modular Publications 7: 1–33.
HALE, M.H. & N.B. TINDALE. 1930. Notes on some human remains in the Lower Murray Valley. *Records of the South Australian Museum* 4: 145–218.
HERITAGE, 1981. *The heritage of Australia: the illustrated register of the National Estate.* Melbourne: MacMillan/Australian Heritage Commission.
JONES, R.M. 1975. The Neolithic, Palaeolithic and the hunting gardeners: man and land in the Antipodes, in R.P. Suggate *et al.* (eds.), *Quaternary Studies*: 21–34. Wellington.
LANGFORD, R.F. 1983. Our heritage – your playground, *Australian Archaeology* 16: 1–6.
LOURANDOS, H. 1983. Intensification: a late Pleistocene-Holocene archaeological sequence from south-western Victoria, *Archaeology in Oceania* 18: 81–97.
MCCARTHY, F.D. (ed.). 1970. *Aboriginal antiquities in Australia..* Camberra.
MACKNIGHT, C.C. 1976. *Voyage to Marege.* Carlton: Melbourne University Press.
MISRA, V.N. & BELLWOOD, P. (ed.) 1985. *Recent advances in Indo-Pacific prehistory.* New Delhi.
MULVANEY, D.J. 1949. Some influences on the early Australian Labor Party, *Twentieth Century (Melbourne)* 3(4): 34–49.
1957. V.G. Childe, *Historical Studies (Australia and New Zealand)* 8: 93–4.
1958. The Australian Aborigines, 1606–1929: opinion and fieldwork, *Historical Studies (Australia and New Zealand)* 8: 131–51, 297–314.
1960. Archaeological excavations at

Fromm's Landing, on the Lower Murray river, *Proceedings of the Royal Society of Victoria* 72: 53–85.
1961. The Stone Age of Australia, *Proceedings of the Prehistoric Society* 27: 56–107.
1962. The Belgae and English economic history, *Historical Studies (Australia and New Zealand)*10: 327–38.
1963. Prehistory, in H. Shiels (ed.), *Australian Aboriginal studies.* Melbourne.
1964. The Pleistocene colonization of Australia, *Antiquity* 38: 263–7.
1966. Beche-de-Mer, Aborigines and Australian history, *Proceedings of the Royal Society of Victoria* 79: 449–57.
1968. *Australian archaeology: a guide to field techniques.* Canberra: Australian Institute of Aboriginal Studies.
1969. *The prehistory of Australia.* London, Thames & Hudson.
1971. The ascent of Aboriginal man: Howitt as anthropologist, in M.H.Walker, *Come wind, come weather*: 285–329. Carlton: Melbourne University Press.
1975. *The prehistory of Australia.* Ringwood: Penguin.
1978a. Future pleasure from the past, *Australia ICOMOS Proceedings, Beechworth*, 59–67.
1978b. Australia before the Europeans, *Bulletin of the Institute of Archaeology* 15: 35–48.
1979. Blood from stones and bones, *Search* 10: 214–18.
1981. What future for our past? Archaeology and society in the eighties, *Australian Archaeology* 13: 16–27.
1983. Towards a new national consciousness, *Australian Natural History* 21: 88–9.
1985a. *A good foundation: reflections on the heritage of the first government House, Sydney.* Canberra.
1985b. A question of values: museums and cultural property, in I.McBryde (ed.) *Who owns the past?*: 86–98. Melbourne: Oxford University Press.
MULVANEY, D.J. & J. GOLSON (eds.). 1971. *much that is new': Baldwin Spencer 1860–1929.* Carlton: Melbourne University Press.
MULVANEY, D.J. & J. GOLSON (ed.). 1971. *Aboriginal man and environment in Australia.* Canberra: Australian Institute of Aboriginal Studies..
MULVANEY, D.J. & E.B. JOYCE. 1965. Archaeological and geomorphological investigations on Mt Moffatt Station, Queensland, *Proceedings of the Prehistoric Society* 31: 147–212.

MULVANEY, D.J. & R.P. SOEJONO. 1970. Archaeology in Sulawesi, Indonesia, *Antiquity* 45: 26–33.

MUSEUMS. 1975. *Museums in Australia, 1975.* Report of the Committee of Inquiry on Museums and National Collections, including the Report of the Planning Committee on the Gallery of Aboriginal Australia. Canberra.

TINDALE, N.B. 1957. Culture succession in south-eastern Australia from Late Pleistocene to the present, *Records of the South Australian Museum* 13: 1–49.

Index